The New Anti-Catholicism

Also by Philip Jenkins

The Next Christendom: The Coming of Global Christianity
Beyond Tolerance: Child Pornography on the Internet
Hidden Gospels: How the Search for Jesus Lost Its Way
Mystics and Messiahs: Cults and New Religions in American History
The Cold War at Home: The Red Scare in Pennsylvania 1945–1960
Synthetic Panics: The Politics of Designer Drugs
Moral Panic: Changing Concepts of the Child Molester in Modern America
A History of the United States
Hoods and Shirts: The Extreme Right in Pennsylvania 1925–1950
Pedophiles and Priests: Anatomy of a Contemporary Crisis
Using Murder: The Social Construction of Serial Homicide
Intimate Enemies: Moral Panics in Contemporary Great Britain
A History of Modern Wales 1536–1990
Crime and Justice: Issues and Ideas
The Making of a Ruling Class: The Glamorgan Gentry 1640–1790
Images of Terror: What We Can and Cannot Know About Terrorism

The New Anti-Catholicism

The Last Acceptable Prejudice

Philip Jenkins

OXFORD
UNIVERSITY PRESS
2003

305.6
J

OXFORD
UNIVERSITY PRESS

Oxford New York
Auckland Bangkok Buenos Aires Cape Town Chennai
Dar es Salaam Delhi Hong Kong Istanbul Karachi Kolkata
Kuala Lumpur Madrid Melbourne Mexico City Mumbai Nairobi
São Paulo Shanghai Taipei Tokyo Toronto

Copyright © 2003 by Philip Jenkins

Published by Oxford University Press, Inc.
198 Madison Avenue, New York, New York 10016

Oxford is a registered trademark of Oxford University Press

www.oup.com

Library of Congress Cataloging-in-Publication Data
Jenkins, Philip, 1952–
The new anti-catholicism : the last acceptable prejudice / Philip Jenkins.
p.   cm.
ISBN 0-19-515480-0
1. Anti-Catholicism—United States.
I. Title.
BX1770.J46 2003
305.6'2073—dc21   2002012488

Book design and typesetting by
Glen R. J. Mules, New Rochelle, NY

9 8 7 6 5 4 3 2 1

Printed in the United States of America
on acid-free paper

Contents

Preface

As always, my main debt of gratitude in writing this book is to my wife, Liz Jenkins. I would also like to thank my friend Marian Ronan for her good counsel—though I am sure she will disagree with much of what follows!

I should say a word about my personal stance toward the issues discussed in this book. Over the past decade, I have worked on a number of controversial topics involving Catholicism, particularly on the theme of child abuse by clergy. During the wave of national concern about that issue during 2002, I argued that the reality of the "pedophile priest" issue was quite different from what was being presented by the mass media, and that the number of priests involved in this behavior was significantly smaller than was commonly assumed. In the context of the time, my attitude was seen by some as a defense of the Church, and not surprisingly it involved me in some lively debates. As a result, I have often been asked about my personal relationship to Catholicism. I was a member of the Roman Catholic Church for many years, but I left, without any particular rancor, and since the late 1980s, I have been a member of the Episcopal Church. (Within that tradition, I define myself as a small-c catholic, a distinction that often puzzles large-C Roman Catholics.) I have never been a member of the clergy in any church, nor a seminarian, nor was I associated with any religious order. I have no vested interest in defending the Roman Catholic Church, nor can I fairly be described as an uncritical defender of Catholic positions.

The New Anti-Catholicism

1 | Limits of Hatred

Depressing thought: every conformist group has its own equivalent of the scourge of anti-Semitism, a scourge inflicted on any minority it dare not understand for fear of having to think things through. Your "Jew" (your "slacker," your spoilsport, your inconvenient non-booster) is whoever distracts you from your television set. Or who asks "why" instead of "how." Catholic-baiting is the anti-Semitism of the liberals.

— Peter Viereck

Catholics and Catholicism are at the receiving end of a great deal of startling vituperation in contemporary America, although generally, those responsible never think of themselves as bigots. Examples are far too easy to find. Recently, the notionally secular *New Republic* published an article on the wartime role of the papacy, in which Pope Pius XII was charged with directly serving the Antichrist. Somewhat less apocalyptically, writing in *The Nation*, dramatist Tony Kushner dismissed Pope John Paul II as a "homicidal liar" who "endorses murder." Catholic bishops, meanwhile, are, to Kushner, "mitred, chasubled and coped Pilates." Responding to a papal appeal about the need to revive civil discourse, Kushner wrote that he would first request the Pope not to "beat my brains out with a pistol butt and leave me to die by the side of the road." In 2002, the furor over child sexual abuse by Catholic clergy provoked a public outpouring of anti-Church and anti-Catholic vituperation on a scale not witnessed in this country since the 1920s. Reasonable and justified critiques of misconduct by particular Church authorities segued effortlessly into grotesque attacks on the Catholic Church as an institution, together with sweeping denunciations of Catholic faith and practice. Large sections of the media assumed that most Catholic clergy were by definition child molesters, who should be viewed as guilty until proven innocent.[1]

Responding to such attacks draws forth still plainer examples of raw anti-Catholic sentiment. Not long ago, *Sister Mary Explains It All,* a televised version of Christopher Durang's play, was attacked as grossly anti-Catholic. Whether or not the charge was fair, the response of the film's director certainly seemed to fit that characterization, since he claimed that "any institution that backed the Inquisition, the Crusades and the Roman position on the Holocaust deserves to be the butt of a couple of jokes." The accuracy or relevance of each of those historical references is open to massive debate, but the director was citing them as if they somehow represented the authentic face of Catholicism. Each term—*Inquisition, Crusade, Holocaust*—is powerfully evocative, so that a suggestion that any group might share guilt for these acts is very damning. A writer in *Slate* magazine effectively blamed Catholics themselves for any stigma they suffer: "If anti-Catholic bigotry exists in America, it might have something to do with the Catholic Church's past conduct. Just this weekend, His Holiness John Paul II conceded as much when he finally got around to apologizing to the world for 2000 years of Catholic wickedness. He apologized for the forced conversions, for the murderous Crusades, and for the Inquisition." The author compared the Pope to "hatemongers" like Louis Farrakhan.[2]

None of these remarks is terribly unusual in contemporary discussions of religion. What is striking about these comments is not any individual phrase or accusation, but the completely casual way in which these views are stated, as if any normal person should be expected to share these beliefs. Responding to criticisms of his attack on the Church, Kushner himself wrote, apparently seriously, "I can't help feeling stung at being labeled anti-Catholic." Complaints about anti-Catholicism are likely to provoke countercharges of oversensitivity, much as complaints about racism or anti-Semitism did in bygone generations. As Andrew Greeley writes, anti-Catholicism is so insidious "precisely because it is not acknowledged, not recognized, not explicitly and self-consciously rejected."[3] The attitudes are so ingrained as to be invisible.

Even more outrageous than verbal remarks have been protests and demonstrations directed against Catholic institutions. Two notorious examples involved protests in venerated churches. In 1989, several thousand protesters led by the AIDS activist group ACT UP demonstrated during a mass at New York's St. Patrick's Cathedral. A hundred and thirty protesters demonstrated in the church itself, stopping mass and forcing Cardinal John O'Connor to abandon his sermon. O'Connor was loudly denounced as a "bigot" and a "murderer." Demonstrators fell down in the aisles to simulate death, while condoms were thrown. Among the slogans chanted by protesters were "You say, don't fuck; we say, fuck you!" and "Stop killing us! Stop killing us! We're not going to take it anymore!" Placards read "The Cardinal lies to his parishioners." Most harrowing from a Catholic perspective, one protester grabbed a communion wafer—to a believer, literally the body of Christ—and threw it to the floor. One enthusiastic supporter of the demonstration boasted that the action "violated sacred space, transgressed sacred ritual and offended sensibilities."[4]

In 2000, a similar outbreak occurred in Montreal, when twenty ski-masked members of a Feminist Autonomous Collective interrupted a mass in the Catholic cathedral of Marie, Reine du Monde. They spray-painted on the church "Religion—A Trap for Fools," sprayed atheist and anarchist graffiti on the altar, and tried unsuccessfully to overturn the tabernacle, which contains the sacred Host. Demonstrators stuck used sanitary napkins on pictures and walls, threw condoms around the sanctuary, and shouted pro-abortion slogans. They also destroyed or removed hundreds of hymnbooks or missals.[5]

Quite as remarkable as the events themselves was the coverage they received in the media, and the general lack of outrage. One would have thought that the element of book burning in the Canadian incident should have aroused powerful memories of religious hatred in bygone eras. Yet remarkably few U.S. or even Canadian newspapers so much as reported this event. Both stories, moreover, have rather faded from popular memory in a way they would not have done if other religious or racial groups had been targeted. Imagine, for instance, that a group wishing to protest the actions of the state of Israel had occupied or desecrated an American synagogue, particularly during some time of special holiness such as Yom Kippur. The act would unquestionably have been described by the familiar label of "hate crime," and the activists' political motivation would not have saved them from widespread condemnation. Depending on the scale of the violence, the political content of the act might even push it into the category of terrorism. The synagogue attack

would be cited for years after as an example of the evils of religious hatred and bigotry, in marked contrast to the near oblivion that has be-
fallen the anti-Catholic protests. This kind of analogy helps explain why
Jewish organizations have been so notably sensitive to incidents like the
St. Patrick's affair, far more so than the secular media.

We can draw parallels with a 1996 incident in which employees of a
Denver radio station stormed into a mosque, playing the national an-
them on bugle and trumpet. Public outcry was enormous, and thousands of citizens gathered to protest the attack; the story gained media
attention both nationally and globally. The radio station issued a grovel-
ing apology and agreed to provide "sensitivity training" for its personnel,
as well as offering reparations to local Muslims. Yet this moronic prank
was probably less traumatic than the cathedral attacks, since it did not
include the same kind of highly targeted assaults on venerated objects as
did the Catholic incidents. (While Muslims have no less sense of the sacred, they do not share Catholic sensibilities about the sanctity of conse-
crated places of worship.)[6]

| The Thinking Man's Anti-Semitism

Almost as troubling as the sheer abundance of anti-Catholic rhetoric is
the failure to acknowledge it as a serious social problem. In the media,
Catholicism is regarded as a perfectly legitimate target, the butt of harsh
satire in numerous films and television programs that attack Catholic
opinions, doctrines, and individual leaders. Arguably, such depictions
are legitimate expressions of free speech and stand within America's long
tradition of quite savage satire, but the same tolerance of abuse does not
apply when other targets are involved. It would be interesting to take a
satirical or comic treatment featuring, say, the Virgin Mary or Pope John
Paul II and imagine the reaction if a similar gross disrespect was applied,
say, to the image of Martin Luther King Jr or of Matthew Shepard, the gay
college student murdered in Laramie, Wyoming, in 1998. What sometimes seems to be limitless social tolerance in modern America has strict
limits where the Catholic Church is concerned.

Since the 1950s, changing cultural sensibilities have made it ever more
difficult to recite once-familiar American stereotypes about the great
majority of ethnic or religious groups, while issues of gender and sexual
orientation are also treated with great sensitivity. At least in public discourse, a general sensitivity is required, so that a statement that could be
regarded as misogynistic, anti-Semitic, or homophobic would haunt a
speaker for years, and could conceivably destroy a public career. Yet there
is one massive exception to this rule, namely, that it is still possible to

make quite remarkably hostile or vituperative public statements about one major religious tradition, namely, Roman Catholicism, and those comments will do no harm to the speaker's reputation. No one expects that outrageous statements or acts should receive any significant response, that (for example) performances of Kushner's *Angels in America* should be picketed.

Assessing the scale or seriousness of any kind of prejudice is extraordinarily difficult, but Peter Viereck described "Catholic-baiting" as "the anti-Semitism of the liberals," a phrase that sometimes appears as "the thinking man's anti-Semitism."[7] At first sight, this analogy seems unnecessarily provocative. It invites the obvious question of whether anti-Catholicism been responsible for the deaths of millions of innocent people in the same way that anti-Jewish prejudice undeniably has. The Nazis murdered millions of Catholics in Poland and elsewhere, but in the vast majority of cases, they acted on the grounds of their victims' nationality or politics rather than their religion. And while Communist regimes in Europe and East Asia murdered and tortured millions of Catholic believers, the persecutions did not come close to the kind of near annihilation that Jews suffered in the Holocaust. Is the anti-Semitic analogy not hyperbolic and incendiary?[8]

Obviously, I am drawing no comparison between modern American cultural phenomena and the exterminationist anti-Semitism of Europe in the 1930s and 1940s. Still, a quite proper analogy can be drawn between the history of anti-Semitism and anti-Catholicism within the United States itself. Let us compare like with like. In some periods, American anti-Semitism has been rampant, and even violent, but religious prejudice in the United States has been directed at least as often against Catholics as against Jews, and anti-Catholic vitriol has more frequently been central to party politics. Viewed against the broad context of American history, the intensity of anti-Jewish hatred in American life during the 1930s and 1940s looks anomalous, an odd departure from the customary cultural themes. Past and present, analogies between the two "antis" are closer than we might think. Yet while anti-Semitism is all but universally condemned, anti-Catholicism is widely tolerated.

Anti-ism

In one crucial area, anti-Catholicism is different from other prejudices, and this difference is commonly used to justify the kinds of remarks and displays described. While a hostile comment about Jews or blacks is directed at a community, an attack on Catholicism is often targeted at an institution, and it is usually considered legitimate to attack an institution. Someone who speaks of "the evil Catholic Church" can defend this view as a comment on the leadership and policies of the institution without necessarily denouncing ordinary Catholic people. That phrase cannot immediately be cited as bigotry in tandem with a slur on "the evil Jewish community" or "America's evil black population." From this point of view, the proper parallel for an attack on the Catholic Church would be (say) with a denunciation of the National Association for the Advancement of Colored People. Since this would not of itself constitute bigotry, neither should an attack on the Catholic Church. This distinction between institution and community also helps explain the relative lack of social reaction to anti-Catholic venom. As Andrew Greeley writes, "The reason that most Catholics are not concerned about anti-Catholicism is that they are not hurting."[9]

Yet this distinction between institution and people is a very weak defense. Unlike those other instances, the institution of the Church is fundamental to the Catholic religion, and it is disingenuous to pretend otherwise. The NAACP is simply not central to black cultural identity in the way that the Church defines Catholicism. The Pope may be the institutional head of a gigantic political and corporate entity, but for hundreds of millions of people, he is also a living symbol of their faith. Moreover, if the Catholic Church as an institution is so wicked, so homicidal, what does that say about the people who believe deeply in it, for whom it provides the vital organizing principle of their lives, the basis of their social identity? Anti-Church sentiment leads naturally to contempt for practicing or believing Catholics, whose faith must reflect emotional weakness, internal repression, or unnatural subservience to authority. The *National Lampoon* once featured a parody of multiple-choice exams, in which one question read "Only a very ___ person believes in Catholicism." There were four possible answers, *a* through *d,* all of which offered the same word to fill in the gap: *stupid.*

At the outset, we need a reliable definition of what is meant by the term "anti-Catholic." Obviously, not every statement attacking a Catholic doctrine or stance is ipso facto a form of bigotry. Not even the most extreme Catholic traditionalist believes that everything the institutional Church does is beyond debate, still less the acts and words of every individual Church leader. Traditionalists themselves are likely to have very hostile words for recent Church policies, and for particular bishops or cardinals. In Boston in 2002, the scandal over sexual abuse by clergy provoked savage criticism of the city's Catholic leader, Cardinal Bernard F. Law, as conservatives and liberals vied with each other to show the greater zeal in demanding his resignation. Even when the Catholic Church was much less liberal than it is today, Catholic writers freely acknowledged that throughout history, particular priests, bishops, and even popes had committed terrible blunders or outright crimes. Catholics have never claimed a privilege against self-criticism.

Of its nature, the Catholic Church is also more exposed to criticism because of the breadth of outlook that in other respects is one of its proudest boasts. Far more than most churches or denominations, Catholicism offers a comprehensive social vision, and claims the right to speak authoritatively on any and all issues affecting the human condition. In a more secular modern world, though, that ambitious position means potentially treading on a great many toes. The Catholic stance is a continuing affront to upholders of the powerful contemporary idea that religion is fine so long as it is held privately, on an individualistic basis.[10]

Many people strenuously oppose the positions taken by the Catholic Church on social and political issues without needing to attack that religion as such or wishing to insult its theology. Abortion, contraception, genetic research, school vouchers, marriage annulments—all are issues on which the Church has positions that are unpopular with substantial sections of the American people. Some of these ideas also provoke strenuous dissent within the Catholic community itself, where a growing number of believers classify themselves as members of a loyal opposition. Within the Church, and passionately committed to its interests, there are Catholics who dissent from official teachings on such key issues as contraception, homosexuality, the ordination of women, and clerical celibacy. It is not anti-Catholic simply to assert that the Church's position on a given issue is dead wrong, nor that Bishop X or Cardinal Y is a monster or a menace to the public good. Just because a given Catholic group is offended by a particular cause or policy stance does not automatically place that idea within the realm of bigotry. This was the position taken by William Donohue, president of the Catholic League for Religious and Civil Rights, who is quick to take umbrage at perceived slurs against the Church. Responding to the media coverage of the clergy abuse scandals, though, he wrote, "There's nothing biased about hanging the dirty laundry of an institution out for the public to see. People who love the Church want to get rid of the problem, and the way to get rid of the problem is to be informed." When confronted with a problem of this gravity, the most effective way to damage Catholic interests would be to withhold or suppress legitimate criticism. This would also be the position of the liberal reformist group Voice of the Faithful, formed in direct response to the abuse crisis in New England.[11]

We also need to recognize that the charge of anti-Catholicism is as

open to misuse as any other accusation of bias or bigotry. To take a hypothetical example, imagine a Catholic diocese that has been repeatedly affected by scandals involving sexual or financial fraud, and in which it is
clear that a bishop has simply ignored the persistent problems around
him. If the local news media were to expose the abuses and demand reform, it is conceivable that diocesan authorities would argue that their
critics were anti-Catholic, and such an argument would have carried a
great deal of weight in most periods prior to, say, the 1980s. The regular-
ity with which Church authorities played this card in bygone days helps
explain modern skepticism about the whole notion of anti-Catholicism.

So when does a statement or act plausibly make the transition from
criticism to bigotry, to "anti-ism"? Once again, we can see a useful parallel in the concept of anti-Semitism. Nobody would complain if a news
outlet accurately reported the criminal activities of an individual who
was Jewish. On the other hand, most observers would complain bitterly
if the media outlet in question proposed that this form of criminality was
peculiarly characteristic of Jews or arose from features of Jewish religion
or ethnicity. It would be still worse to report a given crime or misdeed
alongside real or imaginary instances of Jewish misdeeds through the
centuries, implying that "this is what Jews do, this is what they are like."
That would be frank anti-Semitism.

To take another Jewish example, criticisms of the state or government
of Israel are not of themselves anti-Semitic, even if they allege wide-
ranging crimes or misdeeds by that nation. Human infallibility is a concept unknown to Judaism, and even a Jewish nation can err badly, as can
specific leaders. Many Jews are severely critical of Israeli politicians such
as Ariel Sharon or Benjamin Netanyahu. Yet over the last few years, especially in Europe, criticisms of Israel have tended to develop into quite
vicious anti-Semitic attacks, deploying the full range of traditional stereotypes. This is particularly true in visual displays, in which the Star of
David is juxtaposed with swastikas or shown symbolically dominating
the world. However justified anti-Israel criticisms may be on specific occasions, this rhetoric can serve as a highly sensitive detonator for anti-
Semitism. Again, the core argument is that this is the sort of thing that
Jews can be expected to do.

If we generalize these principles, we can say that is quite legitimate to
attack an individual or an institution, even if these are religious in nature. It is a quite different matter to say that some essential features of
that religion give rise to evil or abuse and that the evil cannot be prevented without fundamentally changing the beliefs or practices of the religion. It is not anti-Catholic to remark that Bishop A or Cardinal B is

dishonest or criminal. It is more questionable to describe these actions as characteristic of a large body of Catholics or to claim that the behavior arises from ideas and practices fundamental to Catholicism.

Perhaps some religious or political systems are so aberrant in their very nature that they do inevitably produce evil consequences. Most of us would happily concur with this view of Nazism, say, and would have no problem in accepting the overarching label "anti-Nazi." But very few would argue overtly that a whole religion is evil in the same way. With few exceptions—such as a handful of notoriously violent cults—religions are usually held to be worthy of respect by outsiders. Condemning a whole religion is commonly, and reasonably, perceived as bigotry. This reluctance to stigmatize religious traditions was evident following the appalling terrorist attacks in the United States in September 2001, when political leaders, the mass media, and civil liberties groups allied to resist attacks on Islam. Any public remark suggesting that Islam was intrinsically connected with violence and terrorism was deemed racist, prejudiced, and unacceptable, while sporadic assaults on Muslim institutions met with widespread condemnation. As with anti-Semitism, public opinion was expected to reject any attempt to denounce a religion on the grounds of the misdeeds of some of its members. Commonly, this kind of bigotry is seen as a fundamental betrayal of American values.

This campaign in the name of tolerance is remarkable when set next to the blanket denunciations all too often visited upon Catholicism. Ironically, the September massacres resulted in some remarkable tirades not against the religion of Islam but against Catholicism, though the actual Catholic linkage to the attacks was nonexistent. In the *New York Press,* Michelangelo Signorile somehow used Islamist fanatic Osama bin Laden as a means of denouncing "the gay-bashing Pope." John Paul, too, was "another omnipotent religious zealot, one who equally condemns us Western sinners and incites violence with his incendiary rhetoric. ... Christian fundamentalist extraordinaire and a man who inspires thugs across the globe who commit hate crimes against homosexuals, a form of terrorism if ever there was one." Signorile later included the Catholic cardinals among the religious right who constituted "the real American Taliban." Writing in the *San Francisco Examiner,* Kimberly Blaker noted, "The irony is that the Islamic terrorists responsible for the September 11 fatalities are merely clones of America's own Christian Right extremists, sheathed in a different religion." She made it clear that she considered the Catholic Church the heart of the lunatic "religious right." It is difficult to know how to characterize these views except in terms of rank anti-Catholicism.[12]

The problem of differential sensitivity is also illustrated by another post–September 11 episode that occurred in a high school in Sharon, Massachusetts. As the school prepared for its 2001 Halloween celebration, teachers were instructed to watch carefully for any costumes that might indicate anti-Arab or anti-Muslim sentiment. Fortunately, no such issues arose, allowing the teachers to relax and enjoy the event. A panel of teachers then gave the "most comical costume" award to a group of three boys, two of whom were dressed as pregnant nuns, the third as their priest and impregnator. The fact that high schoolers can behave obnoxiously need surprise nobody, but what is amazing about this affair is that no adult thought that the display might conceivably be taken as offensive or bigoted.[13]

Shades of Bigotry

Most of the examples of anti-Church sentiment discussed here can be categorized as anti-Catholicism, but in some instances, we should rather be speaking of anti-clericalism. This is a useful concept, though it requires some explanation. The word *anti-clericalism* is vastly better known in Continental Europe and Latin America than it is in the United States. When the word appears in U.S. periodicals, it is generally in the context of the history or contemporary politics of Latin nations.[14] Because of the very different historical heritage of these lands, clergy have traditionally occupied a privileged place in the social and political order, which makes them primary targets of popular discontent. Over the centuries, a body of stereotypes developed to characterize what clergy are generally supposed to be like. Anti-clerical imagery normally included a common package of images and insults, familiar to anyone who has ever read Geoffrey Chaucer's accounts of medieval English society. In this view, priests, monks, and friars are idle, greedy, lascivious, and hypocritical. With a handful of saintly exceptions, popes and bishops not only demonstrate these same faults, but compound them with sins of power such as greed, despotism, and megalomania. In the anti-clerical view, the clergy are not just wicked in themselves, but the enemies of public welfare and of social progress.

It is commonly secularists or socialists who express the most violent anti-clerical views, but often the same opinions can be heard from people who would happily describe themselves as Catholics, lay believers who are deeply unhappy with what they perceive as the abuses of the clergy. Although the Catholic Church has never enjoyed a legally established status in the United States, there have always been anti-clericals. Anti-clericalism is usually associated with churches that enjoy an official established relationship with the state, but it would be difficult to convince most residents of large American cities that the Catholic Church did not possess such a quasi-established status through most of the twentieth century. Catholics, in other words, can be fervent critics of their church and can be strongly anti-clerical.

These distinctions are helpful when understanding a theme that surfaces repeatedly during controversies over writings or artworks that at least some Catholics deem offensive, namely, that the artists or writers under attack objects are themselves Catholics. For many readers observing these cultural battles, the argument sounds convincing, especially when they apply analogies from other religions. It is difficult to imagine circumstances in which, say, a Jew might be described as anti-Semitic, so how can a Catholic be guilty of Catholic-bashing? On the surface, the idea seems absurd. Critics who cry "anti-Catholicism" must therefore be oversensitive and enemies of free expression: they must be demonstrating the familiar Catholic tendency toward repression and intolerance. To the contrary, I will suggest that the religious background of the offending artist certainly does not absolve a work of bigotry or bitter anti-Church animus, although we need to be careful whether we label an attitude as anti-Catholic or anti-clerical.

The argument that "Catholics can't be anti-Catholic" has been a staple of recent cultural controversies. It was heard, for instance, during the 2001 contretemps over Renee Cox's display at the Brooklyn Museum of Art. The artist portrayed herself, nude, in the role of Jesus during the Last Supper, to the horror of conservative critics such as Mayor Rudolph Giuliani and Catholic activist William Donohue. To deflate such attacks, *Salon* magazine responded, "Unfortunately for Donahue [*sic*] and Giuliani, Cox isn't guilty of prejudice (she's a lapsed Catholic herself, after all)." As Cox herself remarked, "I don't know what they're talking about, anti-Catholic. I grew up Catholic and I feel that as a Catholic and having been put through that, I have the right to critique it." A similar defense was heard when artist Andres Serrano displayed his "Piss Christ," a photograph of a crucifix submerged in a jar of his own urine. Though the work was attacked as clearly blasphemous, Serrano's defenders stressed that he was an ex-Catholic who was exploring Catholic symbolism. Commenting on such rows, art critic Eleanor Heartney stresses that "the religious right's favorite examples of 'secular humanist culture' were raised as Catholics."[15]

I have had a personal encounter with this kind of defense. In 2001, my book *Hidden Gospels* criticized radical New Testament scholar John Dominic Crossan for a political agenda that I described as, in some measure, anti-Catholic. A journalistic account of this controversy dismissed any suggestions of anti-Church polemic on the part of "Mr. Crossan, Irish by birth and a former Roman Catholic priest." The journalist clearly thought that this was a knockdown argument: a former priest cannot be anti-Catholic, least of all if he is Irish.[16]

In fact, several critical elements separate the hypothetical instances of the anti-Jewish Jew and the anti-Catholic Catholic. One obvious difference is that Catholicism is an intellectual or emotional stance rather than a matter of genes or skin color, so that it is quite possible for a person to abandon Catholicism, and even to loathe everything associated with that heritage. As Shakespeare remarked, "Heresies that men do leave / Are hated most of those they did deceive." And when people leave religions, especially faiths that demand a great deal of emotional investment, they are all the more likely to revile them as pernicious "heresies." Through the centuries, defectors from particular religions have distinguished themselves by their fanatical zeal against their former friends and colleagues. Once upon a time, there was a monk named Martin Luther. During penal times in early modern England, when the very act of saying the Catholic mass was a capital offense, the most dedicated and ruthless priest hunters were themselves recent defectors from the Church, who could usually count a good number of Catholics in their immediate family circle. Literally, in some instances, brother hunted brother.[17] Adolf Hitler himself offers a prime example of an ex-Catholic turned violent anti-Catholic bigot, one whose hatred of Catholicism led him to an even more comprehensively anti-Christian stance. Of course someone raised Catholic can be anti-Catholic.

Catholics Against the Church?

We are on quite different ground when the person accused of attacking a faith still claims to be loyal to that tradition. But such an individual can certainly be viscerally anti-clerical, accepting the range of prejudices that characterize that lively tradition, and therefore unwilling to see anything but ill in the Catholic Church or its representatives. The concept of anti-clericalism is particularly important in the United States because it reflects a potent strand of American Protestant culture, with roots in colonial times. Americans have often shown themselves resentful of clergy and of clerical attempts to influence politics, and the most successful religious movements have often been those that entrusted most power to the laity. In modern times, we think of the booming self-help and recovery movements that so conspicuously lack any kind of clerical involvement. Anti-clerical attacks find a real resonance in the social mainstream, as well as in Catholic circles.

But can people who describe themselves as loyally Catholic go beyond mere anti-clericalism, to be guilty of outright anti-Catholicism or "Catholic-bashing"? This is a sensitive issue in debates within the Church, since conservative and traditionalist groups sometimes level this charge at their liberal opponents. The most visible activist group is the Catholic League for Religious and Civil Rights, which has sought quite successfully to establish itself as a Catholic counterpart of the Jewish Anti-Defamation League. Whenever a public figure makes an anti-Catholic statement, the Catholic League protests strenuously. Some of the league's main targets, however, are avowedly Catholic, including feminist groups such as Catholics for a Free Choice (CFFC).

In consequence, liberal Catholics themselves have attacked the league's whole view that "anti-Catholicism" constitutes a pressing social problem. Feminist theologian Rosemary Radford Ruether has written that "the mantra of 'anti-Catholicism' from the Catholic Right is primarily a reflection of this internal Catholic conflict. This term is being used by the Catholic Right to claim that they and they alone are 'authentic' Catholics, and Catholics that hold progressive views are not Catholics, are hostile to 'authentic' Catholicism, and hence are 'anti-Catholic.' Furthermore, non-Catholics in the larger society who listen respectfully to the views of progressive Catholics are therefore also 'anti-Catholic.' In short, the charge of 'anti-Catholicism' is being used as a scare tactic by the Catholic Right in the service of repression of progressive Catholic views." CFFC leader Frances Kissling remarks that "for ultraconservative Catholic groups to claim that any criticism of the Catholic Church is Catholic-bashing is part of the game." Writing in the *Village Voice,* Frank Owen presents a similarly hostile view to complaints of "anti-Catholicism": "it's hardly a coincidence that the examples of so-called anti-Catholic culture that most upset activists like Donohue ... were perpetrated not by outsiders but by Catholics, or former Catholics. ... Which suggests that what's actually going on here is a heated debate over Catholic identity—a nasty civil war of ideas among conservatives and liberals, hard-line literalists and relativist semi-believers, about who is a genuine Catholic and who isn't."[18]

Given our modern historical memories of oppressive states and party systems, we have to be very careful about describing loyal critics of any system as outsiders, still less enemies. Depending on the individual case, we might see the person as drawing on anti-clerical ideas while remaining within the broader Church tradition. Throughout history, the Catholic Church has known a wide variety of opinions on quite fundamental matters of faith and practice, including papal authority, clerical celibacy, and the powers of the priesthood. One of the boasts of Catholicism through the centuries is its ability to accept the principle of development: it is always a work in progress. Let us imagine the hypothetical example of a Catholic reformer in the 1940s, say, who criticized many aspects of Catholic worship and liturgy, and advocated extensive reform. At the time, that view might be dismissed as fundamentally anti-Catholic, yet those ideas would be vindicated by the reforms of the 1960s. Far from being anti-Catholic, the reformer might today be regarded as a prophetic voice within the Church. Contemporary advocates of women's ordination or greater lay participation in Church structures assuredly believe that, in the same way, history will absolve them, too.

Yet on occasion, in any institution, internal criticism can become so hostile as to move far beyond the notion of loyal opposition. To return to the Jewish parallel, we might imagine a ludicrous example of someone speaking as a Jew and demanding basic reforms within that religion, including the abandonment of the scriptures, circumcision, the Sabbath, and dietary laws; in addition, Jews should apologize for wrongs done by them over the centuries. Even though claimed as a reform of the religion, most observers would see this critique as simply anti-Jewish and wonder how the speaker could possibly claim any loyalty to Judaism whatever. If the hyperreformer launched intemperate denunciations of every Jew who opposed his dreams, we might not be speaking of true racial anti-Semitism, but we would certainly be dealing with frank anti-Judaism.

Within Catholicism, likewise, some attacks on established doctrine are just as sweeping as this notional example. In his popular recent book, *Constantine's Sword,* James Carroll offers his agenda for the purification of a Catholic Church allegedly suffused in anti-Semitism. Among other things, he rejects virtually the whole of Christian theology, including atonement, "the inhuman idea that anyone's death can be the fulfillment of a plan of God's," and the concept of salvation. ("The coming of Jesus was for the purpose of revelation, not salvation—revelation, that is, that we are already saved.") He declares that any "Christian proclamation that says that redemption, grace, perfection, whatever you call it, has already come is unbelievable on its face." The structures of the Church are fatally flawed, and a future Vatican Council would abolish papal supremacy and eliminate the clergy as a separate caste: bishops would be elected.[19]

By any customary standard, a Catholic Church without Christ, without salvation, or without a clerical structure, would cease to be Catholic, and could scarcely be described as Christian. As the Catholic League's Robert Lockwood observes, "Rather clearly, the objective solution Carroll has in mind already exists: Unitarianism."[20] Yet for Carroll, failure to institute these "reforms" would mean not only that the Church was in theological and historical error, but that it was irredeemably tied to anti-Semitism and the massacre of Jews through the centuries. The main purpose of this reformed "Catholic" Church would be to live in a constant state of apology and penitence for the dreadful crimes it had committed. For Carroll, the Church is founded upon hatred and is in every sense a hateful institution.

If a contemporary writer advocates a total change in the nature of the religion and blames it for such appalling crimes, then it is difficult to see why he or she would continue to use the Catholic label. If that same person uses harsh, sweeping, and vindictive language to denounce the Church for failing to live up to an idiosyncratic notion of Catholicism, then it is reasonable to call that an anti-Catholic attack. While we have to be very cautious in applying the anti-Catholic label to self-described Catholics, on occasion the term is applicable.

| Hate Speech

In commenting on the ferocious attacks to which Catholics and their beliefs are subjected, I am not objecting to the fact that controversialists use stark or intemperate language. Political and religious debate over the last few decades has become anemic compared with that of previous centuries, when writers almost casually classified their opponents as the spawn of Satan. Martin Luther, one of the great heroes of European history, was a master of this slash-and-burn theory of theological debate. There is nothing wrong with polemic as such. The argument of this book is not so much that Catholicism is subjected to unjust abuse, but that it is virtually the only major institution with which such liberties are still permitted.

Just how sensitive many people have become about any kind of attacks on racial or religious groups is demonstrated by some of the legal attempts over the last two decades to regulate so-called hate speech. American courts have never accepted that speech should be wholly unrestricted, since some words might provoke dangerous or violent consequences; courts have thus upheld laws regulating "fighting words." During the 1980s, though, a variety of activists pressed for expanded laws or administrative codes that would limit or suppress speech directed against particular groups, against women, racial minorities, and homosexuals. The most ambitious, and worrying, of these speech codes were implemented on college campuses. Usually, these codes encountered heavy criticism from libertarians, as well as from the political Right, which viewed them as gross manifestations of political correctness. Most codes have since been struck down by the federal courts on grounds of overbreadth: in order to achieve desirable social goals, states and particularly colleges were infringing severely on permissible public discourse and on First Amendment rights. Even so, those who originally advocated speech codes remained unrepentant and attacked the courts for their alleged failure to protect minorities. A substantial section of liberal and radical opinion not only favors limiting the right to criticize minorities and other interest groups, but believes that this regulation should be enforced by stringent legislation.[21]

The relevance of these debates to the anti-Catholicism issue is obvious when we look at the language of some of these recent codes. If these provisions had been upheld in the courts, what would they have meant for recent Catholic controversies? One typical university code defines hate speech "as any verbal speech, harassment, and/or printed statements which can provoke mental and/or emotional anguish for any member of the . . . University community." Nothing in the code demands evidence that the offended person is a normal, average character not oversensitive to insult. According to the speech codes, the fact of "causing anguish" is sufficient. Since the various codes placed so much emphasis on the likelihood of causing offense, rather than the intent of the act or speech involved, the codes might well have criminalized artworks such as Serrano's "Piss Christ."[22]

The element of "causing offense" is generally central to speech codes. At the University of Michigan, a bellwether for the academic world, a proposed code would have prohibited "any behavior, verbal or physical, that stigmatizes or victimizes an individual on the basis of race, ethnicity, religion, sex, sexual orientation, creed, national origin, ancestry, age, marital status, handicap, or Vietnam-era veteran status." "Stigmatization and victimization" are defined less by any objective criteria than by the subjective feelings of the individuals or groups who felt threatened. Though this criterion is not spelled out, these codes imply that the targets of harassment should be groups who have at some point experienced discrimination or violence, so that it would still be legitimate to denounce powerful categories such as the rich or corporate executives. In terms of American history, the obvious categories to be protected on the basis of past discrimination would include blacks, Jews, homosexuals, Native Americans—and, logically, Catholics.[23]

Although these speech codes are probably unenforceable, some sweeping "hate" statutes have been sustained. In 1992, the U.S. Supreme Court upheld a local bias crime statute that prohibited the display of a symbol that one knows or has reason to know "arouses anger, alarm or resentment in others on the basis of race, color, creed, religion or gender."

The implied reference is obviously to a swastika or a burning cross, but as it is written, the criterion is that the symbol causes "anger, alarm or resentment" to some unspecified person. There is abundant evidence that these were precisely the reactions of many Catholic believers who saw or read about "Piss Christ" or the controversial displays at the Brooklyn Museum of Art.[24]

One key justification for hate speech laws is that speech is very difficult to separate from conduct and that creating a hostile climate for a particular group often leads to actual discrimination or violence—for example, to gay-bashing or racist violence.[25] When a violent incident occurs, such as the murder of Matthew Shepard, activists seek to link the act to those who had expressed anti-gay opinions over the previous years, or to those who opposed pro-gay-rights legislation. Hateful words have hateful consequences, and the speakers should not escape the blame. Again, there is no obvious reason why Catholics should be exempt from protection on these same grounds. Although they receive next to no media publicity, attacks on Catholic churches and properties do occur quite frequently, often in circumstances that suggest specifically anti-religious intent. In 1999 and 2000, a series of church desecrations in Brooklyn left religious statues decapitated and defaced, and hate mail left no doubt of the sacrilegious intent. If hate speech contributes to hate crime, why should anti-Catholic speech not be regulated?[26]

In the area of hate crime as much as hate speech, Catholics receive fewer protections than other groups. Many jurisdictions have hate crime laws, which usually carry severe penalties. On the surface, there seems no reason why such laws should not have been invoked in response to the outrageous demonstrations at the Catholic cathedrals in New York City and Montreal, or the Brooklyn church desecrations. In practice though, we rarely hear suggestions that hate crime laws should be invoked in such cases. When Montreal's cathedral was attacked, Quebec police announced that the province's stringent hate crime law would not be invoked against people who "in good faith" attempt "to establish by argument an opinion on a religious subject."[27] Nor were hate crime laws invoked in the Brooklyn case, in which the perpetrator received five years of probation with no jail time. Legally, though, it is all but impossible to define hate crime or hate speech without including these acts, or many others at which Catholics have taken offense. Why are Catholics not judged worthy of protection under these laws?

I am not arguing for the extension of hate speech codes or hate crime laws, which, in my view, are already far too wide-ranging and ill-defined. But the highly selective nature of such regulations amply illustrates the common failure to treat the large and pervasive phenomenon of anti-Catholicism as an authentic social problem.

| The Catholic Problem

For many people in the United States—particularly for opinion-makers in the mass media and in the academic world—Catholicism neither needs nor deserves the kind of protections that apply to other religious traditions. To the contrary, many observers hold the view that Catholicism, and specifically the organized Church, is itself a problem, a major opponent of social progress. In this assessment, the Church is a haven of reaction, especially on matters of gender and sexuality, and it deserves little sympathy when it is attacked because, frankly, it is so dependably on the wrong side.

One goal of this book is to describe just how this notion of Catholicism-as-problem developed, especially over the last thirty years or so. We must distinguish between the general historical fact of anti-Catholicism and its current manifestations. Anti-Catholicism as such has a very long pedigree in North America. Indeed, the idea predates the creation of the United States, and much of the country's social and political development in the nineteenth century would have been radically different had this force not existed. To take one example, the whole American party system would likely have developed on very different lines.[28]

I have spoken of contemporary Catholicism as a social problem not because I personally view the Church as a threat or a menace, but because this religious tradition is so widely viewed in such negative terms. For many activists, Catholicism is indeed a problem to be solved, an obstacle to be overcome. We can learn something here from the large sociological literature on social problems, which are defined not by any intrinsic quality they possess, but by the reactions they inspire in others. If, for instance, most of a society considers witchcraft a pervasive threat, then we can legitimately speak of a witchcraft problem, whether or not we believe that witches really exist. What is it about Catholicism and its enemies that have shaped the "Catholic problem" as it is constructed in the contemporary United States?[29]

Societies differ dramatically on what themes or issues they rank as social problems, and problems can rise or fall over time. One society might consider homosexuality a major problem, another might focus on sexual harassment, another on alcohol consumption. Forty years ago, homosexuality was generally considered a pressing social problem in America, whereas today, far more people are concerned with the problem of homophobia, or opposition to that same behavior. In trying to understand these shifts of emphasis, social scientists pay close attention to the changing role of interest groups and how these use new problems to defend and advance their interests. To take an obvious example, a society in which women have substantial political and economic power is likely to be far more concerned about issues such as sexual violence and abuse than one in which women are largely confined to domestic roles. As we will see, the changing shape of anti-Catholicism tells us a great deal about shifting social roles and expectations in American society.

Theorists also study activists and moral entrepreneurs, those individuals and groups who try to formulate social problems, to tell society what it should be most concerned about at any time. Whether these activists succeed depends on how well they shape their messages according to the groups to whom they are seeking to appeal, and how far they can present these messages in convincing terms. Claims makers use a well-established repertoire of techniques to frame these problems in the most broadly appealing way. These rhetorical themes are amply illustrated by the civil rights struggles waged by African-Americans over the last century, in which activists portrayed injustice in terms of symbolic events and individuals, using richly coded words such as lynching, Scottsboro, Selma, and so on. Problems are presented through mythologized narratives that include starkly dichotomized visions of heroes and villains. Decades after the events occurred, debates about race still commonly invoke the names of figures such as Martin Luther King Jr and Bull Connor, just as gay rights rhetoric harks back to the hallowed name of Stonewall. Ironically, in view of the supposed secularization of American society, the most potent narratives are often those that appeal to underlying religious assumptions, that draw on images of martyrdom or crucifixion, of righteous victims and evil Pharisees. Witness the crucifixion imagery in media accounts of the death of Matthew Shepard.

| Summoning Demons

Often, a hostile organization or group comes to symbolize not just an agglomeration of individuals, but a cause, an enemy, which is labeled with the worst attributes that can be found in the imagery familiar to that culture. This is the process known as stereotyping or demonization, and it is familiar from America's long history of ethnic and religious conflict. Once such stereotypes are established, they become increasingly detached from this or that specific individual and acquire an enduring cultural reality of their own. As interest groups rise or fall in society, they often identify new enemies, so studying a society's changing folk devils is a valuable tool of social analysis.

Against this background, we can trace how the "Catholic problem" has changed its nature over time. In the nineteenth and early twentieth centuries, anti-Catholicism had an obvious class and ethnic appeal, since new ethnic and religious groups represented both an economic and cultural challenge to established groups. Successive activists and agitators could create alarm by warning the native-born how a rising Catholic population could threaten their wealth and their political hegemony. Claims makers employed a well-established common fund of knowledge and stereotypes about Catholic behavior, which drew variously on religious polemic and historical mythology. Popes offered splendid demon figures in this respect, as did conventional nightmare images such as the Inquisition, the seducing priest in the confessional, and the fires in which Catholic states had murdered countless Protestant martyrs over the centuries.

The traumatic changes in American society during the 1960s created a new range of insurgent interest groups, most obviously feminists and gay rights activists. In many areas, these groups found themselves at odds with the Roman Catholic Church, to the extent that they increasingly defined their own ideological positions in opposition to that religious tradition. In seeking to discredit the Church that was their primary political enemy, radicals constructed a new anti-Catholicism that was more relevant to them than the old ideas based on class and ethnicity, and that laid more stress on themes of gender and sexuality. However, the new formulation coincided at many points with the older body of stereotypes that were so ingrained in the public consciousness—inevitably, since these images had circulated for so many years.

Modern anti-Catholicism differs in significant ways from older models. Above all, while the older tradition was primarily nativist, xenophobic, and politically right-wing, the modern distaste for Catholicism is primarily found on the left/liberal side of the spectrum, especially among feminists and gay activists. This liberal coloring has reshaped the tradition in other ways, too. Whereas many earlier critics loathed the Roman Catholic Church for its alleged betrayals of Christian and biblical truth, such an explicitly religious critique is of little interest to modern secular liberals. As we will see, though, some liberal and feminist writings on the early Church do draw on this notion of the Church as the betrayers of the authentic message of Jesus.

And there are other differences. While in earlier eras of intense religious conflict, such as the 1850s or the 1920s, anti-Catholic activists were deeply opposed to mass immigration, modern critics of Catholicism are favorable or neutral on immigration issues. This may seem curious given the fact that so many of the Latino and Asian migrants who have entered the United States in recent years are Catholic. Contemporary anti-Catholicism is not usually directed against Catholics as individuals or as population groups, however, but rather against the ideas and teachings of the Church. This is important because that makes it much easier for anti-Church activists to appeal to dissident Catholics themselves, who draw on the parallel ideology of anti-clericalism.[30] Moreover, the issues of substance in contemporary anti-Catholicism differ greatly from those that troubled previous generations. While traditional anti-Catholic rhetoric addressed issues of national and international politics and alleged threats of Catholic political dominance, the newer concerns are centered on personal and moral dilemmas, issues such as sexual identity, abortion, and contraception. All, of course, have their partisan implications.

Yet having noted all these differences, we can still perceive definite continuities with older ideas, particularly in the stereotypes that emerged during successive controversies. However different the roots of modern anti-Catholic activism, with its liberal and feminist affinities, the imagery would have been broadly familiar to nativist Protestants a century or two ago. In film especially, wicked Catholic clergy look very much like their counterparts in hostile tracts from bygone years, with tyrannical cardinals, homicidal bishops, and depraved priests. Especially in the coverage of child abuse by clergy, the media have presented a panoply of very traditional anti-clerical imagery, attacking clergy as sexually repressed hypocrites. The lesson seems to be that although the political environment may have changed, there is something very powerful, very resonant, in this versatile cultural imagery, which allows it to serve the interests of a remarkable range of constituencies.

The shifting nature of the "Catholic problem" helps explain the very different attitudes that society demonstrates toward this form of religious prejudice, in contrast to other kinds of bigotry that superficially seem so similar. Since the 1960s, American politics has been dominated by issues of identity, conceived in terms of gender, ethnicity, and sexual orientation. In conventional argument, racism, sexism, homophobia, and anti-ethnic prejudice are all social problems, grave manifestations of a broader social phenomenon that is characterized as "hate" or bigotry. In keeping with other social movements through the centuries, rising groups have tried to express their newfound power through legislative change, notably the prohibition of discrimination and hate speech. As we have seen, anti-Catholicism should logically be categorized together with these other species of "hate," but the political context has ensured that this particular kind of bias receives quite different treatment. Often, it is not anti-Catholicism that is presented as a glaring social problem, but rather Catholicism itself, the religion of almost a quarter of all Americans. If only because of the sheer numbers involved, anti-Catholicism must be seen as the great unknown "anti-ism" or phobia, the most significant unconfronted prejudice in modern America.[31]

2 | The Catholic Menace

Abhor that arrant Whore of Rome,
And all her blasphemies;
And drink not of her cursed cup,
Obey not her decrees.

— New England Primer, 1688

The Catholic system is adverse to liberty, and the clergy
to a great extent are dependent on foreigners opposed to
the principles of our government, for patronage and
support.

— Lyman Beecher, *Plea for the West*

In 1977, Andrew Greeley described anti-Catholicism as an "ugly little secret" of American history. Ugly perhaps, but a great deal of scholarship in the intervening years has ensured that this particular form of prejudice is anything but secret. Arthur Schlesinger Sr. has called it "the deepest bias in the history of the American people." John Higham has aptly described anti-Catholicism as "the most luxuriant, tenacious tradition of paranoiac agitation in American history." Over the decades, the grounds put forward to prove just why Catholicism is so pernicious, so threatening, have shifted, but fundamental to all the attacks has been the notion that Catholicism is un- and anti-American. As the notion of Americanism has gone through periodic transformations over time, so has the popular concept of the religious tradition that supposedly represents its darkest negation. Modern anti-Catholicism is built upon these multiple layers of ideological precedent.[1]

Mother of Harlots

Through most of American history, anti-Catholicism has been an exceedingly potent force that often shaped political allegiances. Through the end of the nineteenth century, many Americans believed their country had a specially ordained role in divine providence, and specifically religious critiques of Catholicism enjoyed real force. At least through the nineteenth century, many Protestants accepted that the Roman church was the monstrous creature prophesied in the Book of Revelation, Babylon the great, the "mother of harlots" clothed in purple and scarlet, who held in her hand "a golden cup full of abominations." The Pope, evidently, was the Antichrist. American publishers poured forth books and pamphlets with hair-raising titles such as *The Trial of the Pope of Rome: The Antichrist, or man of sin ... for high treason against the son of God.*[2]

Though now rarely heard in respectable discourse, these ideas have never entirely vanished, and they survive today. Isolated propagandists continue to circulate anti-papal and anti-Catholic mythologies, presenting the Church as the hidden hand behind the world's governments and financial systems. The best-known such activist is Jack Chick, whose tracts and comics continue to promulgate bizarre allegations of Catholic conspiracy and sexual hypocrisy. A little more respectable is the fundamentalist church that sponsors Bob Jones University, in South Carolina, which made headlines in 2000 when it hosted presidential candidate George W. Bush. The school teaches that Mormonism and Catholicism are both cults unrelated to genuine Christianity. Bob Jones Jr describes the Catholic Church as "a Satanic counterfeit, an ecclesiastic tyranny over the souls of men, not to bring them to salvation but to hold them bound in sin and to hurl them into eternal damnation. It is the old harlot of the Book of the Revelation—'the Mother of Harlots.' ... She is drunk with the blood of the saints of God whom she has harassed and persecuted, imprisoned, massacred and destroyed. The monstrous abomination which is Rome has, like a vampire, fattened upon the lifeblood of men and nations. Constantly changing her masks but never her nature, she has infiltrated where she could not command and adapted when she could not enforce." The coming of the World Wide Web has given a new platform to exponents of such radically anti-papist ideas.[3]

Although this kind of hysterical rhetoric is unfashionable among mainstream evangelicals, some nevertheless retain serious suspicions of the Roman church. This became evident during the 1990s, when prominent evangelical and Catholic leaders declared their points of agreement on significant social and theological issues. The very fact that evangelicals were acknowledging Catholics as Christians and as members of a bona fide church was itself a dramatic testimony to the decline of older Protestant hostility. Evangelicals were agreeing that Catholics should be exempt from the kind of missionary endeavors that should properly be devoted to pagans and adherents of other faiths. Even so, these friendly statements drew widespread anger from Protestant fundamentalists. Generally, their anti-ecumenical statements are presented in a sober and reasoned way and cannot be classified with the kind of strident nativist prejudice that so often marks anti-Catholic propaganda. Still, they indicate the continued existence of an anti-Catholic rhetoric with a wider popular foundation than might be suspected from its absence in the mainstream media.[4]

English and Protestant

Explicitly religious arguments against Catholicism were inextricably linked with Anglo-American political ideologies, in which the Catholic Church represented the denial of personal liberty. Already in the seventeenth century, English and American Protestants shared an elaborate mythology about Catholic misdeeds that almost amounted to a national foundation myth. Elements included the burnings of Protestant martyrs under Queen Mary, the Spanish Armada, and the Irish massacres of Protestants in 1641. Catholicism was actively anti-Christian; it was associated with fanaticism and tyranny, oppression and ignorance. The Catholic association with underhand conspiracy was best expressed in the national loathing of the Jesuits. English (and American) freedom was defined against the feared alien force of Catholicism, which was ritually condemned each year in the symbolic November burnings of the Pope and of conspirator Guy Fawkes. When the English passed their Bill of Rights in 1689, the clause that would ultimately become the basis of the American Second Amendment declared "that the subjects *which are Protestant* may have arms for their defense" (my emphasis).[5]

Catholicism was clearly identified as a foreign evil, a dire threat to Anglo-American notions of national identity and independence. As has so often occurred in modern history, an emerging nationalism was strengthened by denouncing an alien force, to which a wide variety of evil characteristics could be attributed. Historian Linda Colley has shown how, through the eighteenth century, the stereotyping of hostile Catholic France and Spain did much to create the whole ideology of British nationalism.[6]

Often, religious prejudice was buttressed by sinister ethnic stereotypes, as the Catholic Irish were denigrated as a treacherous enemy race.
Catholicism was also associated with all the evils that the English credited to people of Latin stock. In Elizabethan and Jacobean plays, Italian
and Spanish settings gave authors full opportunity to explore bizarre
fantasy images of clergy and cardinals as depraved sadists. In John Webster's play *The Duchess of Malfi*, the Cardinal is a vengeful plotter who deploys a legion of spies and assassins:

> Where he is jealous of any man,
> He lays worse plots for him than ever was imposed on
> Hercules, for he strews in his way flatterers, panders,
> Intelligencers, atheists, and a thousand such political
> Monsters.

Such clerical conspiracies produce murder, usually in some outrageously
devious and underhand manner—tools might include the poison ring,
the poisoned crucifix, the stiletto blade hidden in the monk's sleeve.
Anti-Latin stereotypes also had a strong sexual element: in Stuart England, one common euphemism for a pederast was "Italianate." These literary images affected perceptions of actual Catholic believers, who were
seen as un-English in their baffling subservience to the clergy, and the
taste for emotional and foreign imagery and devotional practices. This
observation about classic literature would be of only historical interest, if
strikingly similar imagery of conspiracy and secret murder had not appeared more or less overtly in much more recent portrayals of Catholic
misdeeds, including modern films such as *The Godfather III* or *Stigmata*.
Webster's ghost still walks.[7]

Obvious analogies exist between the British traditions of anti-Catholicism and the common Continental theme of anti-Semitism. In both instances, the imagined outside enemy subverts accepted standards of
decent behavior, including through sexual contamination; he operates
clandestinely in order to take over and destroy the decent Christian society; and he is a sinister cosmopolitan. English Catholics faced very much
the same charge of divided loyalties that European Jews would face
throughout the twentieth century. The enemy is also to blame for unex-
plained catastrophes. While European Jews were blamed for unleashing
the Black Death by poisoning wells, so English Catholics were obviously
responsible for setting the Great Fire of London in 1666. "The treachery
and malice" of the Catholic arsonists were memorialized in a monument
that stood on the site for 150 years afterward. Anti-Semitism lost much
of its power in England during the long exclusion of Jews from that

country, which lasted from 1290 to 1655, but anti-Catholicism emerged to fill the gap. Bigotry abhors a vacuum.[8]

The two movements will often be found moving in parallel, in the United States as much as England. As recently as 2001, the major publishing house of HarperCollins published F. Tupper Saussy's book *Rulers of Evil*. This purports to offer "proof of a vast Roman Catholic substratum of American history—more specifically, that Jesuits played eminent and under-appreciated roles in persuading New Englanders to rebel against their mother country in 1776. ... [T]he American Revolution and its resulting constitutional republic may have been single-handedly designed and supervised by a Jesuit named Lorenzo Ricci—this country's true founding father." Ever since, it is claimed, Catholics have pulled the strings that manipulate American public life. The trade journal *Publishers Weekly* remarked that "most will see [the book] for what it really is—an anti-Catholic version of *The Protocols of the Elders of Zion*."[9]

American Gothic

Americans inherited these anti-Catholic traditions in full, and may in fact have nurtured them even more successfully than their English cousins, because the political culture of the new nation drew so heavily on anti-authoritarian and anti-clerical traditions. Both anti-Catholic and anti-clerical activism contributed mightily to the emergence of opposition culture in colonial America, and thereby to the movement for independence. Through colonial times, religious and political conflicts in the new colonies regularly involved charges that established authorities were leaning to Catholic views or policies. Whenever a colonial governor tried to support an Episcopal church, he was obviously (from this perspective) trying surreptitiously to establish a repressive Catholicism: "priests" (the term for Episcopal as well as Catholic clerics) were ipso facto suspect. In the 1770s, the British government's tolerant policies toward the Catholic Church of the province of Quebec gave a massive stimulus to radical dissidence in New England.[10]

Hostile imagery grew after the Revolution, and in the nineteenth century traditional anti-Catholicism acquired a still more potent linkage with ethnic divisions. From the 1830s, the nation's Catholic population grew swiftly in consequence of immigration from Germany and Ireland; the shifting ethnic and religious balance was especially evident in the major cities. Nativist fury was expressed in writings such as Samuel Morse's *Foreign Conspiracy Against the Liberties of the United States* and William C. Brownlee's *Popery: An Enemy to Civil and Religious Liberty and Dangerous to Our Republic*. In the 1840s and 1850s, the nativist

Know-Nothing movement became a powerful political force that disrupted older party allegiances. The party warned its supporters, "You cannot have failed to observe the significant transition of the foreign-born and the Romanists from a character quiet, retiring, or even abject, to one bold, threatening, turbulent and even despotic."[11]

The anti-Catholic venom of nineteenth-century America is evident in some notorious and much-reprinted cartoons, such as Thomas Nast's "The American River Ganges" (1871). This evocative piece shows Catholic bishops rising threateningly from the river to menace honest Protestants, with their episcopal miters taking the form of crocodilian jaws. Particularly under threat from this assault are the impressionable young, who are being lured into this sinister doctrine (the cartoon is subtitled "The Priests and the Children"). In the background, we see the public schools in ruins, and papal flags waving over the Capitol.[12]

In some ways, urban religious conflicts at this time resemble the black-white confrontation in the United States of the 1960s and 1970s. In both eras, there was fierce economic competition, as established groups were slowly dislodged from what they thought to be their rightful monopoly on jobs and patronage. Between 1830 and 1870, America's great cities were often shaken by riots between Protestant nativists and Catholics, the latter usually Irish, with both sides organizing through armed street gangs. Overt violence subsided in later years (though it did not disappear), but anti-Catholic agitation remained powerful.[13]

Strengthening this racial analogy, the social rhetoric of the time did not initially grant the status of "white" to many of the new immigrants, first the Irish, and later the Italians and Slavs. Literally, through the end of the nineteenth century, American Catholicism was a predominantly nonwhite religion. In the first quarter of the twentieth century, religious prejudice acquired a pseudoscientific tone, as the new science of quantifying intelligence claimed to demonstrate that southern and eastern Europeans represented quite poor genetic stock—not as despicable as blacks, perhaps, but far inferior to Anglo-Saxons or Germans. Low intelligence and lack of initiative easily made these new immigrant groups natural followers, gullible adherents of childish superstition—in short, natural Catholics.[14]

The power of anti-Catholic ideology lay in its broad cross-class appeal. For the social elite, Catholicism was evidently the religion of the ignorant and fanatical, the unwashed masses who were visibly annexing cities such as Boston and New York. Well into the twentieth century, Catholics themselves could scarcely deny that the very poor were overrepresented in the American Church. In the *Baltimore Catechism*, ordinary Catholics are taught to answer "the excuses some give for not becoming members of the true church," including the statement that "there are too many poor and ignorant people in the Catholic Church." In response, Catholics were told to concede the basic fact, but to make a virtue of it. They should go on to argue that "to say there are too many poor and ignorant in the Catholic Church is to declare that it is Christ's Church; for He always taught the poor and ignorant and instructed His Church to continue the work."[15] For educated Protestants, "poor and ignorant" Catholics epitomized everything that was wrong with emerging urban-industrial America, with its blatantly corrupt political machines. Much as Catholics represented the subversion of older religious notions of America, now they signified the betrayal of another idealized vision, this time a secular liberal dream.

For the working classes, meanwhile, Catholics were above all rivals for jobs. Well into the twentieth century, America's booming industries commonly assigned promotions and privileges according to the religious and ethnic hierarchy. When the traditional economic order was upset—for instance, by the importation of Italian and Slavic strikebreakers during a labor conflict—the furious response of established groups often took a religious form. In such circumstances, as in the riots of the mid-nineteenth century, it is all but impossible to distinguish between religious, ethnic, and class grievances.[16]

| Anti-Catholicism as Anti-Cult Rhetoric

Nor can we easily disentangle hatred for the Church as an institution from the popular contempt for Catholics as a community, though the two types of prejudice were expressed somewhat differently. In understanding this, we can usefully draw parallels with the popular suspicion of religious cults during the 1970s and 1980s, when many Americans feared that their young might be seduced by alien cults, which were tarnished by political megalomania and sinister sexual practices. For Protestants of the 1870s, Catholics were quite as aberrant as the stereotypical Moonies or Hare Krishnas of a later age, and in both eras, the leaders and followers of these suspect groups were hated for very similar reasons. Priests, like later gurus and cult leaders, were obviously cynical and power-hungry, and were prepared to use their religious trickery in order to exploit their gullible subjects.

Though the ordinary faithful might be less overtly criminal than the clergy, they were just as dangerous because of their simple fanaticism and their willingness to follow their leaders blindly. As Lyman Beecher claimed in 1836, Catholic priests "at the confessional learn all the private concerns of their people, and have almost unlimited power over the conscience as it respects the performance of every civil or social duty."[17] Or as a Sinclair Lewis character noted a century later, the Church "requires you to give up your honesty, your reason, your heart and soul." In 1934, the *Harvard Journal* described the Legion of Decency as a "Catholic organization, with its regimental draft of blindly obedient underlings on the one hand, and its Machiavellian pontiff on the other." The language is almost what we might expect from accounts of later events such as Jonestown or Waco.[18]

Reinforcing the cult analogy is the centrality of threats to children in anti-Catholic rhetoric. We recall how Nast's cartoon highlighted this theme of "the priests and the children," and for centuries, Catholic clergy have been attacked for their danger to children, whether sexual (molestation) or intellectual (brainwashing). As with the comparable charges against cults, these accusations have a powerful rhetorical foundation. Since religious liberty is so fundamental to national ideals, most Americans accept the right of consenting adult individuals to choose their own faiths, however unreasonable these creeds may appear. From that perspective, the most plausible justification for banning or restricting a religious group is to argue that it poses a threat to those who cannot give full consent, namely, children.

Anti-Catholic Politics, 1870–1930

By the end of the nineteenth century, Catholics clearly had become a strong force in American life, especially in the cities, and it was not fantastic to suggest that they might someday dominate the whole country. Already by the 1850s, the Roman Catholic Church was the country's largest single religious denomination. Between 1870 and 1920, the number of priests in the United States rose from seven thousand to twenty thousand and the number of Catholic faithful from seven million to twenty million, and there was a vast network of clergy, schools, and seminaries. During the First World War the new National Catholic Welfare Conference gave the Church the nucleus of a national organization that critics saw it as a "general staff"—perhaps a provisional government? Enemies of Catholicism were especially troubled that the Church demonstrated no interest in merging or assimilating with the American mainstream. It was determined to maintain a separate and parallel range of structures, most visibly in education. Catholic leaders themselves agonized for years over whether to accept public schooling, but from the 1880s, the Church was committed to keeping children strictly separated in religious schools. Critics viewed parochial schools as centers for brainwashing and intolerance, much as some Americans today see Islamic schools. The controversy raised major doubts about the Catholic commitment to Americanization (and also focused attention on a threat to vulnerable children). Once again, Catholicism seemed opposed to a model of Americanism, this time the whole "melting pot" theory.[19]

Anti-Catholic sentiment repeatedly found expression in organized political movements, including some of the most impressive mass movements of American history. At the end of the century the American Protective Association (APA) briefly threatened to dominate national politics. At its height, the APA had seventy weekly publications nationwide, which presented a steady diet of religious prejudice laced with those tabloid staples of sex and violence. The lurid charges featured in APA's propaganda sheets, such as *The Menace*, were enough "to make any boy wonder if the priest kept beautiful young girls tied up in the confessional booths and if there was really an arsenal in the church basement." The temperance movement also drew heavily on anti-Catholic sentiment, as the drink issue increasingly became a symbolic marker distinguishing Protestant respectability from Catholic immorality. In the presidential election of 1884 Republican supporters coined a famous phrase to attack the unholy Democratic coalition between northern Irish Catholic machines and unreconstructed southerners. Speaking to the Religious Bureau of the Republican National Committee, a party loyalist declared, "We are Republicans, and don't propose to leave our party and identify ourselves with the party whose antecedents have been rum, Romanism, and rebellion. We are loyal to our flag."[20]

Anti-Catholic themes of the late nineteenth century are perfectly summarized in Harold Frederic's 1896 novel *The Damnation of Theron Ware*. When a young Methodist minister meets a genial and cultured Irish Catholic priest, he is puzzled at the force of his reaction, his own "tacit race and religious aversion" to Catholics but specifically to the Irish. He examines the looming tableau forming in his mind: "The foundations upon which its dark bulk reared itself were ignorance, squalor, brutality and vice. Pigs wallowed in the mire before its base, and burrowing into this base were a myriad of narrow doors, each bearing the hateful sign of a saloon, and giving forth from its recesses of night the sounds of screams and curses. Above were sculptured rows of lowering, ape-like faces from Nast's and Keppler's cartoons, and out of these sprang into the vague upper gloom—on the one side, lamp-posts from which negroes hung by the neck, and on the other gibbets for dynamiters and Molly Maguires, and between the two glowed a spectral picture of some black-robed, tonsured men, with leering satanic masks, making a bonfire of the

Bible in the public schools." This vision encapsulates the mingled themes of ethnic, class, and race prejudice plus anti-urbanism, all united through evocative religious symbols.[21]

In the 1920s, anti-Catholic politics again stimulated a mass movement in the form of the second Ku Klux Klan, which in the northern and western states was at least as concerned with keeping the Catholics in their place as with repressing blacks and Jews. The KKK struggled against the "Kike, Koon, and Katholic." For the Klan, Catholicism represented "Alienism," "the unassimilated hordes of Europe," which threatened American racial purity. As a Klan writer argued in 1928, an apocalyptic struggle would unfold between "traditional Americanism and the religious and political invasion of the United States by the champions of European institutions and ideals." Catholics had so often shown themselves the masters of subversion and conspiracy, and now they were using the latest forms of propaganda to initiate "America's Armageddon." One of the Klan's major goals was to combat "the great amount of Roman Catholic propaganda being disseminated through the medium of Press, the stage and the movies." At its height, the Klan of this era had anywhere from five million to eight million adherents. And although they despised the Klan's gangsterism and demagoguery, liberal observers often made remarks that conceded much of the movement's basic argument.[22]

| Al Smith and Afterward, 1930–1960

Like the APA, the Klan quickly self-destructed, but the political sentiments these movements represented survived for many years afterward. Most discussions of American attitudes to Catholicism highlight the 1928 defeat of Democratic presidential candidate Al Smith, who so perfectly epitomized the Catholic danger. In addition to being Catholic, he was also Irish, urban, and "wet."[23] Historians then commonly fast-forward to the parallel debates over John F. Kennedy's campaign in 1960, saying little about the intervening years. Yet anti-Catholicism continued as a subterranean stream through these years, and occasionally surfaced to generate real hostility.

This continuity is important for understanding modern controversies. It explains why attacks on the Catholic Church from the 1970s onward so often echo much older rhetoric. The new generation of anti-Catholics did not need to draw their ideas from archival research into ancient tracts, but could tap into a living tradition. Also, American anti-Catholicism of the mid-twentieth century foreshadowed its modern counterpart in important respects, in often being a middle-class and elite movement that was generally associated with leftist or liberal political opinions. As so often in the past, Catholicism symbolized the forces opposing Americanism, but this time progressives were attacking the Church for its repressiveness and anti-modernity, and its alleged sympathy for totalitarianism.

Through the 1930s and 1940s anti-Catholicism flourished in an impressively broad range of settings, and by no means just among street bigots. Historian John McGreevy has traced an important aspect of the American intellectual tradition represented by the efforts of liberal and secular thinkers such as John Dewey and Walter Lippmann to define the distinctive features of the "American mind." They stressed not just ideas of democracy, individualism, and autonomy, but also philosophical pragmatism and the notion of free scientific inquiry. At every stage, this liberal synthesis defined American culture explicitly against Catholicism: the American mind was not Catholic and, logically, Catholicism was not American. The Church was hierarchical, authoritarian, foreign, European, and hostile to intellectual inquiry—naturally, since it was founded upon a supernaturalistic philosophical system.[24]

Catholicism was also seen as desperately ill-suited for a world of rapid scientific and industrial development. Liberal scholars were still influenced by Victorian anti-clerical and anti-Catholic polemics such as J. W. Draper's *History of the Conflict Between Religion and Science*, in which the struggle between reason and superstition was personified in the heroic images of Columbus and Galileo. Generations have grown up with the picture of Columbus asserting the fact of the round earth, to the scorn of intolerant priests and friars, a legend that attributes the discovery of America to a courageous repudiation of Catholic authority. (In reality, Columbus' clerical enemies knew perfectly well that the earth was round: they just had a far better idea than he did of its actual size. As they rightly told him, sailing three thousand miles west from Portugal was simply not going to bring him to Japan.) In the person of Galileo—according to the same mythology—science itself stood judged and condemned by the Vatican. Though Draper attacked religion and superstition in general, he reserved most of his bile for the Catholics, supposedly the most brutal and obscurantist of sects: "in the Vatican—we have only to recall the Inquisition—the hands that are now raised in appeals to the Most Merciful are crimsoned. They have been steeped in blood!"[25] Twentieth-century liberals were entranced by the theory that traced the whole Industrial Revolution to the growth of Protestant individualism: Max Weber's *The Protestant Ethic and the Spirit of Capitalism* appeared in English in 1930 and had a profound influence on historical writing. Not just in a geographical sense, Catholicism was the religion of the Old World, which fitted poorly with the New.

From the liberal perspective, religion could survive, provided that it was privatized, and made every compromise with the liberal scientific worldview, which the Roman Catholic Church demonstrably was not prepared to do. Through these liberal writings, we repeatedly find the standard stereotypes of Catholicism as the religion of repression and ignorance, the implicit enemy of democracy. Because these ideas had such an impact in the elite universities, they helped form the assumptions of a generation of upper- and middle-class Americans who would have scorned any overt racist or anti-Semitic sentiments. To oversimplify, we might adopt a phrase sometimes used to describe English upper-class attitudes toward religion. There are only two religions—Roman Catholicism, which is wrong, and all the others, which don't matter.

The Continuity of Anti-Catholic Politics

Anti-Catholic sentiment also played an overt political role in the post–Al Smith world. The obvious power of Catholic political machines in the New Deal coalition was a source of continuing grievance for Republicans, and Democrats themselves recognized a need to avoid presenting themselves too blatantly as a "Romanized Democratic Party in the North." Only thus could they maintain the sometimes uneasy alliance that united the Catholic-dominated urban machines with other elements of the Roosevelt coalition, which included middle-class Protestant progressives, Jews, and Bible Belt southerners.[26]

Though nothing like as visible as the Klan, anti-Catholic organizations remained in existence. By far the most important center of formal organization was Freemasonry, which at least in theory condemns all bigotry or hostility based on race or religion, and which notionally permitted Catholics to join. Still, the fact that the Catholic Church rigidly prohibited its members from becoming Masons gave the nation's numerous lodges a strictly non-Catholic, and often anti-Catholic, coloring. This hostility was enhanced by the violent denunciations of Masonry regularly forthcoming from even the more liberal popes and prelates. While anti-Masonic exposés often indulge in the wildest kinds of conspiracy theory, there is substantial evidence that Masons carried out active anti-Catholic propaganda through the mid-twentieth century, focusing especially on the issue of the Catholic schools. At least into the 1940s, meanwhile, Ulster-linked Orange Lodges continued to meet and demonstrate in northern and midwestern cities, though by later years they had become much more social rather than political bodies.[27]

Anti-papist fears in the 1930s were galvanized by the demagogic career of Father Charles Coughlin. Particularly after Coughlin's shift to anti-

Semitic ranting in 1938–39, liberals and mainstream Protestants wrote widely of an explicit Catholic threat, which they viewed as a direct parallel to the Franco movement in Spain. Coughlin himself openly boasted of the analogy, and the need for the United States to follow in "the Franco way." Some urban Catholic extremists organized the Christian Front, an anti-Semitic paramilitary group, sections of which openly trained for urban guerrilla warfare. Aggravating the fears of non-Catholics was the media's failure to report the often terrifying activities under way in Irish and Italian sections of major cities, a silence that suggested the effectiveness of Church censorship. During the long hot summer of 1939, Coughlinite thugs ranged New York, Boston, and Philadelphia, intimidating Jewish and liberal Protestant gatherings, and scarcely a word about these events appeared in any newspaper. In Philadelphia, the press could break their silence only when a riot led to numerous arrests. Even then, the local media did not refer openly to Coughlin or the Christian Front, but could only speak euphemistically of a "German Nazi *Bund*" organization—though all the "Germans" arrested bore names like Gallagher and Murphy. Nor would Boston media say a word about Irish Coughlinite assaults on Jews and liberals in that city, which continued well into the war years—a scandal that was exposed only by the New York leftist newspaper *PM*. Though Jews were the main targets, Protestants also felt threatened by the violence. One Pittsburgh writer pointed to Coughlin's antics as the reason that "ancient fears of the Inquisition, hangings and burnings, and living in caves and dens in the Scotch mountains, racial memories of the hideous Thirty Years War, are stirring again in Protestant breasts."[28]

Memories of ancient battles and massacres now merged with contemporary fears of dictatorship and Fascism, and hard-line Protestants found themselves in curious harmony with leftists and Communists. The left-wing loathing of Hitler and Franco was understandable, but many Protestants shared this hatred because of what they saw as the powerful Catholic tilt of both regimes. A linkage between Catholicism and Fascism seemed to be confirmed by the dictators' savage persecution of Freemasonry. And although the American Catholic Church condemned anti-Semitism, its clergy were largely united behind the Franco cause, to the extent of denouncing American supporters of the Spanish Republic as Communists or their dupes. Catholic authorities organized boycotts against pro-Republic newspapers in the United States, tried to prevent meeting halls being rented to Loyalist supporters, and generally sought to silence anti-Franco voices. Any U.S. media outlet that even described Franco as "Fascist" could definitely expect Church retaliation.

These activities revived charges that the Church was trying to operate as a clandestine government, trampling on civil liberties and the freedom of the press. The depth of liberal suspicion of Catholicism is suggested by the 1939 book *The Catholic Crisis* by leftist muckraker George Seldes, who repeatedly accused the Church of operating in intimate alliance with Fascism and anti-Semitism. He was particularly conscious of threats to the freedom of speech. Seldes described Church pressure on American journalism as "one of the most important forces in American life, and the only one about which secrecy is generally maintained, no newspaper being brave enough to discuss it, although all fear it and believe that the problem should be dragged into the open and made publicly known." The only place where such interference could be openly discussed was in Catholic publications themselves, which occasionally crowed about their successes in silencing hostile views. Also in 1939, the newspaper of the Philadelphia archdiocese noted, "There were in the course of the year sporadic slurs upon the Catholic church in publications in various parts of the country. In at least one instance the offending publication was a secular college paper. The Government found it necessary to ban certain issues of these publications from the mails."[29]

Protestants also found common cause with the left from the late 1920s onward over the issue of Mexico, where a secularist regime with strong Masonic ties launched a violent anti-clerical purge. While American Catholics demanded military intervention against what were seen as Red dictators on the nation's southern border, leftists and Protestants both opposed any such interference and complained about the Catholic Church's dabbling in secular politics. If we think only in terms of secular left and right, it is difficult to understand the Klan propaganda of these years, which preached what sound like familiar left/liberal positions on the evils of Hitler, Franco, and Coughlin, and the need to defend Mexico.[30]

| American Freedom and Catholic Power

Religious tensions calmed during the war years, and memories of interfaith cooperation in the services left an important legacy of "foxhole fellowship." Catholics also gained respect for their staunch anti-Communism. Charles Morris has described how through the 1940s and early 1950s, the Catholic Church, in its "militant, rigorist" version, "was slowly becoming the dominant cultural institution in the country." Throughout the 1940s, Hollywood depictions of the Catholic Church and its clergy were uniformly favorable, to the point of adoring. Thomas Merton's hymn to monasticism in the *Seven Storey Mountain* became a triumphant mainstream best-seller.[31]

Even so, new religious controversies resurfaced in these very same years, with anti-Catholicism once again manifesting in its left-liberal guise. As Communism and international power politics occupied center stage in post-war American life, leftists denounced the Catholic Church as a supporter of global reaction. This served as a useful rhetorical counterpoint to the Red-baiting that was becoming prevalent in the American media. If the right denounced tyranny in the Soviet Union, then the left could gain sympathy by attacking dictatorial and clerical Spain, or the reactionary Vatican. As conservative Peter Viereck argued in 1953, "The Elders of Zion were used by Father Coughlin's *Social Justice* to frighten reactionaries. ... The Elders of the Vatican are being used by the *Nation* to frighten liberal intellectuals."[32] The issue of U.S. diplomatic recognition of the Vatican was long controversial, because it required the federal government to establish formal relations with the hybrid church-state so loathed by Protestants.

Domestically too, a number of sensitive issues mobilized liberal and leftist opinion against the Catholic Church, especially over state support of Catholic schools. Some states allowed public funds to be used to provide transportation for parochial school children, while Catholic pressure groups demanded that any new federal aid to education be shared equally between public and parochial systems. In some areas with large Catholic populations, the overlap between church and state control was so intimate as to create a bizarre hybrid, the "so-called Catholic public school." Meanwhile, hitherto small Catholic colleges flourished on GI Bill funds, which were freely distributed to religious institutions. These developments, and the perceived threat to public education, reportedly inspired "a tremendous revival of anti-Catholic feeling," which manifested among liberals rather than traditional nativists.[33]

In 1947–48, Paul Blanshard published an explosive series of articles in *The Nation*, based on his "ten years of intensive study of the Catholic problem in the United States." This means that his project had begun about the time of the Coughlin furor and, indeed, of Seldes's *Catholic Crisis*. The publication led to *The Nation* being barred from some high school libraries, a decision that in turn provoked a free-speech debate. The articles formed the basis of Blanshard's 1949 book *American Freedom and Catholic Power*.[34] Many newspapers—including the *New York Times*—refused even to advertise the book, while some stores refused to sell it over the counter. This all seemed to confirm Blanshard's charges about Catholic censorship and denial of free speech. Echoing Seldes, he described Church censorship as "a highly organized system of cultural and moral controls that applies not only to books, plays, magazines, television and motion pictures but to persons and places as well."[35]

Older nativist themes are well represented in Blanshard's book, above all the foreignness of the Church and the incompatibility of its authoritarian structure to American society. This makes it all the more striking that the book was published not by a cranky fringe or fundamentalist press, but from the respected liberal firm of Beacon. Blanshard attacks the "Roman-controlled priests" and describes the hierarchy as "an autocratic moral monarchy in a liberal democracy." For Blanshard, America was facing a fundamental clash of culture and values. "The American Catholic problem is this: What is to be done with a hierarchy that operates in twentieth century America under medieval European controls?" "American Catholicism is still a colonial dependency within a complete system of ecclesiastical imperialism, and there are few signs of American rebellion." "Catholic Power" could never truly be reconciled with "American Freedom," a point confirmed by the grim examples of political and cultural repression in contemporary Catholic states such as Spain and Ireland, or the province of Quebec.[36]

Blanshard's chapter on "the Catholic plan for America" envisages what the nation would look like if the Church succeeded in changing the constitution to suit its interests. The resulting picture is suitably grim and totalitarian. His imaginary "Christian Commonwealth Amendment," the charter of a new theocracy, belongs firmly in the long tradition of American dystopian nightmares.[37] While Blanshard does not actually conjure up crocodilian Catholic bishops, the image is certainly implied. To this extent, the book would have been instantly comprehensible in 1850 or 1920. Equally familiar was the hair-raising solution he recommended to the problems he identified, namely, "a resistance movement designed to prevent the hierarchy from imposing its social policies upon our schools, hospitals, government and family organization."[38] While Blanshard stressed that the scheme would not entail a bigoted attack on Catholic people as such, his proposed movement summoned an uncomfortable echo of earlier nativist activism. Whatever his avowed intent, in the aftermath of the Second World War, the term resistance would for most readers have implied the use of violence.

Though in some ways harking back to the days of the APA or the Klan, the book also marks a transitional point in the long story of anti-Catholicism. Blanshard's critique stresses newer ideas, especially the Church's neglect of the interests of women and its disregard of modern attitudes toward sexuality. Blanshard claims that his investigative study was sparked by his shocking discovery of the rules that Catholic nurses and doctors were obliged to follow when dealing with difficult pregnancies, such that women's rights and interests were (it appeared) dreadfully neglected. Even if the fetus was likely to die, the doctor was still obliged to prefer its life over that of the mother. Blanshard thus opens what was then the highly delicate question of abortion, though only in the case of therapeutic abortions deemed medically necessary to save the mother. For Blanshard, the absolute Catholic prohibition on such a procedure represented cruel subservience to impractical dogma. As a result of changing societal attitudes toward both contraception and women's rights, Catholics were now additionally pilloried for their outmoded attitudes on gender issues.

Also foreshadowing more modern concerns, Blanshard attacks the Church's opposition on public education about venereal diseases, a major issue during the mass mobilization of men during the Second World War and, later, the Korean conflict. The Catholic stance rejected any education in what would later be called "safe sex," using condoms, since that implicitly accepted that people would be engaging in extramarital or premarital sex. The only acceptable educational response was, thus, a demand for abstinence. Through the 1940s, educational programs by the government and the military faced a long guerrilla war with the Church and Catholic organizations over this question, which would recur in still graver terms in the 1980s, with the spread of AIDS.[39]

Parenthetically, we should say that Blanshard makes a rather dubious precursor for modern views on sexual liberalism. While his statements on contraception and abortion make him sound congenial to modern social views, the reasons for his positions are jarring. While defending "modern" and even feminist stances on many issues, one of his main grievances against the Catholics is their refusal to support eugenics laws, and especially the sterilization of the biologically unfit. He is contemptuous of the Church's dogmatic insistence on the human quality of severely deformed children, of what he calls "monstrosities," which the clergy nevertheless deemed worthy of baptism.[40] In retrospect, perhaps it is Blanshard himself, rather than the clergy, who sounds callous, though he was only giving voice to the views of many contemporary liberals.

Blanshard's anti-Church views were reflected in the political activism of two major liberal secularist organizations, the American Civil Liberties Union (ACLU) and Protestants and Other Americans United for Separation of Church and State (POAU), founded in 1947. (Blanshard served as a lawyer for POAU.) Though the 1950s, both served as components of his "resistance movement," conducting a brushfire war against the Catholic Church and Catholic politicians over issues such as censorship and state funding of sectarian education. Blanshard and the POAU demanded that all Catholic candidates be confronted with what they regarded as the three key issues in church-state relationship: "the Catholic boycott of public schools, the drive of Catholic bishops for public funds, and the appointment of a Vatican ambassador."[41]

McCarthy's Inquisition

Within a year of the controversy over Blanshard's book, liberal fears were reignited by the career of Joseph McCarthy. Though the postwar anti-Communist reaction is often popularly labeled "McCarthyism," we must distinguish the events of the later 1940s from those of the early 1950s, when Senator McCarthy became the most visible face of the movement. In the earlier period, many liberals were happy to support action against open or covert Communists in government, given the likelihood of actual warfare against the Communist world. "McCarthyism" was a quite different phenomenon. This was not so much a rational response to potential subversion as an irresponsible and demagogic tactic characterized by vague accusations for political ends, the exploitation of hysterical public fears, and the reckless persecution of innocent or relatively harmless dissidents. Also, this more aggressive phase of the anti-Communist movement was led and supported by Catholic figures, both lay and clerical, including McCarthy himself and congressional leaders such as Francis Walter. For liberals, charges of an official "Inquisition" had a strong religious undercurrent.[42]

The nakedly Catholic component of the anti-Red crusade was symbolized by an event that occurred in 1954, shortly after the televised hearings that had done so much to discredit McCarthy, when Cardinal Spellman personally introduced the senator to a raucous gathering of several thousand cheering New York police officers. McCarthyism raised fears that Red smears were being used not just against leftists and liberals, but against virtually anyone who challenged the Catholic political worldview. McCarthyite partisans made no secret of their suspicions that liberal Protestant churches had been thoroughly penetrated by Communist agents and sympathizers. By 1953 Walter's House Un-American Activities Committee was threatening a full-scale investigation of the Protestant churches and the National Council of Churches. One special target was liberal Methodist bishop G. Bromley Oxnam, who was also the founding president of POAU. After Oxnam appeared before the committee, Walter remarked that "the Communists are using well known and highly placed persons as dupes and the bigger the name, the better for their cause."[43] Like Coughlin's career, the whole McCarthy episode raised serious fears about the Catholic potential for repression, and also for fanaticism, which was especially dangerous in a nuclear-armed world.

Seen in this context, we can understand why John Kennedy should have made so many non-Catholics and particularly liberals nervous in 1960. James Michener recorded the fears of his liberal acquaintances that "Irish priests" would manipulate a Catholic president "as if he were their toy." One liberal dignitary (unnamed) feared a Catholic president because his church was "dictatorial, savage in its enmities, all-consuming in its desires, and reactionary in its intentions ... positively brutal in its lust for power."[44] Certainly, the Kennedy presidency quelled most such fears, as did the heroic liberalism associated with his brother Bobby, but imagery and stereotypes built up over centuries could scarcely be expected to vanish in a decade.

The Catholic Difference

We can understand the lasting hostility toward American Catholics in terms of recurrent myths and stereotypes, but underlying all these are some fundamental issues and principles that have repeatedly created tension between Catholics and their neighbors. At least as the Catholic Church has existed since the Counter-Reformation, its most basic values genuinely do appear to be in tension with what we familiarly think of as those of the United States. This is not to justify the nativist movements, to accept the notion of "no smoke without fire," but some quite authentic differences do help to account for the mythical superstructure built by anti-Catholic activists over the centuries.

These rival Catholic values include, notably, theories of hierarchy and obedience, and an ideal of universality. Catholics belonged (and belong) to a global institution that often had good relations with specific nation-states but which could never allow its members to think of themselves primarily as citizens of a state rather than sons and daughters of the Church. Of its nature, the Catholic Church denied the absolute claims of nations and nationalism. Tensions between church and state were generally less under governments that claimed to be Catholic, but the United States posed a specially difficult case because of both its secular government and the overwhelmingly Protestant character of its people and historical traditions. From the first establishment of the Church on American soil, the whole issue of being an "American Catholic" seemed to involve a contradiction, even an oxymoron. How could the subject of one regime—especially with such exalted claims to divine authority—simultaneously be the citizen of another? Speaking in 1959, Harry Truman himself asserted that Catholics could scarcely be trusted in the highest office because "[Catholics] have a loyalty to a church hierarchy that I don't believe in. ... You don't want to have anyone in control of the government of the United States who has another loyalty, religious or otherwise."[45]

Also troubling was the belief that a specific religious institution had unique access to revealed truth. The fact that religious privilege was concentrated in the hands of a special closed caste was a particular offense to Protestant notions. Even when the Church's leaders spoke most warmly of friendly cooperation with other faiths, Catholics were never allowed to forget that they themselves did not belong to a denomination, nor even to *a* church, but to the Church. One of the most damaging charges facing John Kennedy in 1960 concerned an incident some years previously, when he had been invited to speak in Philadelphia at the dedication of a memorial to four naval chaplains of various faiths. The four had perished together in 1943 aboard the *USS Dorchester* in what many saw as a heroic symbol both of self-sacrifice and interfaith collaboration. Kennedy ultimately withdrew from the event at the urging of the city's Catholic leader, Cardinal Dennis Dougherty, who would not countenance any suggestion that Protestants, Catholics, and Jews should cooperate so visibly in religious matters, and on equal terms. This opposition also explains why Hollywood never made the seemingly inevitable film of the *Dorchester* affair.[46]

The existence of religious groups who claim exclusive truth has often posed real problems for societies that are in effect being asked to tolerate the intolerant. Again, we think of modern attitudes toward another powerfully separatist faith, namely, Islam. This toleration issue is not too pressing when the group involved is a tiny sect physically segregated from the mainstream, but that was scarcely the case with American Catholics, who were a visible presence throughout the nation, and usually a dominating fact in the larger cities. Catholics also resembled small sects and cults in the many distinguishing beliefs and customs that segregated them from their neighbors. As Mark Massa observes, "This American Catholic world was a 'total experience,' not unlike being Amish in Pennsylvania or Mormon in Utah, but stretching coast to coast."[47]

Catholics resembled small sects like Mormons or Jehovah's Witnesses in their distinctiveness, but unlike these other subcultural groups, they had both the will and the ability to impose their tastes and standards on the wider population. The Catholic Church was not prepared to limit its influence to a strictly defined spiritual sphere, but claimed wide authority over secular matters. Through much of the twentieth century, Catholic pressure groups had a profound effect on what ordinary non-Catholics could read, the films they could see, and even the decisions they could legally make concerning family planning. Some clerics in particular—

Dougherty in Philadelphia, O'Connell in Boston—had no qualms about throwing their political weight around in urban politics. Campaigning for Kennedy in Pennsylvania in 1960, James Michener found voters who loathed the prospect of a Catholic candidate not because of abstract anti-Catholic charges dredged up from Klan pamphlets, but because of the concrete experience of living under the Dougherty regime in nearby Philadelphia. One friend declared that "I fear the shadow of Cardinal Dougherty over the White House." Even though the cardinal had died years before, "[h]is spirit goes on forever, telling Protestants what they can't do." She felt that her views were shared by "[a]ll the Lutherans. Most of the Baptists. Many of the Presbyterians."[48]

| The Sexual Threat

Reinforcing the analogy with unpopular cults or separatist sects, Catholic ideas differed substantially from the mainstream in the most basic matters of family life, sexuality, and gender relations. These differences go far toward explaining the highly sexualized nature of anti-Catholic polemic over the centuries, a trend that is if anything more powerful today than it has ever been.

Never far from the heart of anti-Catholic rhetoric is an attack on the Church as the purveyor and practitioner of depraved sexuality. In the nineteenth century, the most sensitive issue was that of the confessional, which posed a frontal challenge to conventional middle-class ideologies of family and gender relations. This institution placed ordinary Catholics in the position of having to discuss sexual matters and intimate thoughts with a non–family member who was moreover a single male. It also meant that power over family matters was being placed in the hands of priests rather than husbands—in those of Fathers, not fathers. Clerical celibacy was another delicate issue, as a denial of fundamental assumptions about the supremacy of family life, not to mention received ideas about masculinity and gender roles.[49]

Through the nineteenth century and well into the twentieth, both celibacy and the confessional provided anti-Catholic writers with material for the most elaborate sexual fantasies. Mark Twain claimed that "the confessional's chief amusement has been seduction—in all the ages of the Church. Père Hyacinthe testifies that of a hundred priests confessed by him, ninety-nine had used the confessional effectively for the seduction of married women and young girls. One priest confessed that of nine hundred women and young girls whom he had served as father confessor in his time, none had escaped his lecherous embrace but the elderly and the homely. The official list of questions which the priest is required to ask will over-masteringly excite any woman who is not a paralytic." In 1875, apostate priest Charles Chiniquy published a scurrilous tract, *The Priest, the Women and the Confessional*, which described the sexual exploitation of women parishioners by lustful priests.[50]

The idea of clerical celibacy was subversive enough even if it was taken as a genuine aspiration, but of course the claim to superior sexual virtue attracted charges of hypocrisy. Many Protestants believed that celibacy was a cynical pose adopted to conceal the lascivious deeds of priests and nuns or, just as likely, homosexual or pederastic behaviors. A whole American genre of quasi-pornography claimed to expose the clandestine life of the confessional, the hidden tunnels linking convents and rectories, and the secret cemeteries in which nuns' babies were hidden after they had been murdered.[51]

Most celebrated among such works was the autobiography of the purported former nun known as "Maria Monk," whose memoirs claimed to reveal the inner workings of a Quebec convent of the 1830s. According to this severely disturbed fantasist, nuns were the exploited sex slaves of priests and bishops, and flagellation was a weapon both to enforce discipline and to excite sexual urges. In the 1890s, one of the regular lecturers sponsored by the APA was the alleged ex-nun Margaret Shepherd, whose convent life had supposedly been one long round of "grotesque ceremonies, orgies of sex and sadism" at the hands of "licentious and lecherous priests … seeking to lure young and innocent girls into sin." As late as the 1940s, purported ex-nuns were still making the lecture circuit, retailing pornographic fantasies to entranced Protestant audiences. In 1926, ex-monk Joseph McCabe recounted many scandals involving drunkenness and sexual license in his book *The Truth About the Catholic Church*. As Stephen Marcus writes of this genre, "Roman Catholicism is a pornographer's paradise. … All priests are lechers, satyrs and pimps, all nuns are concubines or lesbians or both. The confessional is the locus of meeting of lubricity and piety."[52]

For nineteenth-century readers, such Catholic fantasies offered one of the few socially approved vehicles for pornographic interests, but this sexual critique survived well into the next century, into a time when sexual themes could more easily be explored in mainstream literature. As late as 1962, respected Presbyterian scholar Lorraine Boettner published the first of many editions of a comprehensive polemic against the Catholic Church, in which he warned that "[f]orced celibacy and auricular confession are by their very nature conducive to sex perversion … the monasteries and convents sometimes became cesspools of iniquity." In the same year, ex-priest Emmett McLoughlin published *Crime and Im-*

morality in the Catholic Church.[53] During the 1960 presidential election, even the most ancient and discredited pornographic fantasies were again pressed into service. In addition to conventional pamphlet attacks on candidate Kennedy, Democrats also had to confront such scabrous titles as *Abolish the Nunneries and Save the Girls*, *Convent Life Unveiled*, *The Convent Horror*, *I Married a Monk*, and those ludicrous old warhorses, *Maria Monk* and *The Priest, the Women and the Confessional*. Other tracts depicted priestly Inquisitors torturing heroic Protestant dissidents.[54]

The power of anti-Catholicism lies in its infinite adaptability. In different times and places, different kinds of anti-papist rhetoric have been more in evidence, but none has entirely vanished from view. Each is ready to rise again when it meets the needs of a particular political movement or interest group. As the United States entered a great age of liberal and radical reform in the 1960s and 1970s, it is not surprising that the dominant aspect of anti-Catholicism should have been a liberal variety that would have resonated with Blanshard and his contemporaries. Yet the rise of new concerns about gender and sexuality would also bring a revival of many of the sexual stereotypes and allegations that would have seemed just too scurrilous for respectable controversy in Blanshard's time.

3 | Catholics and Liberals

*The Roman Catholic Church, it needs to be remembered,
is quite literally an un-American institution. It is not
democratic. The Church's views on due process and on
the status of women, to name just a couple of key issues,
are sharply at odds with those that inform the laws of
American secular society. And its principal policies are
established by the Vatican in Rome.*

— David R. Boldt, *Philadelphia Inquirer,* 1990

W riting on anti-Catholicism in the late 1970s, Andrew Greeley made a statement that seemed quite remarkable in the context of the time. Not only did this kind of bigotry still exist, he claimed, but "it may be even more vigorous now than it was twenty years ago." Greeley was arguing that anti-Catholicism was actually more potent than it had been before the election of President Kennedy, the event that was commonly believed to have laid the ghost of nativism to rest for all time.[1] Yet older prejudices had survived and were reinforced by grievances against the Church that were new, or at least newly redefined. While liberals had long been hostile to the Catholic Church, their distinctive issues now played the central role in defining anti-Catholic sentiment. As liberalism itself changed, so liberals reconceived their enemies, and the Church occupied a critical place in a growing demonology.

The fact that liberals loathed the Church was scarcely news, but other social changes ensured that the new anti-Catholicism would differ substantially from what it had been during the Blanshard era. Especially important were changes within the Catholic Church itself. Whereas in the past Catholics had largely presented a united front against prejudice, new Church divisions greatly reduced the sense of confrontation between Catholics and non-Catholics, between "us and them." In consequence, many arguments that would once have seemed nakedly anti-Catholic now gained an audience among Catholics themselves, giving this rhetoric much greater legitimacy. Catholic divisions contributed to opening the Church to attacks by the mass media that would hitherto have been unthinkable.

The New Liberalism, 1968–1980

The renewed vigor of liberal anti-Catholicism in recent history would probably have surprised observers during the 1960s. From a liberal point of view, the Catholic Church in those years mainly seemed to be on the right side, which is rather to say the left side. Since the New Deal, the Democratic Party had relied heavily on Catholic constituencies in both the urban machines and the labor movement, which provided the driving power for the activist liberalism of the New Frontier and the Great Society. The Church was a dependable ally of liberalism and the Democratic Party on most social issues, including labor organization, interventionist government, social welfare, civil rights, and immigration. Catholic activists such as Michael Harrington deserved much of the credit for formulating liberal agendas.[2]

Kennedy liberalism was an excellent advertisement for the Catholic cause, while anti-Catholicism was increasingly despised. The political passions of the 1964 race led prominent academics to analyze and condemn the forces of reaction and nativism in American history, and anti-Catholicism was clearly a facet of what Richard Hofstadter called "the paranoid style." Catholic clergy were much in evidence among white supporters of the black civil rights movement and, later, of the Latino cause figureheaded by Cesar Chavez. As the Vietnam War came to dominate American politics, Catholics such as Cardinal Spellman became controversial for their hawkish opinions, but they were counterbalanced by prominent peace activists like Charles Owen Rice and the Berrigan brothers. Adding to this benevolent picture of Catholicism was the intense media coverage of Pope John XXIII (1958–1963) and the second

Vatican Council, which was viewed as an epoch-making act of liberalization. So lively was public interest that most secular media outlets now began a broader and more systematic coverage of religious matters in general.[3]

No one single event marked the end of the brief liberal honeymoon with Catholicism, but the one year of 1968 can be seen as a symbolic pivot. This was of course when Pope Paul VI issued the encyclical *Humanae Vitae*, prohibiting artificial means of contraception. The decision marked the first definitive stop on what had previously appeared an unrestricted road toward liberalization and conformity with the American Protestant mainstream. Though the coincidence of timing is often forgotten, the publication of the encyclical was often bracketed in contemporary writing with the Soviet-led invasion of Czechoslovakia, which occurred a few weeks afterward. Both events were seen as panicked overreaction by totalitarian regimes threatened by reform movements. *Humanae Vitae* spawned intense public criticism of the Catholic hierarchy, especially—and this was a vital development—from Catholics themselves. The substance of the attack included many long-familiar themes, above all a questioning of the legitimacy of foreign, Roman authority over American believers. Other, newer themes, though, emphasized gender issues and the rhetoric of sexual liberation. Why should celibate old men presume to tell ordinary men and women how to regulate their sexual lives?[4]

The year 1968 also marked massive changes in the substance of American liberalism that had a devastating impact on the Democratic Party. Since the 1930s, liberal politics had stressed domestic themes such as economic justice and racial equality, and on these issues the Democratic Party could reasonably expect to depend on the working-class and lower-middle-class vote. This expectation was visibly collapsing by 1968, in the aftermath of urban rioting, the upsurge in black militancy, and growing racial hostility. Racial tensions had a special impact on Catholics, who represented an increasing share of the white urban population and were deeply affected by issues such as urban crime, residential desegregation, and busing. When television news showed irate white residents protesting a possible move-in by a black family, the demonstrators were often Catholics. Their entrenched position in city jobs also placed Catholics at the forefront of controversies over affirmative action. Obviously, only a minority of Catholic families fitted the stereotype of being headed by a cop or a firefighter, but it was these working-class and lower-middle-class groups who most drew the attention of the media. Catholics visibly represented the wrong side in a highly polarized nation.[5]

In addition, issues of gender and sexuality were coming to the fore in a way that would have been unimaginable a decade previously. The women's liberation movement was a visible public presence by 1968, and a gay rights movement emerged the following year. An older emphasis on class was rapidly replaced by a focus on the politics of race, gender, sexual identity, and personal liberation. In all these areas, the Catholic Church generally found itself on the side of tradition and thus, however reluctantly, of the political right.

This political sea change was deeply confusing for many Catholic voters who hitherto would have found it impossible to vote for anyone but a Democrat. White ethnic fury at the new liberalism found a voice in 1968 in the third-party presidential campaign of George Wallace, who found an enthusiastic constituency among working-class voters in the North and the Midwest, including many Catholics. Only intense lobbying by union leaderships prevented most of this support from being turned into ballots during the November elections—though even so, Wallace still won nearly ten million votes. Within the Democratic Party itself, conservative ethnic reaction was personified by political leaders such as Chicago's Mayor Daley or Philadelphia's Frank Rizzo. The Nixon campaign wooed disaffected white ethnic voters, a policy that would sporadically win much success for the Republicans through the 1980s. In 1972, Republicans portrayed the Democrats as the hyperliberal party of the three A's: acid, amnesty (for draft dodgers), and abortion.[6]

Working-class Catholics became steadily more disaffected with traditional liberalism. When, in 1976, the Democratic Party held what was billed as its most representative convention ever, organized feminist and gay groups were much in evidence, as were blacks, Latinos and other ethnic minorities, but the traditional urban machines that spoke for "white ethnics" were not to be seen. Inclusiveness had its limits. In the long term, Catholics did not become a Republican constituency as firm in their loyalty as the old Democratic monolith, but they demonstrated a much greater willingness to vote for parties or candidates on selected issues, and in many cases it was Republicans who benefited.[7]

Though this political reconfiguration by white ethnic voters was not explicitly religious, it transformed the attitude that liberals held toward ordinary Catholics, and hence the opinions and stereotypes that appeared so regularly in the mass media. As Andrew Greeley remarks, "The super-patriot of the 1950s was converted into the white ethnic hard-hat racist-chauvinist hawk of the 1960s and 1970s so dearly beloved by professors, educators, editorial writers, clergymen, TV commentators, reporters and national columnists." Archie Bunker may not have been a

Catholic, but he well represented the media stereotype of the reactionary Catholic bigot.[8]

The Myth of the Religious Right

Suspicion of ordinary Catholics did not necessarily translate into hostility to the Church as an institution, but the shift in the substance of political debate increasingly cast the Church and its hierarchy as the most prominent advocates of conservative positions. In most cases, this was not because the Church suddenly adopted rightist or reactionary positions, but because it refused to change its principles to conform to new social norms. Especially from the late 1970s, the Catholic Church came to stand as the single most obvious bastion of social and sexual conservatism.

Through the 1970s, liberals and progressives tried to implement their political agenda through far-reaching legal reforms. For feminists, this meant reforming state and federal codes in matters such as divorce, child custody, and rape and sexual assault. In 1973, the Supreme Court struck down current abortion laws in *Roe v. Wade*. The Equal Rights Amendment (ERA) was easily passed by the U.S. Congress in 1972, and initially there were high hopes of national ratification. Gay groups also won major victories. Between 1971 and 1976, sixteen states repealed their sodomy statutes, and by 1980 a further six had either undertaken repeal or had their laws declared unconstitutional. By the mid-1970s, several jurisdictions proposed to extend gay rights further by prohibiting discrimination on the grounds of sexual preference.[9]

By 1976–77, however, social liberalism was meeting growing resistance at several points. Ironically, this change owed something to the election of the Democratic president Jimmy Carter, whose campaign had drawn many conservative evangelicals into political activism. Catholics were also involved in political campaigns, especially in the anti-abortion movement that sought to reverse *Roe v. Wade* by means of a constitutional amendment. In 1977, Congress refused federal funding for abortions. Meanwhile, moves to legalize marijuana were failing, and gay campaigns were meeting particular resistance. The 1977 ballot that overturned a gay rights ordinance in Dade County, Florida, was followed over the next three years by electoral battles in Minnesota, Kansas, and elsewhere. A California ballot measure sought to prohibit the advocacy of homosexuality in public schools. Though evangelical Christians led the war against gay rights, Catholic authorities played a visible conservative role in all these moral battles.

By the end of the 1970s, the most effective enemy of social liberalism was self-evidently to be found in organized religion, among both Catholics and evangelicals, who together would gain a new political voice during the Reagan administration. The Moral Majority was founded in 1979 to consolidate the tactical alliances between evangelicals and conservative Catholics. For the next twenty years, liberals and feminists would identify their chief enemies under the blanket terms "Religious Right" or "Christian Right."[10]

These labels were misleading. In the event, as its evangelical allies discovered, the Catholic Church was scarcely a bastion of conservatism. While the Church hierarchy was resolute on abortion, on other key issues of the Reagan years it stood well to the left of the administration, and on occasion far to the left. The Church hierarchy retained an old-fashioned liberalism on economic questions such as welfare policy and labor unions, opposed overly stringent immigration controls, and was firmly opposed to restoring the death penalty. On other crucial policies such as the nuclear buildup and confronting Communism in Central America, the mainstream of Church opinion was firmly to the left. In 1983, U.S. Catholic bishops issued the statement *The Challenge of Peace*, an influential critique of Reaganite defense policy. In Central America, too, bishops and clergy protested against the rightist forces with which the United States was allied and which had been responsible for the deaths of Catholic clergy and nuns.[11] With the bishops ranged among the chief banes of the Reagan and Bush administrations, comprehensive terms such as "Christian Right" sounded ironic. The fact that the Catholic Church was regarded as such a reactionary force is stark testimony to how absolutely central matters of gender and sexuality had become to American politics since the 1970s.

A drift toward moral conservatism within the United States coincided neatly with the shift within the Catholic Church itself caused by the 1978 election of Pope John Paul II, whom liberals saw as a perfect symbol of reaction and misogyny. During the 1970s, liberals both inside the United States and overseas could hope that the conservative positions held by the papacy represented no more than a reactionary last stand and that the last vestiges of resistance to change would soon be swept away, perhaps following a new council, "Vatican III." The election of John Paul II showed that such hopes were illusory. In the Church, as in U.S. domestic politics, the progressive advances of the previous decade might yet be reversed. As the Pope enjoyed a long reign, he was able to remodel the Church according to his own thinking, by the careful selection of traditional-minded cardinals and bishops. Critics of the new papal conservatism drew attention to the sinister role supposedly played by traditionalist groups such as Opus Dei, which became the center of elaborate conspiracy theories.[12]

On moral issues as crucial as abortion, contraception, homosexuality, clerical celibacy, and women's ordination, it became clear that the Church was not going to give any more ground. Politically, too, the papacy was entering a much more actively conservative phase, as the new Pope tried to root out the liberation theology that had gained so much influence in Latin America. Commentators drew the obvious parallels between John Paul II and secular leaders such as Margaret Thatcher and Ronald Reagan.[13]

The Media and the Church

As American Catholics became more strongly identified with conservative causes, their depiction in the mass media deteriorated sharply. The political leanings of the media are open to much debate, and general statements that media outlets consistently favor any political party are misleading. If the media have any permanent bias, it is perhaps their uncritical inclination to accept the voices of bureaucratic authority. On particular issues, though, mainstream media do tend to form a solid front, and this was true of the debates over morality and gender in the 1970s and 1980s. Whatever their preference in terms of the major parties, journalists and commentators overwhelmingly supported women's causes such as the ERA and abortion rights just as consistently as they later favored gay issues. Accordingly, by the 1980s, Catholic clergy were seeing quite hostile coverage of their involvement in political matters. Stories about women's ordination, say, would feature the comments of a bishop as part of the journalistic obligation to preserve balance, but the tone of the story left no doubt of the pro-ordination message that the reader was meant to derive.[14]

Indirectly, too, the Catholic Church was tainted by the political legacy of Watergate, which made the American media much more prone to conspiracy theories and raised suspicions about large political institutions. When the Vatican featured in the American news media during the 1960s it was usually in the context of specifically religious issues, such as the Vatican Council or *Humanae Vitae*, or else in the context of international peacemaking. Whether or not one agreed with particular Catholic policies or attitudes, the Vatican itself was not presented as a sinister or suspect institution. Matters changed substantially at the end of the 1970s, when Venetian patriarch Albino Luciani became Pope under the title of John Paul I. The new Pope died barely a month after his election and was swiftly followed by John Paul II. The sudden death became the focus of conspiracy charges, alleging that perhaps Luciani had been murdered to prevent him from undertaking liberal reforms within the Church.[15]

During the early 1980s, observers found another possible context for the death when it was revealed that the Vatican Bank, the Institute for Religious Works (IOR), had been engaged in huge financial irregularities. The Vatican was damaged by the IOR's associations with an international underworld of organized crime figures, drug dealers, terrorists, and political extremists. Though no conspiracy was involved in the death of John Paul I, who perished of natural causes, these scandalous associations probably provided the context for the assassination attempt on his successor, when John Paul II was shot in Rome in 1981. The scandals became still more notorious in 1982 with the baroque death of Vatican banker Roberto Calvi, whose body was found hanging beneath a London bridge. Through the 1980s, Vatican scandals provided material for a number of sensational true-crime books and thriller novels, such as David Yallop's *In God's Name* and Nick Tosches's *Power on Earth*. All presented a harsh view of the upper ranks of the Catholic Church: the blurb for Richard Hammer's *The Vatican Connection* referred to "men in red hats and long robes abusing the power of their religious authority." The whole mythology was popularized through films such as *The Godfather III*.[16]

The Vatican featured more in the secular media than it had for decades, but often in a sleazy and criminal context, which legitimized the revival of the ugliest stereotypes about cynical greedy prelates. These events prepared the way for a new genre of scandalous thriller fiction with church settings, pioneered by Andrew Greeley's 1981 novel *The Cardinal Sins*, which dealt with the scandals of Cardinal Cody's time as archbishop of Chicago (1965–1982).[17] The fact that a book about clerical corruption and hypocrisy was a runaway success, and that the publisher suffered no public backlash, signaled a major shift in standards. By 1980, the Church exercised nothing like the monolithic power it once had.

| Margin and Mainstream

However large the shifts within American liberalism, the new media hostility to the Catholic Church could not have been so openly expressed had it not been for transformations within the Church itself. Before about 1965, the customary definition of what it meant to be a faithful Catholic was very strict, so that public dissent by individual Catholics was a sensitive matter. During the late 1960s and 1970s, though, large numbers of Catholics did dissent, to the extent of forming visible pressure groups frankly critical of the policies of the Church hierarchy, commonly over the familiar liberal issues of gender, sexuality, and personal morality. By the 1980s, conflict was so overt that observers spoke of America's "Catholic civil war." Catholics themselves were now speaking the traditional anti-papist language of "Vatican aggression," using the terms Rome and Vatican as symbols of reaction and ignorance, and frankly challenging the Church's stance on contraception, abortion, and celibacy. This trend removed any scruples that the secular media might have had about confronting the Church or its hierarchy.[18]

The new dissidence within American Catholicism has to be seen in the context of the substantial changes in religious belief and practice within the Church, which occurred so rapidly as to cause observers to speak of a new reformation. The net effect was a dramatic decline in the number and scale of cultural markers that distinguished Catholics from their neighbors, so that there seemed ever less reason for Catholics to maintain their very distinctive stance on doctrinal issues. The extent of the change is masked by the institutional continuity. It would be far easier to recognize the scope of the transformation if indeed the American Church had formally gone into schism and overtly abolished its hierarchy and its links with Rome. Even without such a secession, however, most of the everyday practices and habits that had characterized Catholic life from roughly 1840 to 1960 changed so rapidly that today they are almost unintelligible to practicing Catholics under the age of forty.

To understand this change, we might imagine the life of a typical Catholic parish in the 1930s. At every point, the older Catholic life depended upon beliefs and practices that were utterly distinctive from those of the Protestant or secular mainstream. Masses were then in Latin, and the celebration of Mass was focused on the special sacred role of the priest, rather than on congregational participation. In addition, Catholics prided themselves on a whole culture associated with the liturgy, with hymns and responses sung to the Church's ancient music. For the uninitiated, a Catholic Mass literally looked quite as foreign and baffling as an Orthodox Jewish service. Protestants also found celibacy and the practice of private confession as distasteful as they had ever done.

But just as important to Catholic life were the basket of religious customs collectively known as devotionalism, which led Protestant or secular critics to denounce the Church for its promotion of blatant superstition and sentimentality. In most cases, these practices could claim only tenuous biblical warrant but were justified by long usage and tradition; that distinct claim to authority was itself a major element of the Catholic Difference. Catholic churches looked radically different from their Protestant counterparts because of the abundance of images of the

Virgin Mary, of saints, and of the Sacred Heart of Jesus. A glance inside even a small Catholic church revealed the existence of a quite distinctive aesthetic. To see today what older urban churches in the United States looked like in this period, one would have to travel to a traditional-minded community in Mexico or Central America. These older churches were also the settings for many customary events that Protestants found both embarrassing and difficult to comprehend, such as the saying of the rosary and novenas, First Fridays and benediction. The cults of saints were centered at shrines and churches that promoted their causes through the most modern forms of advertising and merchandising, as well as through older rituals such as processions. Individual Catholics simply behaved differently from other people. Key cultural symbols involved matters as basic as food (fasting during Lent and on Fridays) and attire (saints' medals or scapulars).[19]

For many Catholics today, especially in suburban parishes, most of the visible signs of the older Catholic differences barely exist, or are at best regarded as the habits of the elderly and traditionalist diehards. Changes were already in progress during the 1950s, when attendance at some of the most popular urban shrines began to decline. Perhaps this trend owed something to subtle changes in women's lives and expectations: post–World War II women were less prepared to accept the traditional social ethos that expected them to endure worldly woes and injustices with passive resignation, seeking consolation in devotion to some beloved saint. What has been called the "ghetto Catholicism" that prevailed between the two world wars declined as Catholics moved to the suburbs and their lifestyles and attitudes conformed more closely to those of their non-Catholic neighbors.[20]

The transformation received some official sanction from the second Vatican Council, which met from 1962 to 1965 and caused a revolution in parish life and liturgy. The centerpiece of religious life was henceforward to be the Eucharist, spoken in English, and the rhetoric of the age demanded a new emphasis on congregational participation and the use of the Bible. The practice of confession began a steep decline from the mid-1960s onward, as did the fasting rules that specified fish on Friday.[21]

As churches were reconstructed to meet new liturgical needs, they came to look increasingly like Protestant buildings, while the old devotionalism became ever less important. Even the Virgin Mary is a tangential figure in many churches built since Vatican II. One important case study of a popular Pittsburgh shrine argues, a little sweepingly, that "Catholics all across America appear to have abandoned devotional rituals by 1980." By the 1980s, liturgy and religious practice in an average

Catholic parish looked and felt very much like that in mainstream Protestant denominations such as the Lutherans, Episcopalians, or many Methodist churches. Though Catholics were still distinguished by key elements of church structure and theology, the lived experience of Catholic believers became increasingly harmonized to that of "higher" Protestants.[22]

Today, while Catholic loyalties remain strong, large segments of the laity differ from official positions on many issues that once would have seemed beyond discussion. Especially subject to change has been belief in the core Catholic doctrine of the Eucharist. In 1994, a Gallup survey suggested that only a little over a third of Catholics accepted the teaching that bread and wine become the body and blood of Christ at the Eucharist; almost two-thirds said that Christ's presence was merely symbolic. Obviously, the results of surveys depend enormously on the exact wording of the question, and later polls have indicated a rather stronger belief in the Real Presence. Even so, around a third of American Catholics think that the Eucharist is merely a symbol in which Christ is not really present, and the figure rises to nearly 40 percent among those ages twenty to twenty-nine. With the mass viewed in less supernatural or miraculous terms, the role of the priesthood has declined accordingly. Meanwhile, laypeople have taken to heart the documents of Vatican II stressing that the Church is not merely the clergy, but the entire People of God. In one 1993 survey, three-quarters of Catholics believed that laypeople should have a voice in the choice of a parish priest, rather than leaving the decision entirely to the bishop.[23]

A crisis in traditional Catholic beliefs is indicated by the sharp decline in ordinations to the priesthood, and mass defections among existing priests. The hemorrhage was at its greatest between 1966 and 1976, when thousands left the priesthood, mainly because they wished to marry. Reading an older work such as Merton's *Seven Storey Mountain*, a modern Catholic is amazed to learn about the ease with which the Church of the 1930s could fill its ranks. Wanting to become a novice in a religious order, even someone like Merton had to wait patiently until a vacancy could be found in the next intake of novices; the seminaries were similarly booming. Books and films of this era depict rectories lavishly staffed with a whole clerical hierarchy of senior and assistant pastors.[24]

Today, in contrast, priests are much scarcer. Five hundred fifty-two priests were ordained in 1995, compared to 994 in 1965. And, of course, the number of Catholics requiring their ministry has soared during the same period, to the extent that over a quarter of U.S. parishes either have no pastor or share one with another parish. By the end of the century, the average age of America's diocesan priests had reached fifty-seven, and sixty-three for priests in religious orders: today, more priests are over ninety than are under thirty. A decline in older ideologies is also suggested by the collapsing number of nuns, as many Catholic women rejected the ideals of celibacy and the cloister. There were 180,000 nuns in 1965, compared with 80,000 by the end of the century. Between 1966 and 1976 alone, some 50,000 nuns left their religious vows. Today, half the nuns in the United States today are sixty-eight or older. Ex-clergy and ex-religious were not generally leaving the Church as such, but rather were changing their concept of how one should best live as a Catholic in modern America.[25]

Churches were not the only Catholic institutions that became ever closer to the national norm in the 1960s and 1970s. Changes were also evident in the colleges and universities that had for decades been the flagships of Catholic culture. In 1967, leaders from major Catholic schools gathered to sign the "Land O'Lakes Document," which argued that "the Catholic university must have a true autonomy and academic freedom in the face of authority of whatever kind, lay or clerical, external to the academic community itself." This event has been described as "Independence Day for the American Catholic revolution in Catholic higher education." Repeatedly over the coming decades, conservatives would attack Catholic universities for their toleration of liberal professors and speakers who frankly challenged official Church positions. Even Notre Dame, long the preeminent school of American Catholicism, became a haven for liberal dissidence. In 1977, Notre Dame was the venue for a symposium ostensibly planned to discuss the shape of a future "Third Vatican Council," still more radical than its predecessor.[26]

More than ever, the Catholic Church *in* America looked like it was becoming an *American* Catholic Church, and claims to its unique or exclusive access to truth became ever more tenuous.

A Catholic Civil War

The mainstreaming of Catholic religious life placed a new emphasis on those differences that did remain, which chiefly involved matters of hierarchy and clerical authority. If Catholicism had become so very much like the American religious norm, then special justifications were needed for the remaining peculiarities, such as obedience to an international church, and the high status accorded to clergy and bishops. These matters were not terribly pressing or controversial in normal times, but from the late 1960s, the contraception debate made the issue of obedience crucially important. For most Catholic families, to accept the official

Church position meant pursuing a course that would profoundly affect one's everyday life and prosperity. Many families chose to disregard Church teaching on this vital issue, though without feeling the need to abandon the Church. By 1992, a Gallup poll found that 80 percent of U.S. Catholics disagreed with the statement "Using artificial means of birth control is wrong."[27]

If one could dissent from the Church over birth control, why not over other matters? During the 1970s, as feminist positions became part of mainstream public opinion, many Catholics saw no good reason why their own church should not accept the obvious conclusion that women should be ordained to the priesthood. Such a development was, after all, supported both by secular opinion and by the example of other leading Christian churches. For the same reasons, large numbers of lay and clerical Catholics favored liberal positions on clerical celibacy and on many gay rights issues. If the American Church had been a freestanding denomination independent of Roman authority, it would probably have had married priests since 1970 or so and women priests by about 1980, and would now be debating the ordination of openly gay pastors. The morality of contraception would be a given.[28]

On all these points, though, liberal Catholic opinion found itself in stark opposition to the American hierarchy, and especially to the Vatican. Though the forces for change in American life seemed irresistible, they encountered an immovable object in Rome, and conflict was inevitable. In 1967 and 1968, dissenters frankly challenged the hierarchy in public ways that would have appalled earlier generations, and they naturally made headlines in so doing. This was the era of the struggle between conservative Los Angeles cardinal Francis McIntyre and the nuns of the prestigious teaching order of the Immaculate Heart of Mary, IHM. Among other issues in contention, the sisters demanded greater rights to choose the kind of work to which they would be assigned, wanted greater freedom in choice of clothing and habit, and, above all, stressed the need for individual autonomy rather than unquestioning obedience. The conflict raised fundamental issues about obedience to Church authority and showed the impact of feminist ideas among women religious. It was in conflicts such as these that the media learned the influential lesson that it could easily find Catholics who would speak powerfully, and publicly, against official Church teachings and policies. As Mark Massa observes, Catholic laypeople "now took 'sides' on the proposed IHM reforms: 'sides,' a shocking word, and an even more shocking concept, defining the relationship of Roman Catholics to a bishop of the church."[29]

The dispute over *Humanae Vitae* also dissolved traditional constraints

about openly challenging Church authorities. Very shortly after the encyclical was issued, prominent Catholic theologian Charles Curran announced to a press conference that Catholics were not bound to obey the
papal pronouncement, and his doubts were publicly echoed by hundreds
of other priests and Catholic educators. This was an early manifestation
of what would be a continuing theme over the next thirty years: the repeated clashes between Church authorities and liberal theologians, especially on issues of sexuality. In 1977, the once dependably orthodox
Catholic Theological Society of America (CTSA) published the study
Human Sexuality, which stated that no definitive grounds existed to condemn practices such as contraception, sterilization, and masturbation.
In some cases, the study suggested, premarital and extramarital relationships might be justified. Homosexuals "have the same right to love,
intimacy and relationships as heterosexuals," without forfeiting the right
to communion.[30] Theologians were directly challenging the hierarchy,
which duly condemned the CTSA's statements.

These conflicts attracted attention outside Catholic ranks, partly
because they raised fundamental issues about academic freedom. Repeatedly, the Church would insist that theologians conform to official
teaching on pain of being forbidden to teach theology in Catholic institutions, and Curran himself was at the center of a lengthy struggle over
such a ban through the late 1980s. Throughout, Curran could count on
extensive support in the Catholic intellectual community, including
some of the best-known theologians. Like the IHM affair in Los Angeles,
the Curran Wars were fought in the secular media, as newspapers and
television commentators generally supported the embattled dissidents
against their clerical superiors.[31]

In the mid-1970s, Catholic discontent was manifested in several well-
organized pressure groups. The pro-abortion-rights group, Catholics for
a Free Choice, was founded in 1973 as an offshoot of the National Organization for Women. The same year, discreet gay rights activism within
the Church found national public expression in the movement Dignity.
Corpus (1974) was an organization of men who had left the priesthood
in order to marry (the name was an acronym derived from Corps of Reserved Priests United for Service). In 1975, the Women's Ordination
Conference organized to press the demand for women priests; the group
incorporated in 1977. A national conference of radical, feminist, and
pacifist activists held in 1976 spawned the Call to Action movement,
which has since served as an umbrella for the various shades of the Catholic left. In 1980, Vatican attempts to silence controversial theologians
provoked the formation of the Association for the Rights of Catholics in

the Church, the very name suggesting a liberal approach that would have caused apoplexy in Catholic leaders of earlier years. Liberal reformers found a public voice in Catholic publications, especially the *National Catholic Reporter*, which spoke for the Catholic left much as *The Nation* did for their secular counterparts.[32]

The scale and diversity of Catholic dissidence gained national attention during the years 1986 and 1987, when a number of controversial issues reached fruition more or less simultaneously. These included the suspension of Charles Curran's license to teach theology at American University, the curbing of the episcopal powers of radical Seattle archbishop Raymond Hunthausen, and the Church's attempt to penalize women religious who had put their names to a petition asserting that the official stance on abortion did not reflect the views of all Catholics. In 1986, too, the *New York Times* published a petition signed by over a thousand Catholics, asserting their right to dissent from official Church teaching. When Pope John Paul II visited the United States in the fall of 1987, he found a Church deeply riven by a very public debate about its identity and its sources of authority. The demands of the Catholic opposition were epitomized in a petition published on Ash Wednesday 1990 and signed by over 4,500 individuals. This "Pastoral Letter" called for the ordination of women, an end to mandatory celibacy, revision of Church teachings on sexual morality, adoption of gender-neutral language in the liturgy, and an end to official restraints on academic theologians.[33]

Us and Them

The upsurge of liberal dissidence within the Church meant that the mainstream media had more Catholic controversies to report, and also made it far easier to express views hostile to Catholicism. How could a point of view be anti-Catholic if it was also held by a group that itself claimed to be Catholic, had the word Catholic in its name, and included priests and nuns among its membership? Changes within the American Church helped critics separate their remarks about the Church hierarchy from direct attacks on ordinary Catholic believers.

Now, dissidence within the Catholic community was anything but new. Contrary to some modern stereotypes, there never was a time when American Catholics moved uncritically in lockstep as the Church directed. Anti-clericalism has always existed within the Church and is probably inevitable in any institution that draws on diverse sources of authority. Through long tradition, the Church exalts its hierarchical structure and its clerical institutions, yet the deeply radical and egalitarian picture offered by the gospels often seems to clash with these institutional values. The two value systems can be reconciled, and usually have been—Francis of Assisi never ceased to be a devoted son of the Church —but the potential for conflict is always present.

Anyone who believes that American Catholic dissidence was born in the 1960s should read the now almost-forgotten novels of Harry Sylvester, who clearly wrote as a Catholic (though he later broke with the Church). The faith that emerges from his once-popular writings of the 1940s—such as *Dearly Beloved*, *Moon Gaffney*, and *Dayspring*—is passionate, mystical and socially activist, yet his novels lack few of the criticisms of the institutional Church that have become so familiar from contemporary Church critics and reformers. *Moon Gaffney* portrays the pre–World War II New York Church establishment as thoroughly corrupted by wealth and power. Senior clergy are cynical allies of corrupt politicians and business leaders and are oppressive landlords in their own right: diocesan real estate is handled by "pietistic shysters." The clergy are anti-labor, anti-black, anti-Jewish, and contemptuous of women, and some favor overtly Fascist positions. For Sylvester, clerical support for Father Coughlin's demagogic anti-Semitism was not an aberration, but rather a logical consequence of a culture of intolerance. America has "a priesthood that lacks both charity and humility and has misled and confused its people until they mistake black for white, hate for love and darkness for light." Sylvester writes at this point as a Catholic reformer who was deeply sympathetic to the radical Catholic Worker movement of Dorothy Day. But his strongly anti-clerical work indicates the deep roots of modern critiques of the Church.[34]

What set Sylvester apart from many of his reformist contemporaries was his willingness to air dirty linen in public and to publish in mainstream secular outlets. Prior to the 1950s, many Catholics might have resented the behavior of the hierarchy, but they were deeply sensitive to any public criticisms because these were all too likely to be taken up by outsiders. And it was all but impossible to separate those external attacks from direct assaults on the Catholic community, on families, neighborhoods, and the fabric of religious life. An attack on the hierarchy was an assault on the Church, on the religion, and believers often took it personally. Catholics accepted a highly organic view of the Church, in which it was impossible to distinguish between the hierarchy and the lay membership.[35]

This made it easy for Church authorities to portray virtually all attacks on official Catholic positions as ipso facto anti-Catholic, a view that gained credence from the long and bitterly remembered record of nativist agitation. The long memories of ordinary Catholics are suggested by James Farrell's *Studs Lonigan* trilogy, which portrays Chicago life in the 1920s. Catholic characters automatically assume that, as a liberal intellectual establishment, the University of Chicago must be "an APA school," though by this point the anti-Catholic APA had been defunct for a generation.[36]

Many real-life examples demonstrate how Church authorities invoked the threat of "bigotry" to defuse legitimate media attacks. In the 1940s, a scandal developed in Washington when a teenage girl was injured trying to escape from what was presumably brutal treatment in a Catholic reformatory. A secular newspaper that reported the affair was confronted by a highly successful boycott, after priests declared that the publication was "opening its columns to bigots who are insulting the purity of our Catholic sisterhoods." The paper lost 40 percent of its circulation in two weeks.[37] Fears of such retaliation explain why American newspapers never gave the Coughlinite violence of 1939–40 anything like the exposure it merited. In *Moon Gaffney*, diocesan authorities know they can act with impunity because of their intimate ties to media and government, and because ordinary parishioners are too intimidated to move against the clergy in court.

Genuine instances of anti-Catholicism contributed mightily to promoting solidarity within the Catholic community, which was made to feel ever more embattled after the debacle of the 1928 presidential election. Philadelphia's Cardinal Dougherty was one of many prelates who regularly referred to the embattled status of Catholics: "By many, the Catholic Church is here ridiculed, scoffed at, despised and persecuted; not by sword, but by hatred and opposition."[38] For ordinary lay Catholics, the customary response was to cleave all the more loyally to the Church authorities, and to resist temptations to assimilate. In Harry Sylvester's novels, any expression of criticism of clerical misdeeds, however justified, is greeted with a horrified response on the lines of "What kind of Catholic are you to attack a priest?"

| Uncircling the Wagons

Such a staunchly loyalist response to criticism was barely imaginable by the 1970s and would be quite impossible today. From abundant experience, the vast majority of ordinary Catholic laity know of individuals or groups who have complained of abuses by Church authorities while apparently remaining within the Church. If to attack the Church on one point is to exclude oneself from the community, then that would probably disqualify every Catholic family that practices birth control. Alongside the pluralist recognition of legitimate diversity, there is a willingness to distinguish between criticism directed against the hierarchy and that aimed at the Church as a community. When a prelate is widely criticized, as New York Cardinal O'Connor was through the 1990s or Boston's Cardinal Law was in 2002, an ordinary lay Catholic does not generally take the attack in personal terms, as if his or her own religious identity is under threat. When the attack involves issues of gender or sexuality, a good number of Catholics might well see the critique as reflecting their own grievances.

As a concrete example, we might take the issue of sexual misconduct by Catholic clergy, a theme that has often surfaced in recent years. If we imagine a case in which a priest molested a child, then multiple reasons suggest why such an incident would not have come to public attention before the 1970s. For one thing, litigation against any church was severely limited by the doctrine of charitable immunity. This made it unlikely that charges would come to light through lawsuits. Moreover, the Church would make every effort to deal with the problem within its own ranks, and it could count on the support of police and media, and by no means just Catholics. Apart from reasonable fears of the consequences of the Church's anger, media standards condemned scandal-mongering against people in respected professions: clergy of all denominations enjoyed some protection from media prying, as did Scoutmasters and teachers. If a story had surfaced about a pedophile Catholic priest, most lay believers would probably have rejected it as, more or less, an "APA lie," an even more unsavory version of *Maria Monk*.[39]

In the 1980s, however, Catholics themselves were the first to trumpet the news of such offenses, partly in order to promote their own ideological positions in the ongoing internecine struggle. When cases of priestly child abuse came to light in the mid-1980s, they were given front-page treatment in Catholic publications. Liberal media such as the *National Catholic Reporter* devoted special issues to the "pedophile priest" crisis: in fact, this term was popularized by a special issue of this publication in 1985. (I will discuss the accuracy of this "pedophile" language in chapter 7.) Liberal reformers publicized the abuse theme because it so aptly illustrated their major concerns. The argument was that priest pedophilia occurred in a church that refused to ordain women or married men and in which the strict notion of hierarchy encouraged a culture of secrecy. On the other side of the political divide, conservative papers such as *The Wanderer* publicized the abuse cases for exactly opposite reasons. In their eyes, clerical abuse scandals were just what might be expected in a church that tolerated gay priests and in which episcopal discipline was scorned.[40]

But for whatever reasons, once unspeakable issues of clerical scandal and sexuality were brought into public eye, often in the most sensational terms. Secular publications took up these themes with gusto, licensed by the precedents offered by Catholics themselves. If Catholics and even Catholic clergy were themselves complaining of a sexual crisis within the Church, of an epidemic of clerical perversion, then how could reporting this news possibly be considered anti-Catholic? Time and again, we find that internal Catholic feuding ignited scandals and causes célèbres that provided rich opportunities for the expression of blatant anti-Catholic stereotypes.

This changing coverage suggests a significant change from bygone years in the very notion of what is religious. While Catholics still generally believe that the Church is a sacred institution, there is greater willingness to distinguish between the holy institution and its worldly structures. Scurrilous mockery of the Eucharist or sacred figures such as Jesus or Mary would still be widely seen as anti-religious, but a critique of Church policies would not. While criticism of a venerated figure such as the Pope would probably be seen as anti-religious, some might feel that it fell on debatable ground. The distinctions are subtle and must be understood on a case-by-case basis, but most Catholics no longer place the clergy beyond criticism. A broad shift in the assumptions of American Catholic culture opened the door to much more overt criticism of the Catholic Church, especially on the liberal social issues that now provided the major grounds for anti-Church polemic.

In the 2000 presidential election, candidate George W. Bush was roundly criticized for speaking at Bob Jones University, the fundamentalist institution that dismisses the Catholic Church as a "Satanic counterfeit." In early 2000, as the contest for presidential nominations was gaining momentum, charges of anti-Catholic bias were flying freely, in most cases directed by Democrats or liberal Republicans against Bush. Andrew Sullivan complained that "the bigotry of Bob Jones is morally indistinguishable from that of the Nation of Islam."[41] This charge is reasonable as far as it goes, but the further suggestion was that such atavistic anti-Catholic attitudes reflected the views of large sections of the conservative right. Although Bush himself was forced to make public declarations of his sympathy for Catholicism, the charges may well have cost him votes in some important states and contributed to making the 2000 contest one of the closest in American history.

The critics were suggesting not only that anti-Catholicism still existed, but that it flourished in its old religious and nativist guise, as a weapon of the political right. This charge was ironic in that over the previous three decades, anti-Catholic and anti-Church opinions were far more likely to be expressed in liberal, feminist, and gay rights circles, which were strongly committed to the Democratic Party. On most issues, moreover, these groupings regarded the Republicans as implacably hostile and reactionary. The short-lived furor over the Bob Jones affair masked the basic reality that since the 1970s anti-Catholicism had become firmly anchored in liberal politics, to the extent that it constituted a significant ideological component of the new liberalism.

4 | The Church Hates Women

Although the horse of sexism still dominates the Vatican
table, the mare of Catholic subservience has long ago
bolted from the church stables.

— Joanna Manning

Recently, feminist activist Eleanor Smeal has suggested that mainstream denominations tended to underplay the blatant evils of the Catholic Church, for fear of appearing anti-Catholic. Specifically, she has said: "We have to be tougher on the Catholic Church—we are letting them off the hook."[1] This suggestion is astonishing in view of the constant barrage of feminist attacks on the Church and its leaders. In recent years, women's groups such as Smeal's Feminist Majority Foundation have been among the most vocal critics of Catholicism, to the extent that the mass media have almost without question accepted the notion of "Catholic misogyny." On many occasions, the feminist critique of the Church has crossed the line into strident anti-Catholicism. Recall the demonstrations in Montreal's Reine du Monde Cathedral in 2000, in which radical feminists scattered bloody used tampons. The symbolism of the attack was straightforward. Protesters believed that the Catholic Church was profoundly hostile to women and their interests and that they were recolonizing this enemy space, this "no-woman's-land," with female symbols.

Of course, there are many shades and varieties of feminist opinion, and an incident such as that represents a distant fringe of feminist activism, but suspicion and hostility of the Catholic Church are commonplace across the spectrum. The notion that the Church is a deadly enemy of women is commonly accepted in the news media and in popular culture, never more so than in responses to the clergy abuse cases that filled the headlines in 2002. This sense of total enmity is curious because, although the Church leadership has opposed aspects of organized feminism, Catholic positions are nothing like as reactionary or obscurantist as the cartoon vision would suggest. Indeed, repeated surveys indicate that on many divisive moral and sexual issues, Catholic stances are much closer to the popular mainstream than are those of the anti-Church militants. For its critics, though, Catholicism is "a weary, dated religion where women are incubators and servants." For a self-described Catholic feminist like Joanna Manning, Pope John Paul II "has promoted sexism to the level of a cult in the Church. As a result, the Catholic Church remains today one of the few institutions in the world whose policies and procedures provide a sanction for the discrimination against and oppression of women."[2]

The Church Against Women?

For observers with a historical perspective, the idea of the Church being anti-female has a certain irony, since for several centuries Protestants denounced Catholicism as appallingly effeminate in its aesthetics and worship style, for practicing a kind of emotional sentimentalism that was clearly "womanly." This critique often had racial undertones. Latin or Celtic emotionalism was overtly contrasted with the sober rationalism of northern European peoples, who were more comfortable with the austere deity of the Old Testament. The regrettable Catholic tendency to favor the feminine was most evident in the Church's exaltation of the Virgin Mary. Today, in contrast, it is exactly the veneration of Mary that is often taken to symbolize the Church's anti-feminine stance; this figure, so quintessentially passive and virginal, negates any positive or realistic view of womanhood. For Catholic theology, it is claimed, the only good woman is a mother, ideally one who has never had sex. Feminist critics of the Church find it only predictable that archconservative Pope John Paul II should be such a passionate advocate of the cult of Mary and a devoted patron of her shrines and apparition sites. The underlying grounds of anti-Church rhetoric may have changed, often in ways that seem capricious, but issues of gender continue to be at the heart of anti-Catholic rhetoric.[3]

The fact that women's causes are so much more central to anti-Catholicism than they were fifty or a hundred years ago does not mean that the Church's attitudes have necessarily changed. Western societies have simply experienced a revolutionary upsurge in women's expectations, which has transformed the substance of political debate. For various reasons, official Catholic positions have been far slower to change, chiefly because of the Church's global character. Many in the American hierarchy may wish to bring Catholic stances on social or moral issues into accord with the secular mainstream, but they are overruled by the Vatican, which has to consider the more conservative attitudes held in other parts of the world. Although American Catholics rarely acknowledge the fact, they make up only a very small component of the global Church—no more than 6 percent out of a Catholic community of over a billion.[4]

But whatever their roots, the Church's traditional attitudes have provided a vitally important weapon for feminists and liberal reformers, who have for decades found Catholicism an immaculate enemy and thus an invaluable propaganda tool. In saying this, I am not trying to understate the authentic hostility that exists toward the Church, much of which stems from a quite genuine fear of Catholic political power. Yet as we have seen, social movements often find it useful to identify and demonize their leading enemies, who can be repeatedly cited as the reason why their cause meets any opposition. This is all the more useful if the enemy in question is already unpopular or can be associated with other causes of which the public is already suspicious. For feminists or gay rights activists, opposition is generally attributed to a stereotyped "Religious Right," a term that in popular usage connotes ignorance, reaction, prurient busybodyism, and hypocrisy. Demonization of this sort has the advantage of discrediting other types of opposition, which might rest on more respectable grounds.

On women's issues, the Catholic Church offers a ready-made demon figure that automatically symbolizes sexism and reaction. The Church's leadership is all male, and the fact that the institution refuses to ordain women seems to commit it to continuing male supremacy of a sort that most other social institutions abandoned decades since. In addition, the supernatural grounds on which the Church bases its social positions invite criticism from an American public that is largely hostile to breaching the wall of separation between church and state, and which takes a negative view of terms such as dogma and orthodoxy.

If a conflict over social issues can be framed in terms of a battle between feminism and the Catholic Church, then feminists have every reason to expect not just that they will win support, but that they will be seen as representing the social mainstream. Imagine a debate between, on one hand, women speaking the language of progress, secular values, and individual tolerance and, on the other, men who are using otherworldly religious rhetoric and whose very clothing seems archaic and foreign. It is very much in the interest of women's groups to portray opposition to their issues as specifically religious and Catholic, and also to represent these religious interests in the most obnoxious and oppressive way. For feminists, anti-Catholicism is an effective strategy for seizing the ideological middle ground of public debate.

Birth Control Debates

In modern America, the Church's supposedly anti-woman attitudes are often illustrated by its condemnation of contraception and abortion. According to critics, the official Catholic position indicates how very far the Church has fallen behind any kind of social reality, and suggests that the Church sees no role for women except as wives and mothers. If the Church denies women a right as basic as the control of their own fertility, then it can scarcely hope to speak plausibly of any other social or political rights. Catholic attitudes are all the more distinctive because the Church is now the only major religious or cultural body in North America that opposes the idea of birth control. (Catholic views on abortion are more widely shared.)

Such accusations are so familiar that it is a little surprising to realize how relatively recent they are, and how new the Catholic Difference is in this area. At the start of the twentieth century, contraception was a deeply controversial subject, and its main advocates were radicals and socialists on the extreme political fringe. Legally, contraceptives were in the same category as pornography, and neither could be advertised freely. Not until the 1920s did the birth control cause gain a substantial following among respectable medical and educational groups, and then largely because contraception was seen as an effective weapon in promoting eugenics, rather than as a women's rights issue. By the mid-1930s, contraception began to achieve legal recognition as well as social respectability, but even then, mainstream Protestant churches continued to be divided about the moral questions involved.[5]

In the early part of the century, then, Catholics were scarcely unusual in their opposition to contraception. What distinguished Catholics from other religious groups was that they had the determination and the ability to enforce their will by deploying their secular power. Long notorious in the anti-contraception campaign was New York's "Battle of Town Hall" in 1921, when Church pressure led the police to shut down a pro-birth-control meeting that was to be addressed by Margaret Sanger. This became a public scandal, but less because of the specific issue to be discussed than the flagrant exercise of Church power: the archdiocese apparently felt that the New York Police Department should act as temple guards when summoned. In later years, though, the absolute Catholic prohibition on birth control became more sharply defined. In 1930, the Pope issued a strongly worded encyclical on the matter under the title *Casti Connubii*. Catholics increasingly stood out by their forceful opposition to the slightest weakening of the laws prohibiting the sale of contraceptive devices and even the distribution of relevant information through the mails. Anticontraceptive rhetoric also became more hyperbolic, as Catholic literature described even contraceptive use within marriage as leading to sex that was no more than "mutual masturbation or unnatural lust," or actual prostitution. In 1935, New York's Cardinal Hayes described birth control as "diabolic," its advocates as "prophets of decadence."[6]

The birth control issue gradually became a cultural marker separating Catholic and non-Catholic populations, as obvious as fish on Friday— though with much more sweeping consequences. Paul Blanshard wrote in 1958, "The Church's opposition to birth control has now become the most important part of its sexual code." Once again, critics charged that Catholics were letting themselves be slavishly subordinate to church and clergy, even in the most intimate matters of life. Yet at the same time, official commands were meeting lay Catholic resistance. Already by the 1950s, Catholic liberals were attacking the prohibition of birth control in language that we normally associate with the aftermath of *Humanae Vitae*. For Blanshard, the prohibition was "the greatest blunder in the history of the church. ... Almost all well-to-do people in the country practice it to some extent, including well-to-do Catholics." From the 1930s onward, survey evidence suggests that a majority of Catholic women disagreed with the Church about whether contraceptive information should be made available to them, even if they were not actually using those devices themselves. By the mid-1950s, Blanshard was describing "the growing defiance of Catholic women, as well as men." (The degree of disaffection is open to some debate: a 1963 study by Andrew

Greeley indicated widespread Catholic support for Church teachings, especially among the better-educated.)[7]

While the Catholic teaching on contraception was not too far removed from the social norm at the start of the century, the gulf became vast in the 1950s and 1960s. One factor was the growing fear of a global population explosion, which led U.S. policy makers to propose the active sponsorship of family planning programs overseas. In 1961, President Kennedy—a Catholic himself, of course—spoke of the "staggering" problem of overpopulation. These fears soared in the next decade, stimulated by enormously influential books such as Paul Ehrlich's *The Population Bomb*. In 1974, the Club of Rome's (wildly inaccurate) study *The Limits of Growth* linked population worries to fears of environmental catastrophe and resource exhaustion, an equation that the Western media generally accepted without question. Since these dangers were so evident to most educated people, the obvious question was why the Catholic hierarchy remained obdurate. Church behavior seemed inexplicable except as a fanatical obedience to outdated dogma. For population control advocates, the Catholic Church was becoming quite literally the primary obstacle to human survival.[8]

The growing popularity of contraception also raised critical questions about women's status. The spread of the contraceptive pill beginning in the early 1960s made effective contraception much more widely available than hitherto, and in a form that gave women the decisive voice in controlling their own fertility. By the 1960s, contraception came to be seen as normal, customary, and familiar, an essential prerequisite for women's social equality. The National Organization for Women was founded in 1966, and an explosive new feminist movement acquired national visibility during the red year of 1968. This rapid change in social sensibility goes far toward explaining the shock caused by *Humanae Vitae*, which the media presented as a callous insult to women, especially those in the Third World.

As contraceptive use has become even more widely accepted in later years, including by Catholics themselves, the Church's stance permits critics to dismiss it as dogmatically anti-modern and above all, anti-woman. This indictment gained still more force in the 1980s and 1990s as the prohibition of contraception was restated just as definitively by Pope John Paul II. The birth control issue opens the Church to attack on feminist grounds, and in an area in which most lay Catholics are likely to sympathize with the critics.

Abortion

The perception that the Church is out of touch with reality on contraception did much to undermine Catholic teachings on other matters in which they might otherwise have enjoyed more impact. This is especially true in the debate over abortion, in which, again, the Catholic Church is commonly presented as the deadly enemy of women's life and health. Only recently, though, has the Church acquired its role as the chief standard-bearer of traditional morality. At least up to the mid-twentieth century, a wide social consensus condemned abortion as a form of murder, and this was even the opinion of most birth-control activists. Not until the late 1950s did the U.S. legal profession begin to advocate easing the law on abortion in special cases involving rape, incest, or deformity of the fetus. In the early 1960s, this last exception became a central argument in a new campaign for liberalizing the law when the drug thalidomide produced a large number of grotesque deformities. By common consent, women in such cases desperately needed abortions in order to prevent the birth of badly deformed children, and yet they faced massive legal obstacles. Notorious cases such as these helped the widespread legalization of abortion—by California in 1967, and by fifteen more states between 1967 and 1970. The National Association for the Repeal of Abortion Laws was founded in 1969. In 1973, the Supreme Court affirmed the new liberalism in its *Roe v. Wade* decision.[9]

Significantly, a substantial number of Catholics favored liberalization, at least in very limited circumstances. A 1965 poll showed that half of U.S. Catholics would support abortion if it was necessary to save the life of the mother. More-sweeping legal reform gained support among the emerging generation of Catholic feminists, notably Mary Daly, whose 1968 book *The Church and the Second Sex* became the movement's foundation text. In 1972, she wrote an important article in the Catholic journal *Commonweal*, arguing that Church opposition to abortion "should be seen within the wider context of the oppression of women in sexually hierarchical society." The continued prohibition was part of the "sexual caste system" upon which the Church was founded. She warned of "a situation in which open war is declared between feminism in this country and official Roman Catholicism"—a fair description of what would in fact develop over the coming decades. In 1973, three NOW activists founded the pressure group Catholics for a Free Choice (CFFC).[10]

Taken aback by the speed of the social change with respect to abortion law, the U.S. Catholic Conference promptly organized the National Right to Life Committee (1970) in order to campaign for recriminalization. In

1974, the Church sponsored the first of what would become annual Marches for Life. Certainly the Catholic Church has not stood alone in its subsequent campaign in the name of "life"; Protestant evangelicals have been well represented. But Catholics can be seen as the mainstream of the pro-life movement. As such, they have borne the brunt of feminist criticism, which has become ever more powerful as pro-abortion views have gained support among the American public.[11]

Catholics have provided useful demon figures in the abortion debate because of their perceived extremism. The common attitude seems to be that if the Church is not prepared to see reason on as basic an issue as contraception, how can it speak sensibly on other matters involving women? Repeated opinion surveys over the years have shown that a substantial majority of Americans favor abortion laws less restrictive than the absolute prohibition called for by the Catholic Church, yet which still fall far short of anything approximating abortion on demand. A consensus seems to favor granting women broad latitude to decide the fate of their pregnancies within the first three months or in cases when the pregnancy poses a danger to the life or health of the mother, though those polled become much more dubious under other conditions. To use President Clinton's influential formulation, many moderate Americans believe that abortion should be "safe, legal and rare," a formula that in theory opens the way to quite extensive legislative restrictions on the practice. For the Catholic Church, however, all abortions are wrong in all circumstances, and any law that fails to acknowledge this fact is simply immoral and unacceptable.

It is easy for pro-choice advocates to discredit virtually all opposition to abortion as the work of the Catholic Church and the "religious right," as an expression of religious dogmatism. Once again, the fervor of religious opposition to abortion allows the pro-choice movement to present themselves as the authentic social mainstream, advocates for the popular causes of individual liberty and public secularism. This approach has been much used in the bitter debates over hospitals providing services involving contraceptives or abortion. Catholic hospitals naturally refuse to be involved in such services, but so also do secular hospitals that merge with Catholic institutions. The charge is that ever-growing numbers of non-Catholics are becoming subject to unreasonable and anti-woman Catholic sexual teachings. NOW complains of "the vast expansion of the Catholic healthcare network, in which religious dictates can take precedence over individual preference."[12]

Particularly when Catholics are involved, religious opposition allows the abortion debate to be framed more clearly in terms of women's rights, as defined against patriarchal oppression. In 1993, for instance, when U.S. Surgeon General Joycelyn Elders addressed a crowd of pro-choice activists, she charged that pro-lifers were conducting a "love affair with the fetus" at the behest of "a celibate, male-dominated church."[13] The more feminists found themselves in direct confrontation with the Church, the more central to their rhetoric became anti-Catholic and anti-clerical statements.

| Protesting the Church

As Daly had prophesied, warfare between feminists and the Catholic Church was already well under way by the mid-1970s, with ferocious mutual denunciations. In 1976, the National Organization for Women asked the Internal Revenue Service to audit the National Conference of Catholic Bishops and the U.S. Catholic Conference, in addition to each individual diocese, on the grounds that the deep Catholic involvement in anti-abortion politics should end the Church's immunity from taxation. In this view, the Church had become a right-wing political party, rather than a religious organization.[14]

Once again, we have to draw a sharp line between criticisms of Church policies and overt anti-Catholicism. It is scarcely surprising that once the Church had become so active in a major public debate, neither the institution nor its leaders should escape attack. Reasonable people can differ about the proper scope of political activism by a tax-exempt organization. Having said this, the abortion debate also produced some grotesque manifestations of anti-Catholic rhetoric pure and simple, direct attacks on the religious system rather than solely against the hierarchy or particular leaders. Feminists had a long tradition of using demonstrations and mass actions, and it was inevitable that such protests would be directed against what was believed to be such a hostile institution as the Catholic Church.[15]

Demonstrations often crossed the line between targeting specific policies or individuals and attacking the cherished ideas and symbols of the faith, moving into active anti-Catholicism. In the mid-1970s, feminists picketed the cathedral of the bishop of San Diego, who had denied communion to members of pro-abortion groups, including NOW. In 1974, on the first anniversary of the *Roe v. Wade* decision, one of the co-founders of CFFC crowned herself "Pope" on the steps of New York's St. Patrick's Cathedral. In 1985, Church attitudes toward abortion and contraception were the target of NOW-organized protest rallies in Washington and other cities, in a campaign entitled "Witness for Women's Lives." Such protests regularly used slogans such as "Keep your rosaries off our ovaries." When the Pope visited the United States in 1987, his appearances were widely picketed by feminists, and both NOW and CFFC protested at the Vatican embassy in Washington. In California, one typical demonstrator was "a self-described 'recovering Catholic,' [who] wore a mock maternity dress, carried three baby dolls and had written on an apron the words: 'My uterus, property of the Vatican.'" By this point, feminist demonstrations against Church properties and offices had become almost commonplace. These events walked a very thin line between protest and blasphemy, and some assuredly caused offense to believers.[16]

| Ordaining Women

In a third area, too, that of women's ordination, the Church became the target of feminist anger, from women both inside and outside its ranks. Since its emergence in the late 1960s, the new women's movement had enjoyed enormous success in removing structural obstacles to women's progress in most aspects of business and government, and this campaign gained broad public support. By the 1970s, a common opinion held that only a belief in women's inherent inferiority led institutions to exclude women from high office, and this exclusion automatically constituted sexism. Gradually, most churches accepted this view, permitting women to be ordained as clergy and bishops or senior leaders, though initially reformers faced intense controversy. In Lutheran denominations, the first ordinations occurred in 1969 and 1970. In the Episcopal Church, the decisive move came in Philadelphia in 1974, when eleven women were ordained in an irregular proceeding. Their position was regularized in 1976, when that church made the official decision to ordain; it acquired its first female bishop in 1989. By the end of the 1970s, women clergy were active in most of the large Protestant denominations. Between 1983 and 1996, the number of women clergy in the United States increased from sixteen thousand to forty-four thousand. By the end of the decade, almost fifty thousand women were serving as ministers and rabbis in America, and the proportion of women clergy in particular Protestant denominations varied between 10 and 20 percent of the whole.[17]

Not surprisingly, given the large constituency of articulate and educated women in its religious orders, the Roman Catholic Church faced early pressure to ordain women as priests. As early as 1971, American Catholic bishops received the report from an investigation they themselves had commissioned, which found no theological barriers to the ordination of women. In 1974, a pro-ordination motion was passed by the National Leadership Conference of Women Religious, one of the most prestigious organizations representing Catholic women. The pressure group that would become the Women's Ordination Conference dates from 1975. Through the 1990s, most opinion surveys showed that a substantial majority of American Catholics supported the idea of women as clergy—67 percent, according to a 1992 Gallup poll.[18]

What prevented American Catholics from following the liberal Protestant denominations was, of course, Catholicism's global dimension, the fact that authority in the Church ultimately resided in Rome and the papacy. In increasingly uncompromising terms, the Vatican made it clear that it was not prepared to consider female Catholic priests. In 1977, a papal commission decisively ruled that a male priesthood represented the clear intent of both Christ and the early Church. Thus thwarted in the attempt to see women ordained, many Catholic feminists developed far more radical views challenging the whole basis of the existing priesthood and of the wider Church. In 1983, a conference in Chicago heralded the formation of "Woman Church," and between 1982 and 1986, Catholic feminist ideas were disseminated at a series of meetings, conferences, and retreats, often held on the premises of Catholic institutions.[19]

As in the case of contraception, the American Catholic Church was massively out of step with most secular opinion. The Church's stance on women priests was multiply infuriating for feminists, who could nevertheless use the conflict to their own ideological advantage. The distinctive Catholic position was possible only because the Church stood outside the law in matters of internal governance and could not be legally compelled to promote women, as could a secular corporation. This immunity made Church interference in secular affairs all the more intolerable: the bishops were claiming the right to influence worldly affairs, though without themselves being subject to the conventional rules and structures of secular society. Also, the Church could be attacked for its submission to foreign reactionary pressures. The Church thus appeared to be anti-democratic, culturally and politically alien, and, above all, misogynistic. The ordination issue provoked anti-Church demonstrations over and above those inspired by birth control issues. As early as 1970, NOW members publicly burned a copy of the Roman missal that prohibited women from serving as lectors.[20]

Culture Wars

Earlier attacks on Catholic misogyny, such as Blanshard's, had been of limited effectiveness because they apparently represented external assaults on the Church and its faithful. The feminist critique since the

1970s has been far more potent because it has been led by Catholic feminists themselves, usually women who remain within the Church and proclaim their loyalty to the faith. This places non-Catholic critics in the far more sympathetic position of external allies trying to assist other women in a struggle against oppression. Since the early 1980s, the cultural war between feminists and the Church has erupted repeatedly, often in ways that have integrated the various causes and grievances.

One confrontation began in 1984 when Geraldine Ferraro, a Catholic, became the first woman to be nominated as a vice presidential candidate by one of the two major parties. Her pro-choice views were attacked by the hierarchy, which was in turn criticized by liberal Catholics such as CFFC. The ensuing controversy raised some traditional anti-Catholic fears about the Church attempting to impose its bigoted opinions upon the mainstream—though, as Catholic writers noted, the same concerns were not raised when liberal clergy spoke freely on their cherished issues, or even ran for office in their own right. Mainstream media rarely so much as remarked on the strongly church-based nature of black politics, still less the overwhelmingly clerical cast of the black leadership. Catholic interventions in politics, however, attracted a very different response. Typically, the *New York Times* claimed that "the bishops' effort to impose a religious test on the performance of Catholic politicians threatens the hard-won understanding that finally brought Americans to elect a Catholic president a generation ago." The language suggests that Catholic politicians can be tolerated so long as they are not too visibly enthusiastic about their religion.[21]

This crisis, and the suspicions of clerical power that it produced, was reflected in Lawrence Lader's 1987 book *Politics, Power, and the Church*, which in many ways can be seen as an updating of Blanshard's polemics. Lader's approach is strongly liberal, and most of the issues he cites are close to feminist hearts, but the core idea is a much older dichotomy between Catholicism and Americanism. Like Blanshard, Lader posed a diametric opposition between Church power and what he called "American pluralism," what earlier generations had termed "American Freedom" or "Americanism."[22]

These controversies also sparked conflicts within the Catholic Church itself. When the *New York Times* printed a CFFC-sponsored advertisement declaring that "a diversity of opinions regarding abortion exists among committed Catholics," the document was signed by a number of nuns and other religious (the "Vatican 24"). The clergy signatories faced Church disciplinary proceedings, including possible expulsion from their orders. The Vatican also began a general investigation of American religious orders—mainly women's orders. Hostilities flared again in 1986 over the question of granting platforms to pro-abortion politicians in premises associated with the Church, such as Catholic colleges.[23]

| Gender Crisis, 1988–1993

The period between 1988 and 1993 marked an acute intensification of gender politics in the United States, as issues long central to feminist rhetoric came to the center of mainstream discourse. Such conflicts could not fail to have an impact on attitudes toward the Catholic Church, which was commonly seen as the chief opponent of organized feminism. It is not surprising that feminist groups should have opposed the Church and its hierarchy, but in practice, they consistently went beyond mere political confrontation to preach a sweeping and overt anti-Catholicism.

As so often, abortion was at the forefront of these battles. For both sides of the debate, abortion is a deeply emotional issue, one of the few areas of mainstream politics in which each side regularly accuses the other of murder or of acquiescing in the deaths of the innocent. The controversy became ever more embittered under the conservative political administrations of the 1980s, when pro-choice advocates feared that a new Supreme Court might reverse *Roe v. Wade* and take American women back to the prohibitive abortion policies of the 1950s. In the event, the major Supreme Court decision (*Webster v. Reproductive Health Services*, 1989) was far less restrictive than many had feared or hoped, but abortion remained a fundamental dividing issue. By the early 1990s, anti-abortion fervor was mobilized in large-scale demonstrations and obstruction operations, "rescues" intended to bring clinics to a standstill. Violence against abortion facilities escalated to the use of arson, bombs, and (by 1993) the assassination of doctors and clinic workers.[24]

Other controversies in these years allowed feminists to portray a pervasive danger from male injustice and oppression. This was, for instance, the era of the Senate hearings to determine whether Clarence Thomas was suited to be a justice of the U.S. Supreme Court, an encounter that brought the matter of sexual harassment to the headlines. The same issue was central to the Tailhook affair, in which servicemen were accused of the mass molestation of female colleagues. Concerns about rape and sexual assault were publicized through several high-profile criminal trials during these years. Meanwhile, the mass media reported sympathetically on extreme charges about the sexual abuse of children, including numerous instances in which abuse was first recalled in adulthood. Whatever the truth of the charges (and most would today find them shaky), the picture was once again of men committing sexual atrocities against women and girls. Together with the real violence outside the abortion clinics, it is not surprising that feminists by this point thought themselves seriously embattled, and under attack specifically by the forces of organized religion. In 1995, terrorist attacks on abortion clinics in Massachusetts and Virginia led to protests against Catholic churches and institutions in various cities. In San Francisco, hundreds of pro-choice supporters demonstrated outside St. Mary's Cathedral, blocking streets. "Protesters mocked the Church by wearing religious apparel."[25]

In retrospect, we know that a liberal Democratic regime would be elected in 1992 and that the political balance would swing back quite far in favor of feminism and the left. At the start of the decade, though, such an outcome seemed quite unlikely, especially given the astronomically high poll numbers enjoyed briefly by the first President Bush after the U.S. victory over Iraq in 1991. Commentators were suggesting that if the Republicans won in 1992, Democrats would have to move to the political center if they ever hoped to regain the White House. The prospect of sixteen or twenty years out of office seemed agonizingly likely. Some Democrats advocated a more conservative policy on public morality that would mean renouncing the party's support of abortion, under the leadership of a pro-life figure such as the Catholic Pennsylvania governor Robert Casey. Though such schemes became moot in the aftermath of the Clinton victory, they aroused real concern at the time, and help explain the passionate opposition to any expansion of Catholic political power.

Though it has been largely forgotten, overt public anti-Catholicism was as much in evidence in these years as at any time since before the 1960 election. One focus of agitation was the confirmation hearing of Clarence Thomas. Among the many reasons liberals opposed Thomas was his Catholicism. Virginia Governor Douglas Wilder expressed concern that Thomas "has indicated that he is a very devout Catholic. ... How much allegiance is there to the Pope?" The remark naturally began a vigorous public debate. A flurry of hostile cartoons depicted the sinister nuns and conniving bishops who would influence secular policy in matters such as abortion once Thomas was seated on the highest court. One image depicted the new justice being hymned to the bench by a group of chanting nuns, with onlookers commenting, "Well, there goes *Roe v. Wade*." When these attacks were criticized as religious bigotry, liberals blamed the furor not on anti-Catholic sentiment, but on the aggressions of the Catholic Church itself. Columnist Ellen Goodman wrote, "It isn't liberals, and it certainly isn't Douglas Wilder who have reopened the can of worms marked religion. It's the Catholic hierarchy." The campaigns of these years raise real doubts about the popular belief that the election of John Kennedy had ended the charge of "double loyalty." In the case of Clarence Thomas, some of the liberal media were not prepared to consider the possibility that a Catholic public official might dare to oppose the edicts of his church.[26]

Contempt for Catholic sensitivities was apparent during the controversy over the political role of Governor Casey, a Democrat who was impeccably liberal on most social and labor issues and who tried to establish universal health care within his state, yet he held strongly to the Church's position on abortion. A Pennsylvania law he had favored was the subject of an important Supreme Court decision in 1992, which permitted states to impose limited restrictions on the practice of abortion. In his views on this issue, Casey reflected a large section of Catholic and moderate opinion. Nevertheless, he was refused the right to address the 1992 Democratic Party convention, because his views on abortion were considered too outrageously extreme for the group's feminist majority. In itself, this incident confirms how far the Democrats had moved from the days when Catholics were a substantial portion of their strength. At the convention, abortion rights activists sold buttons depicting Casey dressed as the Pope.[27]

Shortly afterward, the convention affair was complicated when, in a gesture to free speech, the *Village Voice* invited the governor to speak in New York and to deliver the address that he would have given at the convention. Casey was greeted by a hundred protesters, including both feminist militants and members of the AIDS advocacy group ACT UP. Demonstrators shouted slogans such as "Racist, sexist, anti-gay, Governor Casey go away" and "Murderers have no right to speak"—both astonishing in the light of Casey's liberal record. Casey was eventually forced to abandon his speech. Remarkably, what might have seemed like a significant political event received virtually no attention in the news media, and attracted only strictly limited coverage even in the *New York Times*, suggesting a signal lack of outrage at the silencing of a prominent national politician. As Casey himself said, "If it had been a right-wing group shutting down a pro-choice speech by the governor of a major state, it would have been splashed across page one in the *Times* the next day." Conceivably, it would have been labeled a hate crime. That a hundred people could mobilize against a prominent Catholic politician is scarcely surprising, but the fact that so few editors or journalists were disturbed is far more troubling.[28]

Anti-Catholic hostility in these years went well beyond partisan politics. One new grievance was the continuing scandal about the sexual abuse of children by clergy, the so-called pedophile priest cases. As we will see, much of the reporting of these incidents was tendentious and exaggerated the distinctively Catholic element in abuse cases, but during the early 1990s, the media had no doubt that the Church had systematically concealed massive crimes by its clergy. The menacing figure of the "pedophile priest" acquired a terrifying public face in 1992 with the exposé of the long record of criminal activity by Massachusetts priest James Porter, who had abused hundreds of children over the previous three decades. Such cases gave powerful additional ammunition to feminist critics of the Church, who found it unsurprising that a male clergy would abuse women and children and that a male-dominated Church institution would cover up or trivialize these acts. Since the early 1990s, one of the commonest phrases in media reporting of the scandal has been the "sins of the fathers," a biblical allusion that specifically refers to "patriarchal" crimes. Charges of Church hypocrisy helped to undermine the claims of the hierarchy to speak with moral authority on other sexual matters such as abortion.

Clergy abuse stories became weapons in anti-Church and anti-Catholic polemic, and many cartoons and satirical stories now revived the Victorian stereotype of the priest as sexual exploiter. Even newspapers such as the *New York Times* ran opinion pieces under titles like "Priests Who Prey," and the coverage in women-oriented magazines such as *Ms, Vanity Fair,* and *Redbook* was hair-raising. According to one polemical book on the abuse episodes, the Church itself was teaching a "gospel of shame," following patterns of clerical criminality that authors Elinor Burkett and Frank Bruni traced back to hoary tales of the crimes of the Borgias. (Bruni himself went on to become one of the *New York Times*'s leading commentators on Catholic issues.) This first national wave of clergy abuse stories legitimized the public expression of anti-Catholic stereotypes in media outlets, from the most sensational to the normally sedate. And when a new set of scandals erupted a decade later, feminists would again take the lead in denouncing the Church for its alleged sexual hypocrisy.[29]

Between 1992 and 1994, the media showed themselves willing to present anti-Catholic themes and events that they would have treated much more circumspectly in bygone days, when they would have faced the threat of boycott by a unified Catholic audience. From any number of instances, we might take the moment in 1992 when singer Sinead O'Connor denounced Pope John Paul II on the television program *Saturday Night Live.* She tore up his photograph, inciting the audience to "fight the real enemy!" Both the Pope and Cardinal O'Connor had by this point acquired real demon status among feminists. This context helps explain the strong hostility aroused by the Pope's 1994 statement *Ordinatio Sacerdotalis*, which not only rejected women's ordination outright, but asserted that the issue was entirely closed to further debate. Feminists saw particular significance in the date of this letter, the anniversary of the burning of Joan of Arc.[30]

Population Politics

This polarization helps to explain the deep hostility to the Vatican's international role, which became powerfully evident in the mid-1990s. In the nineteenth century, the Vatican was especially disliked because it represented a sovereign state, making Catholics vulnerable to charges of divided loyalty. During the 1990s, these political themes were much in evidence because of the Church's participation in international conferences on the role of women, which naturally addressed issues of population control, including contraception and abortion. In 1994, the Cairo conference stressed that population control could be achieved only by enhancing women's political role and expanding access to contraception. Conference-related controversies gave a platform for a good deal of overt anti-Catholic and anti-Vatican venom, as feminists portrayed the Church as the main enemy of women's progress worldwide. This event provoked a torrent of anti-papal and anti-Catholic cartoons in the U.S. media, generally targeting the Pope or bishops as callous enemies of all women: for critics, this was "the World Pope-elation Conference." Compounding anti-Catholicism with newer prejudices, protesters denounced Church authorities for their tactical alliances with highly stereotyped "Muslim extremists," as cartoons depicted the Pope literally in bed with drooling Islamist fanatics.[31]

The Church was as anxious to present its agenda as feminist groups were to state theirs, and each side attempted to exclude their opponents. For feminists, Church attempts to limit their participation were seen as manifestations of Catholic misogyny, and this theme attracted wide media support. In 1994, a syndicated cartoon depicted a senior Catholic cleric stating, "We strongly condemn increased participation by radical groups in the upcoming UN population conference," while the priest at his side adds, "For example, say ... women!"[32] The anti-Vatican movement led to the formation of See Change, a U.S.-based feminist campaign to end the special permanent observer status held by the Vatican at the United Nations, a category that allows the Vatican full voting rights in UN deliberations. See Change has subsequently become a center for intemperate anti-Vatican activism.

Both feminists and population control supporters condemned the Church hierarchy in extremely hostile terms. Joanna Manning harks back to still older Roman imperial imagery, referring to the attendance of "the Pope and his praetorian guard of all-male cardinals, bishops and clergy." One pressure group, the Population Institute, has expressed concern about "how one small political entity, the Vatican, in pursuing its own interests, has managed to control U.S. population policy and to thwart freedom of the press. It has also undermined not only our own national security but that of other countries and endangered the earth's environment and its inhabitants." The Holy See, the institute said, was acting as "an anti-contraceptive Gestapo."[33]

| Catholics for a Free Choice

The organization CFFC has often served as a focus for feminist protests against the Church. Conservative critics dismiss the group as the main public voice of overt anti-Catholicism. This is a sensitive charge. As we have seen, many Catholics differ from Church authorities on specific issues, and sometimes criticize the hierarchy quite sharply: think of dissident groups such as Call to Action, Dignity, or the Women's Ordination Conference. However much the Church hierarchy might dislike these groups, the reformers do not usually attack Church doctrines or beliefs in a way that would raise questions about their Catholic credentials. CFFC is the only one of these groups that the National Conference of Catholic Bishops has singled out as crossing the line into active anti-Catholicism. The charge is that CFFC (together with the closely affiliated group See Change) serves very much the same political purpose as the anti-Church "resistance movement" that Paul Blanshard outlined half a century ago.

CFFC has been headed since 1982 by Frances Kissling. For conservatives, CFFC's very title is an insult and an oxymoron. Since the Church has repeatedly declared itself fundamentally opposed to abortion, anyone who opposes such a basic tenet of belief cannot plausibly claim to be a Catholic. Moreover, rejecting the teaching authority of the Church on an issue such as this places one far outside the official standards of that institution. Having said this, a substantial number of Americans who declare themselves to be Catholics also support abortion laws more liberal—often far more liberal—than those permitted by official Church teaching.[34]

For present purposes, though, it is irrelevant whether or not one can be a pro-choice Catholic. Quite apart from its basic stance on abortion, CFFC is also a public voice for opinions that can only be described as anti-Catholic, not merely anti-hierarchy. In 1991, Kissling told *Mother Jones*, "I spent twenty years looking for a government that I could overthrow, without being thrown in jail. I finally found one in the Catholic Church."[35] Her group addresses the familiar themes of anti-Catholicism, and does so using a rhetoric that borrows explicitly from that tradition—usually in a hyperbolic style. When the television magazine program *60 Minutes* reported on the issue of Catholic takeovers of secular hospitals, the main critic of Church behavior interviewed was Frances Kissling, who said, "It's not like the old days. Doctors are no longer gods. Now we have bishops who are gods." In a recent advertising blitz, CFFC claims that "Catholic people care. Do our bishops? Because the bishops ban condoms, innocent people die." In this view, the Church hierarchy is made up of callous megalomaniacs who epitomize patriarchy. In 1994, she described the Church as full of "hatred of women and fear of sexuality ... Misogyny is alive and well at the Vatican ... women's lives still rank at the bottom when it comes to respect, much less value."[36]

Kissling herself wholeheartedly enlists historical anti-Catholic traditions in explaining why the Church has adopted the positions she opposes. In a resuscitation of solid seventeenth-century anti-popery, Kissling explains the continued survival of the Church hierarchy in the modern world: "They're good—they're intelligent, suave, sophisticated, tenacious. These people have been doing diplomacy for 1,500 years. This is the former Holy Roman Empire we're dealing with: they've made and unmade kings." That is a modern version of Thomas Hobbes's seventeenth-century charge that the papacy was "no other than the ghost of the deceased Roman Empire, sitting crowned upon the grave thereof for so did the papacy start up on a sudden out of the ruins of that heathen power."[37]

Another familiar manifestation of anti-Catholic rhetoric can be seen in Kissling's leadership in the See Change movement. The anti-Vatican movement draws on the long-standing critique of the Catholic Church as a sinister cosmopolitan body. Recall that in the 1940s, the question of U.S. diplomatic recognition of the Vatican repeatedly aroused anti-Catholic passions, and was indeed a special grievance of Paul Blanshard's. The best argument in favor of this observer status is that the Vatican is in fact a major diplomatic presence worldwide and has often played a significant mediation role, so in this sense it deserves recognition far more than many of the petty states that are full UN members. This role also distinguishes Catholicism from other religions, which have no comparable diplomatic activity. For Kissling, however, the Vatican is simply the foreign enemy, which deserves no more than mockery. It is "in essence 100 square acres of office space and tourist attractions in the middle of Rome." Stressing the tiny size of the Vatican statelet, Kissling says, "Some of us have been wondering whether or not Euro-Disney had as many qualifications for permanent observer status as the Vatican State." The Web site of the anti-Vatican campaign—at *Seechange.org*— offers a depressingly predictable mélange of anti-Catholic quotes.[38]

The nature and scale of CFFC are both open to some question. The organization has enjoyed real success in presenting itself as a major Catholic pressure group, and television news sources such as CNN and *60 Minutes* regularly feature Frances Kissling as a liberal critic of Church positions. She is accorded enormous respect and sympathy, while the Church representatives who present the official position are equally likely to be attacked as reactionaries. The gender element promotes this perception, since an articulate woman is generally placed in opposition to a conservative male. Yet there is no evidence that CFFC is in any sense a mass organization with a popular membership, and only rarely are CFFC positions stated by anyone other than Kissling herself. The organization's Web site is largely devoted to her thoughts and writings, together with adulatory biographical sketches and samples of "What Kissling Says." Despite her lack of any obvious power base, the media has largely accepted Kissling's claim to speak for millions of liberal or radical Catholics opposed to the obscurantist Church leadership.[39]

Repeatedly, Kissling's own avowedly Catholic positions are starkly opposed not just to official Church teachings, but to most commonly accepted definitions of what constitutes Catholicism. When she disagrees with Church teaching, that teaching is usually framed not as a broad consensus, but as the capricious ideas of one man, namely, the Pope, who serves as an all-purpose demon figure. Rejecting Church teaching on sexual morality, Kissling states, "I think that Catholics have given up expecting to receive moral guidance from the pope on issues of sexuality and reproduction. They make up their own minds." The Pope speaks only as a representative of "Vatican misogyny." When the late Cardinal O'Connor made statements on moral issues, he was acting not as "a loving and concerned pastor" but rather as "a bully." In her view, neither Pope nor institutional Church nor bishops have any authority to make or enforce doctrine, and the Church cannot make statements or even recommendations about morality or personal behavior.[40]

In this context, it is very difficult to see what is left of any kind of Catholicism. The nearest Kissling has come to citing a rival source of authority was in a controversy with the Protestant televangelist Jerry Falwell, who attacked her for betraying Catholic loyalty. In answer, she declared, "The Catholic Church is not a club. Membership is not based simply upon the following of certain set rules and regulations. The Catholic Church is a church of the people. [My faith] is a contract and a covenant that I have with God personally." I do not exactly know how to characterize that doctrine of the personal covenant, but the word Catholic would not come close.[41]

Looking for the Women's Church

Though feminist anger against the Catholic Church is normally focused on specific secular grievances, we can also see a distinctly religious element that forthrightly challenges the whole basis of the Church, and which often provides a platform for frank anti-Catholicism. This is, however, quite different from the religious anti-Catholicism that long prevailed among Protestants and evangelicals. In the feminist view, misogyny is not just a result of the personal prejudices of Catholic leaders and churchmen, but is rather built into the structure of the religion. This idea grows out of the upsurge of women's studies in the universities since the 1970s, especially in fields such as history and religious studies, in both of which women now occupy a large proportion of academic posts. The *Journal of Feminist Studies in Religion* dates from 1985. Feminist critiques of Christianity reach a mass public through means over and above the normal range of stories in the media, because they are so widely taught in humanities departments in colleges, in seminaries, and often in church groups. Hostility to organized Christianity, and especially to Catholicism, is integral to much teaching of women's history, and of the allied topic of feminist spirituality.[42]

As feminist scholars tried to reconstruct the story of women, long "hidden from history," at many points the Catholic Church was targeted as a chief villain. The Church was accused of silencing women who had played a vital role in early Christianity, and concealing records of their achievements. Allegedly, Jesus headed a radically egalitarian and proto-feminist movement, which venerated female leaders like Mary Magdalene. According to this account, this radical Jesus movement was in time annexed by sinister figures such as St. Paul, a misogynist and homophobe, who imposed his dark, repressive vision on the emerging Church. As Christian theology became more elevated and complex, so the mechanisms of the Church became hierarchical, bureaucratic, and oppressive. By the fourth century, when the Church effectively became an arm of the Roman Empire, Christianity was inextricably linked with social and political elites. Among the main victims of this transformation were women, who lost their positions and prestige within the Church.

Much feminist writing on the early Church seeks to rediscover those lost early women leaders and their texts—often, I have argued elsewhere, placing wildly inflated hopes in late and spurious documents such as the Gnostic *Gospel of Mary*. In these reconstructions, the heroic woman apostle Mary Magdalene is glorified in place of the seemingly passive Mary, the Virgin Mother, who offers women such a dreadfully unattainable role model. A great deal of contemporary scholarship on Gnostic heretics and their "hidden gospels" depends on the theory that the Catholic Church has been from its foundation a patriarchal conspiracy to suppress women and their spiritual gifts. From its origins, Catholic Christianity has been fraud, delusion, error.[43]

These approaches to early Christianity contain a powerful and sometimes overt anti-Catholic agenda, denouncing the historical Church for its "clerical and patriarchal" orthodoxy. In a television program on Christian origins, best-selling author Elaine Pagels discussed the writings of the second-century bishop Irenaeus, who had been engaged in controversies with Gnostic heretics. Pagels explained the rift in these terms: anti-Church critics were labeled as "heretics, which means people who make choices about what to think. Irenaeus didn't want people making choices. He wanted them thinking what the bishop told them to think." In her view, the orthodox obediently followed irrational supernatural dogmas, while heretics continued to exercise their intellect freely. The Catholics, who followed Irenaeus, are thus ignorant sheep, while the Gnostics are viewed as the predecessors of modern feminists and New Agers.[44]

Similar views are expressed by Rosemary Radford Ruether, who speaks from a Catholic feminist position. Writing of the Gnostics, she explains, "Christians with these [feminist egalitarian] views were declared heretical and expelled from churches increasingly dominated by male clergy who modeled themselves after the patriarchal rule of families and the governors of Roman cities and provinces. The bishop of Rome would come to see himself as spiritual heir of the Roman emperor and as supreme ruler of the church." That again is Hobbes's idea of the Church as the phantom Roman Empire. Ruether's *Womanguides* claims that the *Gospel of Mary* validates "the church as an egalitarian spiritual community over against that patriarchal church which identified its episcopal hierarchy with an apostolic descent from the prince of the apostles, Peter."[45] The Roman Catholic Church is patriarchal, and ultimately founded on error. Though they would have rejected the feminist assumptions, nineteenth-century Protestants would have identified with contemporary notions that the pristine truth of early Christianity was polluted by the sinister bureaucracy of the emerging Catholic Church, with its evil innovations of celibacy and papal authority. This is good, traditional anti-papist stuff.

The Burning Times

Catholic sins against women reputedly continued through the Middle Ages. Of course, women were excluded from clerical office, though we do hear occasionally the legend of "Pope Joan," the woman who became Pope until she gave birth during a papal procession and was duly murdered by the irate faithful. The return of this legend in recent years is itself fascinating testimony to the enduring power of anti-Catholic and anti-papal legend. Though it has not the slightest foundation, the story was already circulating as a quasi-serious anti-clerical joke in the thirteenth century. From the sixteenth century through the nineteenth, the tale was beloved by Protestants, since it testified to Catholic stupidity, and even suggested that the apostolic succession might have been broken. If a woman could not legally ordain, then anyone she raised to the rank of bishop or priest could not claim the authentic link to the church of St. Peter. Serious scholars had little difficulty, though, in removing Pope Joan from the realm of history, culminating in the definitive work by Bishop Döllinger in the 1860s.[46]

In the last twenty years, the Joan legend has enjoyed a new life, especially in feminist history and polemic. The discredited *pontifica* has returned to public debate through books such as Donna Woolfolk Cross's popular novel *Pope Joan* and Peter Stanford's *The Legend of Pope Joan*. Pope Joan is a character in Caryl Churchill's play *Top Girls*.[47] A film of Cross's novel is currently in the works (a disastrous British version of the tale appeared in 1972). Pope Joan also enjoys a lively presence on the Web, where feminist anti-Catholics celebrate her existence much as did seventeenth-century Calvinists, or Enlightenment rationalists. What better precedent could there be for women's ordination? Cross herself professes herself outraged at the plight of "women of deep spirituality and faith with wonderful leadership qualities" who are denied the Catholic priesthood. The Pope Joan legend is a venerable staple of the anti-Catholic mythology, though it is a little surprising that even the most optimistic activists would try to deploy this blatantly bogus tale.[48]

Among its other crimes, the Church was reportedly guilty of massacring many thousands of real or alleged witches during the "Burning Times," a kind of women's holocaust. Some activists drew direct comparisons with the Jewish Holocaust of the 1940s, to the extent of claiming that some nine million women had perished during these events. (Most historians place the number of those executed far lower, certainly less than a hundred thousand all told, over several centuries.) According to some versions of the Burning Times theory, many of those executed were indeed witches, members of an ancient woman-oriented pagan cult that was subjected to a papal "final solution." The whole structure of the Catholic Church was thus built upon the bones of murdered women. These ideas circulate not just through feminist scholarship but through popular novels such as Marion Zimmer Bradley's *The Mists of Avalon*. A 2001 television film based on this book presented a whole alternative pseudo-history of medieval Europe, in which evil and ignorant Christian priests represent the forces of repression in conflict with woman-based Goddess-worshiping paganism.[49]

For radical feminists, the Burning Times represent a historical warning analogous to the Holocaust for Jews, and for women as for Jews, the lesson is "never again." Executions of witches merge rhetorically into burnings of abortion clinics and draw on other perceived Catholic crimes. One feminist Web site claims that "culturally and religiously a Christian Coalition led by the Catholic Church on one hand and the 'Moral Majority' on the other have used every weapon in their well-financed arsenal to mis-educate and browbeat fear and guilt into us about sex; and now the abortion facilities that exist are under paramilitary attack by the Army of God. ... On all fronts the storm troops of patriarchal property attack—yet as Pagans we know this is not new to their ways."[50]

The historical foundations of these claims are, to say the least, dubious: for one thing, few scholars accept that accused witches represented any authentic pagan tradition. Ironically, it is the surviving pagan and primal religions themselves that to this day remain most enthusiastic about pursuing witch-hunts on the classic model, and often on a terrifying scale.[51] Yet the Burning Times mythology has been highly influential in its own right, and has contributed to the strong anti-Catholicism of some contemporary feminist spirituality. In 1993, for instance—during what I have termed the years of gender crisis—a large gathering of feminist theologians convened in Minneapolis to celebrate an event called Re-Imaginings. The event became controversial because of its daring revisions of Christian theology, but anti-Catholic themes were also much in evidence. Throughout, speakers were defining their views in opposition to what were plainly seen as the patriarchal evils of Catholicism. The meeting borrowed heavily from scholarly reconstructions of Gnosticism and celebrated the divine principle of Sophia, Wisdom, who was presented virtually as a goddess. Describing her theology, Mary Hunt—

avowedly a Catholic lesbian feminist—remarked, "Whether it is Christian or not is frankly, darling, something about which I no longer give a pope." Hunt has also denounced much traditional Catholic teaching on sexual matters as constituting "theological pornography" in its own right. At the same event, theologian Beverly Harrison denounced the Roman Catholic hierarchy as "the pedophile capital of the world."[52]

Only a very small number of feminists would be active in gatherings such as Re-Imaginings, have anything to do with the activities of CFFC, or be closely involved even with a national group such as NOW. These various opinions are important not because they are expressed by a few activists, but because they gain credibility by frequent repetition, especially in the news media and popular culture. As so often in bygone years, the Catholic Church has provided an endlessly useful symbol for everything that America is not, an object lesson and awful warning. As Americans have come to see the notion of women's equality as a fundamental component of the nation's values, so the Church is stigmatized for what is seen, however questionably, as its failure to conform to that goal. The consequence is that feminists have come to provide a solid and enthusiastic audience for anti-Catholic polemic.

5 | The Church Kills Gays

*In other words, the church doesn't engage in gay-bashing,
it engages in homosexuality-bashing. (See any difference?
Me neither.)*

— Michelangelo Signorile

In addition to feminists, gay activists have been among the leading contemporary critics of Catholicism and the Church. Since the Church is so
visibly opposed to so many gay political causes, it has become a symbol
not only of repression, but also of hypocrisy, as it is accused of harboring
within itself such a strong homoerotic culture. As with feminists, opposition to Catholicism has become a major component of gay political organization, a powerful symbol of "what we are fighting." And as in the
case of feminism, controversies over specific political issues have escalated to produce a much broader and more visceral kind of anti-Catholic
polemic. As the mass media has become ever more sympathetic to
gay causes, so anti-Catholic rhetoric has become progressively more

commonplace, and (often) more strident. As gay writer Andrew Sullivan
has remarked, "Some of the most virulent anti-Catholic bigots in America are gay."[1]

The Church and Homosexuality

Catholic opposition to gay rights causes needs little explanation. Since
the foundation of Christianity, churches have varied widely in their attitudes to social and moral issues, so it is not difficult to assemble radically
divergent quotes from Christian leaders on issues such as war, slavery,
usury, or the position of women. On other issues, though, there really is
no such disparity, at least until very recent times, and one of these is sexual acts between individuals of the same gender. "Homosexuality" as
such may be a modern construct, but through the long Christian centuries, no church or Christian tradition prior to modern times regarded
homosexual acts as other than sinful.

This uniformity is not surprising given the explicit biblical condem-
nations of the behavior. The Old Testament abounds in disparaging
statements about same-sex contacts. Also, unlike many other prohibi-
tions of the Jewish law, this one is restated in the New Testament. The
most celebrated passage is 1 Corinthians 6:9, which declares that neither
malakoi nor *arsenokoitai* will enter the kingdom of God. By common
scholarly consent, these terms can be translated roughly as "effeminate"
and "men who abuse themselves with other men." For all the ingenuity
devoted to reinterpreting these words in recent years, the passage unequivocally condemns sex between men, behavior that is placed in the
same moral category as theft, adultery, and idolatry. (Another passage,
Romans 1:26–27, is equally stern in condemning homosexual relations,
and specifically denounces lesbianism). Since these lines are assuredly
the work of St. Paul, written even before the gospels were in existence, we
can reasonably presume that they represent the stance of the earliest
Church.

In practice, Church authorities varied over time in how seriously they
responded to homosexual behavior, and also how aware they were of homosexuality within the clergy, but the official position was always reso-
lutely anti-gay. Occasional attempts to show otherwise have been
embarrassingly inaccurate. A prize example was John Boswell's eccentric
work claiming to show that medieval churches had blessed same-sex
"marriages." The documents on which Boswell based his claim were records of religious services designed to end feuds between factions and
families, in which the respective leaders would pledge to live together in
peace and love. That Boswell could report his research as evidence of

Church-approved gay marriage can charitably be put down to his extreme overoptimism, as can the favorable reception of the book in the media.[2]

The fact that the historic Christian tradition is hostile to homosexual conduct gave rise to significant conflicts when the modern gay rights movement began in the 1960s, and especially as it made such dramatic advances in North America during the 1980s and 1990s. During this relatively short period, the nature of the movement also changed substantially, from simply urging the decriminalization of homosexual behavior to demanding a sweeping restructuring of society. Negative views of homosexuality were to be eliminated, and gay and lesbian orientation presented as in every sense equal to heterosexuality. By the 1990s, pressure for equality had reached a stage unimaginable only twenty years earlier, with the widespread granting of health benefits to gay partners and a serious movement for the legitimization of gay marriage. This change constituted an authentic social revolution.[3]

In the new social climate, it was *anti*-homosexual behavior that was seen as a grave social problem, rather than homosexuality itself, and legislators turned their attention to restricting anti-gay deeds or words by means of hate crime laws and hate speech codes. Social acceptance of what would once have been viewed as a very radical movement was enormously helped by the attitudes of the news and entertainment media. From the 1980s, fictional depictions of homosexual characters in movies and television series were strongly favorable, almost without exception. Anti-gay characters, meanwhile, were generally one-dimensional cardboard villains whose homophobia commonly expressed their own inner psychoses and religious obsessions. The new stereotypes can be seen clearly in a film like *American Beauty* or the wave of docudramas about the murder of Matthew Shepard.

Adapting to the new social climate has posed problems for most religious organizations, since tolerating and accepting homosexuality demands the repudiation of both scriptural authority and long tradition: the problem is all the greater where churches face the issue of ordaining openly gay clergy. Nevertheless, most mainline Protestant churches have achieved some kind of working accommodation with the gay issue, as theologians argue (for instance) that the older condemnation of homosexuality reflected the social prejudices of the ancient world, rather than any defensible moral absolute. In this view, texts denouncing *arsenokoitai* were artifacts of their age, just like neighboring verses urging slaves to remain contented with their lot or passages implying a pre-Copernican view of the solar system. This approach means taking a relativist approach to biblical authority, but that is scarcely a new principle. For many Protestant churches, "moving with the times" in this way does not imply betraying the fundamentals of faith.[4]

By the end of the century, two major Christian traditions in North America had chosen not to change their views to coincide with the revolution in secular attitudes. One was the very influential evangelical or fundamentalist strand, which asserted the permanent quality of the moral values stated in scripture. The other religious body was of course the Roman Catholic Church, which believed that homosexuality was condemned by its philosophical traditions, in addition to the Bible.

In the United States and Europe, some theologians have since the 1960s called on the Church to adopt a more liberal position in keeping with other Christian churches, and the group Dignity acted as a gay pressure group within the American Catholic community.[5] These efforts, however, met firm opposition. In 1977, the Vatican ordered the silencing of Jesuit priest John McNeill, one of the co-founders of the New York City chapter of Dignity, and an influential writer on homosexual issues. The assertion of orthodoxy was, naturally, even more forthright under Pope John Paul II. In 1986, the Church ordered McNeill to give up his ministry to gay people entirely, on pain of expulsion from the Jesuit order; the expulsion took effect the following year. Also in 1986, Dignity chapters were barred from operating on Church premises, a practice that had given the impression that its operations enjoyed a degree of official approval. In 1999, the Church ordered the discontinuation of New Ways Ministry, which was also directed toward gays, under the leadership of Father Robert Nugent and Sister Jeannine Gramick. After a decade-long official examination of their work, both were forbidden to speak or write further on issues relating to homosexuality.[6]

Partly, the Catholic refusal reflected its general conservatism, its character as a strongly hierarchical church preaching principles of obedience to authority, but more important was its international character. For better or worse, the Catholic Church is a global institution that does not necessarily follow the social trends of any particular region or society and claims to base its opinions on universal concepts of natural law. The Catholic position today remains that "[a]lthough the particular inclination of the homosexual person is not a sin, it is a more or less strong tendency ordered toward an intrinsic moral evil; and thus the inclination itself must be seen as an objective disorder." At the same time, the Church condemns any form of anti-homosexual persecution or violence.[7]

By the 1980s, it was the churches, and above all the Roman Catholic Church, which had emerged as the most visible institutional opponents of gay causes across the political spectrum. In one area, the Catholic stance became even more controversial than that of evangelicals because the Church preached strictly against the use of condoms in any context, heterosexual or homosexual. Logically, it opposed any "safe sex" instruction involving condoms, or any public education beyond chastity and abstinence. As the AIDS virus spread rapidly during the 1980s, the Catholic hierarchy was accused of opposing basic social hygiene measures, enforcing irrational dogma even at the cost of losing thousands of lives. Catholic authorities also emerged as the leading opponents of legislative measures to prohibit discrimination on the grounds of sexual orientation, and later of "gay marriage" initiatives. As in the case of women's issues, the Catholic Church achieved its villain status not because it had suddenly adopted a fiercely reactionary or anti-modern rhetoric, but because it refused to conform to new secular standards.

From a gay or liberal perspective, though, these disputes signaled that the Catholic Church was the primary anti-gay villain, the respectable voice of homophobia and gay-bashing. To quote one AIDS activist, "The church sanctioned social violence against [gays and women] and refused to allow their sexual difference." One cleric in particular, New York Cardinal John O'Connor, came to be regarded as the public face of anti-gay politics. In 1991, the gay magazine *The Advocate* awarded him that year's Sissy Award, given to those seen as the most blatant oppressors. In 1989, the catalog for a publicly funded exhibition of paintings on the subjects of AIDS described O'Connor of New York as a "fat cannibal" and a "creep in black skirts." St. Patrick's Cathedral was termed "that house of walking swastikas on Fifth Avenue."[8] Through the 1990s, O'Connor continued to antagonize gay and lesbian groups on numerous emotional issues, including the highly charged symbolic issue of gay participation in the annual St. Patrick's Day Parade that is so central a cultural event for New York City. When he died in 2000, his death was hailed in the gay and lesbian section of *Time Out New York* as the year's best single event. The paper offered this obituary notice: "Cardinal John O'Connor kicks the bucket. The press eulogized him as a saint, when in fact, the pious creep was a stuck-in-the-1950s, anti-gay menace. Good riddance!"[9]

Besides O'Connor, the Pope was also demonized by gays as much as by feminists. When the Pope visited the United States in 1993, protesters in Denver described him as "the biggest homophobe in the world" and accused the Catholic Church of "sins of sexism, homophobia and abuse of power." In *The Advocate* in 2000, Michelangelo Signorile dismissed a papal address as "pure, unadulterated hate speech—grade-A homophobia and bigotry couched in religious theology ... by uttering these words so vehemently and so publicly, he revealed before the whole world that he is a hateful man with little regard for the discrimination and violence he brings upon people's lives. ... the pope is a virulent hate-monger." The Web site StopthePope.com leads to a series of frankly anti-Catholic links, under headings such as "Victims of the Christian Faith," "The Case Against Catholicism," and a "Huge Anti-Catholic Links Page."[10]

I might add a personal comment here. In the aftermath of the terrorist attacks of September 2001, I was talking with some academic colleagues about the recent history of anti-American terrorism, and I mentioned that one Islamist plot in the mid-1990s had planned the assassination of the Pope. The remark inspired high humor, not because my listeners doubted that such a scheme had existed, but because everyone else present agreed that killing such an obviously pernicious figure would be a highly desirable act. I make no assertion that this depth of hostility is in any way representative of academe, but it is a useful reminder of the incredible loathing that the Church and its leadership inspire in some liberal circles.

The Sisters

Whether as individuals or organized groups, homosexuals have been among the most visible critics of Catholicism in the last three decades. Anti-Church hostility has been evident in the repeated lampooning of the Church in gay rights parades and demonstrations. The number of anti-clerical posters and mocking costumes indicates the centrality of anti-Church and specifically anti-Catholic rhetoric in the contemporary gay movement.

Conservatives—and not just Catholics—particularly denounce the activities of the Sisters of Perpetual Indulgence, a group of flamboyant transvestites dressed vaguely as nuns, with beards and fishnet stockings. (The group was founded in 1980.) They boast names such as Sister Hedra Sexual ("The Nun Too Straight"), Sister Anita Blowjob, Sister Chrystina Vampyra Embellisha Hellavallotta, and Sister Hellena Handbasket. Among other events, the Sisters host their annual Easter Bonnet and Hunky Jesus contest. Good Friday is the occasion of Hot Cross Buns, a fetish fashion show that provides "a chance to get spanked." One desperately sensitive point is the group's parodies of the Eucharist, which are calculated to offend even moderately loyal Catholics.[11]

For conservative viewers, the Sisters offer wonderful visual proof of both the blasphemy and the decadence that supposedly characterize homosexuality, and they are a regular staple of right-wing propaganda videos such as *The Gay Agenda* and its successors. Conservatives are all the more disturbed when demonstrations by the Sisters receive the slightest public acknowledgment. In 1999, the city of San Francisco granted the Sisters a parade permit and closed a street to assist the event—on Easter Day. Controversy over the group reached the national stage in the late 1990s when conservatives protested the approval of James Hormel to serve as an openly gay U.S. ambassador. Though the controversy was often framed solely in terms of his sexual orientation, Catholic conservatives were appalled that in 1996 he had offered radio commentary on a gay pride event, in which he had remarked approvingly on the Sisters.[12]

Again, it is instructive to compare attitudes to the Sisters to lampoons of other groups, when the media react with conspicuously less tolerance. Occasionally, news stories come to light of college fraternities organizing events that parody racial stereotypes. Participants may dress in blackface, with accessories such as watermelons and cotton, and some outrageous events have involved pseudo-Klan garb and jokes about lynching and slave auctions. When such an event comes to light, it usually generates a public furor, and official reprisals can be expected. City authorities need not be expected to issue parade permits for such events. They are more likely to insist on mandatory sensitivity training.

Yet having said this, the Sisters are far from being the most pernicious or offensive face of contemporary anti-Catholicism. While this kind of activism is clearly meant to shock, it draws on centuries of carnivalesque parody of the powerful that would have been recognizable in any European Catholic city of the Middle Ages or the early modern period. The whole Sisters phenomenon is meaningless except as a raucous Catholic in-joke: how many non-Catholics would understand the name of Sister Nicene Easy, still less find it funny? Not coincidentally, the Sisters were founded in San Francisco, which in addition to being the nation's gay capital is also traditionally a strongly Catholic city. While explosively anti-clerical, the displays lack the raw malice that characterizes much modern anti-Catholicism.

Also in the realm of the provocative, rather than the hateful, has been the phrase "recovering Catholic," which gay and feminist activists began using during the mid-1980s, and which became popular on T-shirts and buttons. At its inception, the term certainly carried no goodwill toward Catholicism, and it infuriates groups such as the Catholic League. In popular usage, one "recovers" from alcoholism or some other pernicious addiction, which is considered so toxic that real cure will demand lifetime dedication. Yet the term has enjoyed a rather more benevolent career than these bitter origins might suggest. Since the mid-1990s, the phrase has become a wry self-description for people who do not consider themselves faithful or orthodox Catholics, but whose attitude to their religious upbringing retains some affection.[13]

| Stopping the Church

Far more serious than the carnival figures of gay pride parades have been the frontal assaults on the Church, in which Catholic authorities are denounced literally as murderers and their accomplices. As with the feminists, the venom of gay anti-Catholicism must be understood in the context of the rhetorical tactics that social movements use in order to advance their cause. Centrally, the gay rights movement stresses the extreme and direct danger posed to its community, showing that the movement is an urgent necessity, a basic form of self-defense. The message is that gay rights is not an optional or whimsical cause; it is an essential means of saving lives. That idea means emphasizing threatening issues such as hate crimes and AIDS, in which lives are at risk. Once the seriousness of these issues achieves widespread public recognition, they can be used rhetorically to stigmatize other political enemies through a kind of guilt by association. If AIDS and hate crime are such a pressing danger, then any cause that can plausibly be seen as contributing to these dangers must be seen as lethally threatening.[14]

The claim is that anti-homosexual views and activism are not just wrong or misguided, but actually threaten lives. Signorile has argued that the Pope's moral and intellectual position constitutes violence in its own right: the Vatican believes that "homosexuality is 'evil' and 'intrinsically disordered,' terminology that in my view amounts to gay-bashing." Signorile is by no means unique in deploying this line of argument. When in 1992 the Catholic Church spoke out against gay rights legislation, *The Nation* headlined its report "Pope Backs Hate Crimes." The magazine claimed that "[m]ost fundamentalist, patriarchal sects of what Gore Vidal calls the 'sky-god' religions bash gays in theory and practice, but the Vatican's decree is an extraordinary attempt to organize a political campaign to support discrimination. It is akin to the Church's assault on women's reproductive freedom, and to the Iranian *fatwah* against Salman Rushdie. But those religious crusades have been condemned by civil libertarians and the liberal press. No audible cry has been raised against the Vatican's latest hate crime. Once again, Silence = Death." If someone believes that Catholic religious or moral beliefs are so intimately connected with violence, then even the most confrontational or even violent protests against "homophobia" are justified as a form of counterviolence or self-defense.[15]

This helps to explain some of the forceful attacks on religious targets over the last two decades. If in fact the Catholic Church was a leading enemy of gays, and moreover seemed callous on the AIDS threat, then radical gay activists thought themselves justified in using extreme tactics against Church institutions. Though the parallel seems ironic, gay protesters were in these years adopting much the same tactics against churches that pro-life militants were directing against abortion clinics. In both cases, the rationale was the same: the desperate need to save innocent lives superseded legal niceties.

Just how extreme protest methods could be became apparent during the ACT UP protests against Catholic churches between 1989 and 1992, the Stop the Church movement. On the same day as the "storming" of St. Patrick's in New York in December 1989, members of a gay arts group defaced San Francisco's St. Mary's cathedral. They decorated the doors with posters and red handprints, the red of course suggesting that the Church had blood on its hands. Over the next few years, anti-Church actions became almost commonplace, though rarely featuring such overt blasphemy as the New York attack. In 1990, abortion-rights activists joined gay protesters in a noisy walkout during mass at St. Patrick's, and similar actions occurred in Boston, Washington, and elsewhere. Meanwhile, December became a time for regular annual commemoration of the St. Patrick's event. In December 1990, protesters disrupted a Christmas mass in a Washington church.[16]

Gay pride events also acquired dependably anti-Church overtones. In 1994, a gay protest march in New York was described by horrified critics as follows: "When the marchers reached [St. Patrick's] Cathedral, they yelled—in unison—four-letter epithets and pointed their middle fingers at those on the steps of the church. Some were dressed as Cardinals, others as nuns and priests, and many wore nothing at all. They sat down in the street, did satanic dances and generally showed as much disrespect as they could. No one was arrested, not even those who went fully naked through the streets." Every June, gay pride marches could be counted on to produce their share of grotesquely anti-Catholic imagery. "Among the flagrant attacks were men in jock straps simulating oral sex in front of St. Patrick's Cathedral during Sunday mass. Further, there was Catholic Ladies for Choice, a group of gays and lesbians dressed as nuns, carrying wire coat hangers. There was also a man wearing a black bra and jock strap with a nun's veil and a huge pair of Rosary beads." In 1992, the group Queer Nation demonstrated at the National Shrine of the Immaculate Conception in Washington. "The demonstration featured a scantily clad lesbian 'crucified' on a mock cross, to which was affixed a sign that read, 'Christ Loves Women and Queers / Why Does O'Connor Hate Us?'"[17]

Though gay protests against the Church reached their height in the early 1990s, they continued sporadically throughout the decade, organized by groups such as SoulForce and Dignity. (These groups, incidentally, employed none of the shocking or aggressive tactics of ACT UP or Queer Nation.) In 2000, hundreds demonstrated against the annual meeting of the National Council of Catholic Bishops, held in Washington. Protesters blocked the entrance to the National Shrine of the Immaculate Conception.[18]

Many of these actions could easily fit definitions of hate crime, and the more extreme demonstrations represented a direct physical attack on Catholic churches not really paralleled since the nativist riots of the 1840s and 1850s. Nevertheless, activists argued that the attacks were justified as self-defense, as a response to the literally homicidal consequences of Catholic moral teachings. As ACT UP members implied, the Church itself invited the protests when it decided to "meddle in public affairs." In a remarkable logical leap, ACT UP member Michael Petrelis wrote in 1999 that "church policy continues to cause the infections and deaths of hundreds of New York teens who don't have access to lifesaving condoms and safer-sex information. ... The message we send to the Catholic hierarchy is simple: curb your dogmatic crusade against the truth." The Church supported the "murderous policies" that prevented condom distribution in schools. "Cardinal O'Connor has contributed from the pulpit at St. Patrick's Cathedral to the genocidal spread of AIDS."[19]

| Why Not Hate Crime?

ACT UP was, and remains, an extreme fringe group within the gay community, and its tactics disturbed even liberal supporters. Yet even if we dismiss ACT UP as unrepresentative, anti-Catholicism has provided a significant force in gay political and social organization, an instantly recognized rhetorical hot button. And the underlying ideas and rhetoric of ACT UP have enjoyed a wide influence. The key issue was not whether the Church was deeply, even homicidally, opposed to homosexuals—that proposition was taken for granted—but whether direct protest action was justified. ACT UP's views and demonstrations received strikingly little condemnation in the mass media, which were generally sympathetic to radical gay claims.

Crimes against religious and cultural institutions occur with some frequency in the United States, but the anti-Catholic movement was treated very differently from what are conventionally viewed as hate crimes. Remarkably, the mainstream media largely accepted the activists' claim of self-defense against outrageous Catholic policies, or at least felt that the Church attacks were well within the scope of legitimate self-expression.

Of course, there were some exceptions, and conservative correspondents such as John Leo denounced the attacks. Notably, some gay activists themselves were appalled by the outrageous and explicitly anti-religious content of the movement. Andrew Sullivan explicitly categorized these acts as hate crimes and condemned "the hateful act of desecrating Communion hosts at a mass at St. Patrick's Cathedral." In San Francisco, Randy Shilts wrote, "If I didn't know better, I'd swear that the AIDS protesters who have been disrupting services and vandalizing Catholic churches in San Francisco, New York and Los Angeles were being paid by some diabolical reactionary group dedicated to discrediting the gay community. To say the least, these protesters are embracing a disturbing double standard. Just imagine how inflamed the gay community would be if militant Catholics burst into the gay Metropolitan Community Church in the Castro area, scribbled anti-homosexual Bible verses on the walls and stopped the sermon until the police showed up." Another liberal critic was Alexander Cockburn, who thought the ACT UP protests were "a dumb idea. Much of what Cardinal John O'Connor says is imbecilic, but that's no reason to cause offense to a bunch of Catholics on their knees or lining up to take communion." Yet most newspapers and media outlets gave the church attacks nothing like the coverage they surely merited, or denounced them as they would have done other attacks. Normally, a particular protest was reported briefly and then forgotten.[20]

Nor was the language used in such stories what would have been found in attacks on other institutions. In the Catholic instance, the newspapers spoke of "protests" rather than "attacks" or "hate crimes," even though ACT UP itself used much more militaristic language—they had avowedly "stormed" St. Patrick's. The media were also careful to present the viewpoint of the activists in order to balance the complaints of the religious authorities. In a 1990 case, the *Washington Post* concluded its coverage of a Stop the Church event in New York by quoting an ACT-UP representative. The gay spokesman "said the protest was organized to focus attention on church policies. The protesters say O'Connor and the Roman Catholic Church are obstructing the dissemination of safe sex information and advocating 'hatred and violence' against homosexuals and abortion-rights supporters." Though this sounds like laudably balanced reporting, an analogy suggests the flaws of the argument. When a group of youths paint swastikas on a synagogue, journalists do not devote a large part of the story to letting suspects explain in detail why they chose to protest against Israeli policies in the Middle East. The assumption would be that the crime arose from irrational hatred and that granting the offenders a platform would be to aggravate the deed. Quoting the protesters in such detail implies that the action was legitimate.[21]

Significantly, the media tended to report each new anti-Catholic incident as a discrete event, rather than contextualizing them as part of a national "wave" or a pressing social problem that needed to be confronted. This was in marked contrast to what occurred in the mid-1990s when media and political leaders expressed enormous concern over what was perceived as a national wave of arson attacks on black churches. The reality of such a wave was very dubious, and subsequent examination suggests the whole affair was mythical. In many instances, arson was not involved, and in only one or two cases might "hate groups" have participated. This was scarcely plausible material for the national race crisis that was so widely credited. In this instance, the media could plead ignorance, since so many of the reported arsons were occurring in remote corners of the South, far away from the usual media centers. In contrast, the anti-Catholic actions were taking place within blocks of newspaper offices and broadcasting facilities, and there was no excuse for failing to know what was happening or to make these events headline news. Another significant difference between the two "waves" was in terms of the historical context. With black churches, the alleged attacks recalled racist violence of bygone years: as the *New York Times* lamented, "As arson cases mount, the burning of Southern black churches causes outrage and recalls a violent past." Yet nobody drew the obvious analogies between the gay anti-Church protests and the nativist violence of bygone years.[22]

The media also showed their sympathy for the gay protests by their coverage of their later commemoration. In 1991, the St. Patrick's protests were depicted heroically in *Stop the Church*, a documentary that was slated for inclusion in PBS's series of independent films, *POV* (Point of View). Some PBS channels were strongly pressured not to broadcast the film, and most acquiesced. In Los Angeles, Cardinal Roger Mahony complained to KCET, the local public television station, arguing that showing *Stop the Church* would encourage "hate-mongers" to "burn, loot and vandalize houses of worship." The Catholic position can be easily understood, especially if we think of the comparable cases involving synagogues or black churches. Yet it was the Catholic protests that were now denounced, rather than the original Stop the Church movement. The Church was widely attacked in the media for trying to suppress free speech.[23]

| Matthew's Passion

In other ways too, activists enjoyed much success in blaming violent actions on Christian and specifically Catholic anti-gay attitudes, and these ideas received wide coverage in mainstream media. In 1998, the movement found its martyr in Matthew Shepard. However revolting his murder, the incident was rather less simple than it was presented at the time, and the "gay-bashing" element may have been peripheral. Briefly, a pair of petty criminals with a methamphetamine problem went on a crime spree in which they attacked and robbed several men and women before targeting Shepard, who had reportedly propositioned one of the offenders. He was robbed, beaten, and left tied to a fence in a remote field. The affair could have been presented in many ways, and the violence arguably owed as much to class hatred and jealousy as to anti-homosexual sentiment. Gay activists, however, immediately focused on Shepard as a victim of homophobia, motivated by repressive religion.[24]

One extreme manifestation of this outrage was Tony Kushner's article "Matthew's Passion," which appeared in *The Nation*, a magazine with a long-standing distaste for organized religion. (It was in these pages that Paul Blanshard had originally published his anti-Catholic pieces in the 1940s.) Kushner's rant denounced the Republican Party for its opposition to gay rights causes and concluded that "Trent Lott endorses murder, of course … his party endorses discrimination against homosexuals and in doing so it endorses the ritual slaughter of homosexuals." Kushner then proceeded to denounce Catholicism: "Pope John Paul II endorses murder. … And so, on the subject of gay-bashing, the Pope and his cardinals and his bishops and priests maintain their cynical political silence … denouncing the murder of homosexuals in such a way that it received even one-thousandth of the coverage his and his church's attacks on homosexuals routinely receive, this would be an act of decency the Pope can't afford, for the Pope knows: Behind this one murdered kid stand legions of kids whose lives are scarred by the bigotry this Pope defends as sanctioned by God." If the Pope would not condemn discrimination and anti-gay violence, then "won't you excuse me if I think you are not a friend at all but rather a homicidal liar whose claim to spiritual and moral leadership is fatally compromised."[25]

Kushner's article had a powerful public impact, and was later excerpted in *Harper's*. The piece received high praise from many *Nation* correspondents, who found it "very moving," "incredible," "a truth too bold to state its name." Responding to Catholic critics, Kushner denounced them (as well as figures such as Cardinal O'Connor) as "flagellants, fanatics, fundamentalists and cynical political strategists whose utter lack of genuine spiritual inspiration and imagination, not to mention simple human compassion, is cloaked in inept, selective, antiquated misreadings of the Scriptures."[26]

In addition to drawing attention to the evils of homophobia, Shepard's death acquired religious and even mystical significance. Above all, the manner of his passing—left to die on a wooden bar—echoed Christ's crucifixion. Kushner spoke of Shepard as "this crucified man." Playwright Terrence McNally has explicitly drawn this analogy, arguing that "Jesus Christ died again when Matthew Shepard did." After "Matthew's Passion," denunciations of religious homophobia offered Shepard as a martyr figure, definitive proof that anti-gay feelings or ideas could literally kill. Just as Jesus's disciples lived to spread his message, so "it is this generation's duty to make certain Matthew Shepard did not die in vain either."[27] This theme has been much exploited in anti-Church rhetoric, in which we find not just a rejection of Catholic ideas, but an explicit attempt to interpret the conflict in quite contrary religious terms. In effect, the gay cause is being held up as a sacred movement, with its own martyrs and even its own Christ figures. For gays, like feminists, contemporary anti-Catholicism has developed a strong religious framework.

This figure of gay martyrdom or crucifixion has become a common rhetorical device. Gays and gay activists appropriate the role of Jesus, while the Catholic Church becomes the evil priests and Pharisees. According to one supporter of ACT UP, "Jesus' action in the Temple is the model for the transgressive Stop the Church actions at St. Patrick's Cathedral." In an ACT UP demonstration in St. Louis in 1991, protesters created "an action in front of the Catholic cathedral on Easter Sunday to proclaim that they were crucified by the church and that Easter was their day of liberation." On this occasion, demonstrators carried three crosses, to symbolize the triple crucifixion undertaken by the Church—"of lesbians and gays, of women, and of people living with AIDS."[28]

| Corpus Christi

The image of gay martyrdom is central to McNally's controversial play *Corpus Christi*, first produced in 1998. This work is staged as a kind of medieval mystery play in which Jesus is presented as Joshua, from Corpus Christi, Texas. This Jesus, however, is homosexual, flamboyantly and promiscuously so. Equally gay are all his apostles and associates, and there is a good deal of gender crossing among the all-male cast: the actor who plays Peter also represents the Virgin Mary. In one scene, Joshua passionately kisses Judas; in another, he blesses a marriage between two of his apostles. McNally's core message is that homosexuality does not make an individual any less close to God, any less divine, and that logically, homosexuality is in no sense sinful. Hearing enemies cite the biblical texts condemning homosexuality, Joshua responds by deploying another and far more positive scripture: "And God saw everything that he had made, and behold it was very good." To deny the possibility of a gay Jesus would be to restrict the idea of God. "Such a God is no God at all because he is exclusive to His members. He is a Roman Catholic at best, and a very narrow-minded one at that."[29]

In addition, McNally is offering a political statement about the lethal effects of homophobia. Ultimately, Jesus is crucified for his "queerness." At his trial, Pilate asks him, "Art thou a queer, then?" Judas betrays Joshua with the cry "Sold to the fag-haters in the priests' robes!" It does not take too much imagination to appreciate that that phrase is meant to apply as much to modern-day Catholic clergy as to the servants of the ancient Jewish Temple. Regardless of the time period, priests remain priests.

Such a presentation places the author in a powerful rhetorical position, because the opposition generated by the play helps reinforce the statements he wishes to make. The more people denounce him and his work, the more he can argue that they are demonstrating irrational homophobia. Naturally, Catholics and other Christians protested strongly against the image of Jesus presented in *Corpus Christi*, since in the terms of Christian tradition, to portray Jesus as actively homosexual is to represent him as a grave sinner, and this is a fundamental offense to the overwhelming majority of Christian believers. The play depicts Jesus and other venerated figures doing and saying things that, according to the doctrines of all churches from the earliest eras, are morally wrong. (Far less significant, the play contains a grievous violation of historical fact. Had Jesus's circle had any such homosexual currents, it is unthinkable that the documents of the New Testament would have preached so powerfully against the behavior; nor would the movement's Roman and Jewish enemies have ignored the potential for slander.) When the play premiered in 1998, it met fierce public opposition, including bomb threats, which induced one theater to cancel its run. But from the author's point of view, the outrage stirred was taken to prove the unreasoning hatred that Christians supposedly feel toward homosexuals in general.

Generally, the mass media accepted McNally's view of the critics. Instead of condemning *Corpus Christi* as anti-religious polemic—as hate speech, if we prefer—the media chose instead to denounce the reaction of those who found their faith under attack. A common tactic was to imply that opposition to the play could only be confined to religious extremists. In the *Village Voice*, one critic noted dismissively, "One or two scenes may be blasphemous by strict Catholic standards, but no more so than most twentieth-century novels, contemporary movies, or even modern paintings." In *USA Today*, David Patrick Stearns wrote, similarly, "The core issue is whether homosexuality is a sinful lifestyle choice (as some Catholics believe) or a God-given state that can't be negotiated (as the play suggests)." This sentence makes the startling claim that opposition to homosexuality is confined only to "some Catholics." Accepting claims about gay martyrdom, Stearns continues, "Drawing parallels between the clandestine early Christians and semi-closeted gays might have seemed dramatically intriguing before the controversy began; now it seems like genius. The recent murder of a gay youth in Wyoming further underscores the play's message."[30]

Corpus Christi is one of the best-known recent examples of a literary work stirring controversy for alleged blasphemy, but it is by no means alone. Through such controversies, we often find this same pattern: that protests against anti-Catholic or anti-Christian works are never deemed legitimate, and indeed that the act of protesting is itself seen as a manifestation of Christian fanaticism. In 1998, Paul Rudnick's play *The Most Fabulous Story Ever Told* offended Catholic (and Jewish) sensibilities at several points. The play tells the story of the creation of the world and its original inhabitants, two gay men, Adam and Steve, and two lesbians, Mabel and Jane. Mabel becomes pregnant by divine intervention and is to bear the messiah. This scene draws heavily on Catholic symbolism, including a traditional Nativity scene and the use of the Ave Maria prayer. Catholics denounced the play, though according to Rudnick, the campaign consisted largely of cards and scrawled letters using phrases such as "you disgusting kike cocksucker." Quite possibly, Rudnick did receive some "fundamentalist hate mail" of this sort, but as he tells the story, the implication is that all the protesters were motivated by homophobia and anti-Semitism, founded upon simple stupidity—hence the reference to scrawled letters. Absent from his discussion is any sense that people of normal intelligence and sanity might have any reasonable grounds for criticizing a presentation that shocks their cherished beliefs. A similarly dismissive reaction occurred when an off-Broadway production of Jean Genet's *Elle* depicted a Pope as a flagrant drag queen. Anticipating the inevitable criticisms, *New York Times* reviewer Ben Brantley alerted his readers to the play "before the blasphemy police bring out their brass knuckles."[31]

What Does the Church Have to Fear?

One way social movements establish their position is to undermine arguments made against them or, ideally, to deny that any such arguments can be valid. In the case of gay rights, activists have enjoyed enormous success in public debate by invalidating opposing arguments as solely based on homophobia. The fact that this term has entered popular speech is in itself a rhetorical triumph, because the very word contains within itself a highly loaded psychological interpretation. Literally, homophobia simply means "fear of the same," and logically, it should be a term for people who favor change of any sort. In modern parlance, though, it means far more than this: it means someone who is *afraid* of homosexuals and homosexuality. And a generation of pop psychology suggests clear roots for this fear, which in fact comes from denying one's own inner sexual turmoil. To be homophobic is by implication to be a self-hating, self-denying homosexual.[32]

If religious leaders oppose homosexuality, then (logically) they must themselves be suffering from this inner contradiction. To quote Mark Jordan, author of the book *The Silence of Sodom*, "Some of the worst homophobes are guys in the clergy and hierarchy who are gay." If an entire church is "homophobic," then the whole institution is by definition denying its own homosexual tendencies. "The Roman Catholic Church has long been both fiercely homophobic and intensely homoerotic." Jordan again: "There is indeed a silent Sodom. It is housed in the structures of churchly power. Its silence must be disturbed before there can be mature Catholic teaching on 'homosexuality.'" "The exercise of power in the Catholic church enacts some of the unhappiest forms of suppressed desire between men." Since many clergy are allegedly homosexual themselves, it is doubly unacceptable for the Church to criticize overt expressions of gay behavior. Michelangelo Signorile has condemned "the many twisted, personal sexual hypocrisies that envelop the increasingly tainted, lying bishops and cardinals who are running the church."[33]

Gay anti-Church rhetoric has made much use of this theme of clerical hypocrisy. When several thousand protesters interrupted an ordination held by Boston's Cardinal Law, they chanted, "Two-four-six-eight, how do you know your priests are straight?" On its surface, this charge has substance. Homosexual priests certainly do exist, and some studies have suggested that the number of gays in the clergy has risen steeply since the 1960s and now represents a proportion far higher than in the population at large. Evidence occasionally surfaces of active gay subcultures among priests, and some critics speculate about the existence of highly placed gay networks, a "Lavender Mafia."[34]

Yet though clerical homosexuality is a real issue, its exploitation in anti-Church polemic is often so outrageous as to constitute blatant anti-Catholic polemic. Attacking the culture of the all-male priesthood, *New York Times* columnist Maureen Dowd writes, "It may be a news flash to the Vatican, but it's been clear for years that the Church is in a time warp, arrested in its psychosexual development. The vow of celibacy became a magnet for men trying to flee carnal impulses they found troubling. In some cases this meant homosexuality, in others pedophilia."[35] The priesthood is, in this view, an institutionalized closet. The constant stress on (and exaggeration of) clerical homosexuality harks back to a millennium-long tradition of anti-Catholicism, denouncing priests as unmanly, effeminate, and therefore unworthy. Fifty years ago, a mob yelling that Catholic priests were queer would be mouthing the familiar epithets of gutter anti-Catholic bigotry; today, the same charge often stems from gay activists themselves.

The portrait of Catholic clergy as overtly gay appears in Paul Rudnick's 1993 play *Jeffrey*, which concerns the dilemma of a gay man contemplating a relationship with a HIV-positive partner. When he goes to a Catholic church to pray, he becomes the target of a frank sexual advance by the priest, who is himself flagrantly promiscuous. No stereotype is lacking. The priest, Father Dan (played by Nathan Lane in the 1995 film version), declares that he feels the presence of God only when he is having sex, or during a great Broadway musical. He admits to particular difficulties while hearing confession, since he is so stimulated by all the accounts he hears of sex between men; his response is "Where are the Polaroids?" He also has gay pinups in the confessional box. Though he might be considered a sex addict, he responds to criticism by pointing to his parishioners who believe in the Resurrection and the Virgin Birth: "And *I'm* nuts?" Jeffrey is shocked by this outrageously campy character, but Father Dan suggests that he is hardly unusual: "Maybe you didn't hear me. I'm a *Catholic priest*. Historically, that falls somewhere between a chorus boy and a florist." The scene ends with him singing show tunes from the sanctuary. In terms of reproducing ancient stereotypes, this is roughly on a par with images of Jewish moneylenders, or blacks eating watermelons.[36]

Implicit Prejudice

Consistently, gay writers offer a deeply ugly picture of Catholicism, which is viewed as a religion of hatred, violence, repression, and hypocrisy. In trying to explain what has gone wrong with the Church, some gay writers produce frankly bigoted accounts. As with other kinds of prejudice, quite as bad as the detailed polemics are the casual remarks which reflect these very hostile ideas. One of the most persistent offenders from this perspective is Bruce Bawer, a former *Advocate* columnist who is presently a member of the Episcopal Church. In his book *Stealing Jesus,* Bawer complains about the "fundamentalists" and "legalists" who have succeeded in imposing their perverted view of Christianity as if it is the only one, and he claims to describe a more authentic version of Jesus's message. In his work, though, the damning terms fundamentalism and legalism refer to basically every Christian belief or tradition that prevailed before the late twentieth century.[37]

He presents a picture of Catholic ignorance that would have won instant agreement among nineteenth-century nativists. Based on conversations with some Catholic friends, he reports that Roman Catholics "who regularly attended mass didn't make any attempt to get into the experience of it; the very idea was alien to them. They had been taught that they had to show up every week and take communion. ... As long as you performed the act, you had carried out your side of the deal, and God would carry out his."[38]

In trying to explain this puerile religion, Bawer blames the stupidity of women and poor people. He notes that "during the nineteenth century, members of the educated upper classes, and men of all classes, ceased attending services in droves, leaving behind a church composed mostly of women and the under-educated. To appease these members' sentimental superstitions, the Vatican added new doctrines about the Virgin Mary," namely, the Immaculate Conception (1854) and the Assumption (1950). Both ideas—"which, to a thinking believer, were meaningless—had their basis not in scripture but in folk piety."[39] Could there possibly be a more damning indictment of Catholicism than this: that it takes into account the views of women and the poor, no matter how contemptible such people are? Bawer does not realize, or more likely does not care, that his words are almost identical to those of bigots through the centuries, who despised Catholicism on these very same grounds. As with a similar account written in 1880, it is impossible to disentangle the strands of religious and class prejudice that shape his views.

The worst point about Bawer's anti-Catholicism is that, quite likely, it shocked or surprised so very few readers. The assumption today is that homosexuals regard the Catholic Church as a principal enemy and can find nothing too bad to say about it. We are long past the stage when gay activists felt the need to argue an anti-Catholic position. For some years now, anti-Catholicism has simply become part of the scenery, an unexamined commonplace. In 1999, Signorile wrote critically in *The Advocate* about the public adulation of media stars such as Princess Diana, whom he compares to other figures who did a great deal more practical good. "Not to lionize Mother Teresa—she was, after all, an effective PR flack for the often evil Catholic Church—but the woman did devote her life to changing the bedpans of the sick and the poor."[40] Even when praising a venerated Catholic figure, the author must include obligatory nods to Catholic evils in order to avoid giving the impression of saying a good word about her dreadful, homicidal church.

6 | Catholics and the News Media

Get over it! Why can't a woman be Christ?

— Renee Cox

Though it retains many of its traditional characteristics, anti-Catholicism in modern America has changed many of its political overtones, with the decisive movement to the left-liberal end of the political spectrum. Equally significant is the shift in the means by which anti-Catholic rhetoric is generally expressed. In marked contrast to the situation fifty years ago, stridently anti-Catholic themes today are widely present in popular culture and the popular media. This does not necessarily mean that the sentiments themselves are any more powerful than in bygone days, but the overt way in which they are expressed in mainstream media is novel. Partly, the change reflects what most observers would consider a healthy development, namely, the collapse of any threat of effective Church censorship, though the rise of vocal dissent within the Church has also played a role. Whatever the cause, the consequences have been depressing. For newspapers and newsmagazines, for television news and in movies, for major book publishers, the Catholic Church has come to provide a grossly stereotyped public villain.

This is not to say that the news media are uniformly hostile to Catholicism on every occasion. In particular cases, the media can report very positively on the Church as an institution, and on the doings of particular clergy. Following the World Trade Center catastrophe of 2001, media outlets reported movingly on the heroism of Fire Department chaplain Father Mychal Judge, who was killed alongside the firefighters. (The fact that Father Judge was widely believed to be homosexual may have made him a more palatable figure in media circles, but I do not believe that the coverage of his death would have been much different if his sexual orientation were less well known.) Generally, too, Chicago's Cardinal Bernardin was as universally esteemed as his New York counterpart Cardinal O'Connor was controversial.

In some cases, newspapers and television programs have criticized outrageous instances of anti-Catholic behavior. In Oregon in 1996, a prosecutor devised the astonishing idea of secretly taping an accused inmate in the act of making a sacramental confession to a priest. National news media uniformly condemned the scheme as a gross intrusion into religious liberty, and this consensus helped persuade the prosecutor to back down on his plan to use the tape as evidence in court. Although it sometimes appears this way, the news media are not always engaged in a war against the Church.[1]

Overwhelmingly, though, media coverage of Catholic issues over the last quarter century has been hostile to mainstream Catholic positions, and sometimes sharply critical of central tenets of that faith. Quite often, this coverage ventures far into territory that we can unhesitatingly call anti-Catholic. Usually, journalists and editors adopt a strongly *parti pris* position on Catholic matters, and emerge as participants in anti-Church struggles, rather than as mere observers. For most of the media, a knee-jerk response holds that the Catholic Church and its hierarchy are always wrong, especially on matters of gender, sexuality, and morality.[2]

Often, too, the anti-Catholic slant emerges not just from editorial or opinion pieces, but from reporting. In theory, such a partisan slant should be grossly contrary to proper journalistic standards, which emphasize the need for balanced reporting. All journalism schools teach that news is, or should be, rigidly segregated from editorializing. In practice, though, such objectivity is an illusion. Newspapers and television reports signal their positions in many different ways, notably in the degree of respect given to people speaking for particular positions and in the choice of commentators and pundits. This directs the audience's attention to a specific way of understanding and contextualizing the problem. As we saw in the case of gay protests against Catholic churches, activists received balanced coverage in a way they would not if the media considered the incidents straightforward hate crimes.

For all the purported commitment to balance, bias is reinforced by the loaded language used to describe the sides in a given conflict. "Heroic Woman Defies New Inquisition" is only a slightly exaggerated illustration of the kind of headline that has been commonplace in recent reporting of Catholic issues. A pretense of objectivity can be preserved by placing incendiary words in quotes. Imagine a Church critic denouncing a Catholic bishop who is accused of dragging the Church back into the Middle Ages. If the remark was actually made, then a newspaper would not violate the principle of objectivity by running the headline "Bishop X 'Trying to Drag America into Middle Ages.'" In practice, highlighting this kind of potent remark inevitably shapes the reader's interpretation of the story that follows. Even using quotes, no newspaper would run the headline "America Endangered by 'Jewish Greed.'"

News stories favor a narrative format in which heroes and villains are clearly identified, and the media present the events chiefly from the point of view of some protagonists rather than others. Often, the favored side in a story can be identified simply on the basis of who gets the last word, of whose views provide the memorable conclusion that the reader will likely recall as the core message. The heroes-and-villains approach helps make stories intelligible to a popular audience. In a religious dispute, the media is not likely to delve too deeply into any theological or scholarly issues concerned, but will rather present the conflict through analogies familiar to the general public, and those analogies will often dredge up ancient anti-Catholic stereotypes of oppressive bishops, heresy trials, and so on.

Though the underlying issues in each controversy are quite different, pervasive media bias can be illustrated from the response to two themes that recently have attracted widespread media coverage. These involve, respectively, the silencing of Catholic theologians and conflicts over artworks that many consider blasphemous or offensive.

Silencing Theologians

The media demonstrate a strong animus against the Catholic Church over its attempts to regulate clergy or teachers who express opinions contrary to official policy. Such cases have occurred regularly since the 1970s, and reporting of these stories generally follows a familiar pattern. An individual arouses controversy for his or her opinions, which Church authorities attempt to restrict or silence; this was, for instance, the case with Charles Curran, suspended from teaching theology at Catholic University in 1986. In reporting the case, the media invariably take the side of the individual, who is usually labeled with a title that more commonly indicates resistance to political tyranny, such as "dissident." On the other side, the actions of Church authorities are discussed in the language of Inquisition, heresy hunt, or witch-hunt. Regardless of the substance of the issue at hand, the Church's conflicts with its dissidents are invariably portrayed in terms of good and evil, day and night, enlightenment and ignorance.[3]

The notion of disciplining a person who dissents from a religious organization is considered strange and alien by contemporary standards, and the act conjures some very undesirable historical analogies. We think of the Church's trial of Galileo for asserting that the earth revolved around the sun, or of the persecution of American dissidents such as Anne Hutchinson. In any modern representation of such an incident, an audience will always sympathize with the heroic dissident, and regard even the use of the word orthodoxy as indicating intolerance and fanaticism. In popular parlance today, heretics are bold, independent thinkers, while orthodoxy suggests mindless obedience to conventional authority. Orthodoxy is at best boring, at worst oppressive. In its origin, the word heresy just implies "difference," and thinking differently is regarded as a virtue.

Yet whatever impression we get from the mass media, the churches— Catholic and otherwise—are far from unusual in their actions against dissidents. Most organizations enforce some kind of standards for behavior or action on their members, especially where any kind of public criticism is concerned. Businesses, universities, and the armed services all react sharply if an employee publicly attacks cherished company policies, and might well discipline or dismiss the obstreperous person. News organizations themselves have a notoriously short fuse when employees voice criticism of the companies themselves or of their corporate allies. In this setting, though, suppressing dissent is not usually regarded as censorship, still less heresy hunting, since employees are free to express their views elsewhere.

This principle also holds for private organizations united to support common beliefs or principles, since these groups are quite free to remove people who reject those basic ideas. We can imagine a society dedicated to proving that the plays attributed to William Shakespeare were actually the work of his contemporary Francis Bacon, an idea that (however odd) is held by a number of well-informed people. We can easily predict what the response would be if the president of this society made public statements and published books declaring that Shakespeare had indeed written the works that bear his name, that Bacon had nothing to do with them, but nevertheless, by whatever bizarre definition, the president still considered himself a true Baconian. Other members of the society would demand his resignation on the grounds that he was directly contradicting the fundamental goals and beliefs of the society—indeed, making nonsense of them. All kinds of organizations exercise controls on opinions that can be expressed in its name, including the most liberal. Recall the refusal of the Democratic Party to permit Governor Casey to address its national convention. When the media focuses solely on religious organizations as suppressors of "heresy," they are guilty of serious partiality.

Equally, some Catholic "dissidents" undoubtedly do stray quite as far from any reasonable interpretation of Church teachings as our hypothetical rogue Baconian. One long-running saga in the 1980s and early 1990s concerned Dominican priest Matthew Fox, who, according to a sympathetic Web site, is "a liberation theologian and progressive visionary ... silenced by the Vatican and later dismissed from the Dominican order." In modern terms, that sounds like a stunningly good resumé.[4]

Yet on closer examination, his views appear so extreme that his dismissal was scarcely surprising. Since the 1960s, Fox had become increasingly radical and indeed eccentric in his exploration of theological ideas. He set his Creation Spirituality against the traditional Christian notion of the Fall and sought common ground with exponents of nature religions. His Institute of Culture and Creation Spirituality in Oakland, California, included on its staff the neo-pagan witch Starhawk, who popularized the view that the Church-inspired Burning Times claimed the lives of millions of innocent women. Meanwhile, Fox's "provoking style and outlandish claims (such as that he took spiritual advice from his dog) led even former sympathizers .... to distance themselves." Fox became outspoken in his attack on Catholicism, accusing the Vatican of "spiritual sloth" and "creeping fascism." As his superiors became ever more unhappy with his views and public statements, he was repeatedly ordered to leave his institute and enter a monastery, and on each occasion he refused. This placed the issue of his vows of obedience at the center of the controversy. Following his departure from the Dominicans, Fox also left the Catholic Church, and in 1993 became an Episcopalian priest.[5]

The Fox case should remind us that not every exercise of the Church's disciplinary power constitutes an Inquisition or heresy hunt. These subtleties were lost on the media, which spent several years applying the familiar script of "heroic priest battles repressive Church." In 1988, for instance, the *New York Times* reported the conflict entirely in Fox's own terms, citing in the opening paragraph his analogies to Galileo, Thomas Aquinas, and other dissenters silenced by the Vatican. Subheadings stressed that Fox was "criticized by conservatives," giving the impression that no one other than hard-bitten reactionaries could resent Fox's speculations. Fox was also left to deliver the story's concluding lines, in which he complained of the Church's structural injustices: "Did Jesus intend a monarchy? Did Jesus intend a fascist state?"[6]

Sister Joan

Other dissidents are in a very different category than Fox in terms of their attitude to the Church, but they also receive highly favorable media treatment in accordance with the editorial tendency to frame Church battles in terms of heroes and villains. One example of this occurred in 2001, when Benedictine nun Joan Chittister spoke out in favor of women's ordination to the priesthood. She became the focus of an adulatory media campaign, which is all the more surprising in the context of her political views. Unlike Fox, Chittister remains firmly loyal to the Church and her religious order, and is widely esteemed for her writings on spirituality and social justice. Yet by any conventional standard, Sister Joan stands far to the left of the normal range of American political opinion, holding the kind of views that very few media outlets will normally treat with respect. She is a long-serving veteran of left-wing and pacifist causes, and champions the kind of utopian ideas that Europeans sometimes call "68-ism." Even in the aftermath of the terrorist attacks on the United States in September 2001, she urged a pacifist response, focused chiefly on fighting the "social inequities" of "raw capitalism."[7]

During 2001, though, Sister Joan became a media darling when she spoke publicly on the issue of women's ordination, most visibly at an international conference held in Dublin. What attracted the media to her cause was that her act directly challenged Vatican orders, although Benedictines are particularly pledged to observe vows of obedience. Complicating the story, Chittister's Benedictine superior refused to obey Church orders to silence her. Unhesitatingly, the American media identified Chittister as a heroine for her act of conscience, her assertion of freedom of speech and women's equality. For the *Los Angeles Times*, she was performing "a radical act of conscience." The *Milwaukee Journal Sentinel* headlined "Nun Makes Plea for Equality of Women." Though press stories followed the tradition of presenting rival points of view, there was no doubt that throughout, the story was that of Joan Chittister's heroic defiance. In the *Los Angeles Times*, the story's subheadings offered such inspiring language as "Sisters Vow to Work for Peace, Social Justice" and "Speaking Out on Feminist Spirituality."[8]

Consistently, too, the stories concluded with words either by Chittister, reinforcing her view of the conflict, or by her supporters. When the *San Francisco Chronicle* reported Chittister's conflict with authorities alongside those of other dissidents, the saints-and-demons quality of the tale was evident in every line. The article was by Stephanie Salter, who had earlier termed Chittister "a modern-day Joan of Arc for Catholics." This story began, "Although they are looked upon as disloyal heretics by conservative Catholics and much of the Vatican curia in Rome, Jeannine Gramick, Joan Chittister and Christine Vladimiroff have logged 135 years among them as nuns in the service of their church." The story's point was driven home by the closing paragraph, which quoted Jeannine Gramick, criticized by Church authorities for her ministry to gays and lesbians: "We're all victims of a terrible system. We have to find the ways to change the structure so that those poor men in the Vatican can have life." The headline: "They Will Not Be Silenced." Such objective journalism is a wonderful thing to behold.[9]

The media was unquestionably favoring Sister Joan, if not canonizing her. The *Los Angeles Times* ended its story by quoting her as follows: "It took 400 years of debate to end church support for slavery, she notes. It took extended debate on whether to abolish bans on usury, declare Jesus divine, and separate church and state. 'How can you say you know what the Holy Spirit is thinking,' she said, 'until you have heard it in everyone, everywhere?'" *Time* ended with her remark that "I worry for me. I worry for the community. And I worry for the church, whom I love." In perhaps the most dramatic such conclusion, the *Milwaukee Journal Sentinel* permitted Sister Joan to state her hyperbolic vision of Church evils through the centuries, which were contextualized with the worst crimes in human history. She states, "No pious, 'I'm sure that God will lead the church in the way it is meant to go' is ever going to satisfy for our spiritual responsibility now any more than it did for those who sat by while someone else engineered slavery and colonialism, the Crusades and the Inquisition, the Holocaust and the killing fields of Cambodia." We might reasonably ask how Cambodia found its way into this picture.[10]

For the mass media, the dichotomy is straightforward: Joan Chittister is Joan of Arc, and her church represents the Inquisition, the saint burners. We should not expect equally sympathetic treatment of dissident Catholics on the traditionalist end of the spectrum, who are at least as numerous as the liberals. For the media, the traditionalists are simply flaky reactionaries. In terms of the contemporary moral consensus, their views do not merit discussion.

Art Wars

Over the past decade, media hostility to Catholicism has been evident during controversies over the visual arts, particularly over major exhibits that have been denounced as blasphemous or anti-Christian. These disputes demonstrate a strong tradition of media bias and selective partisan reporting, and here too, the central theme is the Church's alleged repressiveness. Whenever an art exhibit outrages Catholic sensibilities, no matter in how extreme a fashion, the automatic response of the news media is to defend the art and condemn the critics.

At first sight, critics of such exhibits seem to be in a very weak position, because the notion of censorship is so widely condemned. For Catholics or other Christians to condemn an artistic display conjures images of the prudery of bygone centuries, when popes ordered fig leaves added to overexposed statues and Catholic bishops regularly intervened to prevent the public from gaining access to sexually frank books and films. Looking at the history of art and literature, it almost appears that official condemnation is a necessary stamp of approval for any significant or experimental work. In the United States, the idea goes back at least as far as the Armory Show of 1913.[11]

A popular image of artistic censorship suggests that it is something of the bygone past, and that the modern world—especially modern America—is far more liberated. "Book-burning"—or the banning of paintings—belongs to the benighted past, and so do the protests of offended religious believers. Only Catholics, with their cynical leaders and sheeplike believers, still dare to attempt such a thing: it must just be part of their strange totalitarian mind-set. Yet the idea that censorship is obsolete is seriously misleading. Americans still have quite rigid standards about what can and cannot be displayed in art, so that censorship today is quite as fierce as in the past. Any suggestive image involving children, for instance, is likely to draw legal sanctions, far more readily in the United States than in Europe. Also, Americans are hypersensitive about images or books that might offend particular racial or religious groups, so the notion that Catholics should demand respect for their sensitivities is less anachronistic than it might otherwise seem.

A widespread opinion holds that some art is so shocking that it must be removed or destroyed, even at the cost of violating the law, and both courts and media will support this position. In 1988, a painting displayed at Chicago's Art Institute gave rise to a city-wide furor and demands for instant removal. Though the gallery refused, citing free-speech rights, several aldermen took the law into their own hands and physically seized the picture. As one of the group declared, "We will not tolerate that picture hanging on the wall, Constitution or no Constitution. There is a higher moral law." Apart from the moral issue, critics complained that the painting constituted incitement to riot, and police responded by impounding the work. This act of suppression ignited a legal controversy that lasted into the mid-1990s, when the city agreed to pay financial compensation to the artist—but not to rehang his work. The vigilantes had won. The offending picture was removed from view, and the Art Institute actually issued a public apology for its bad taste in displaying such an insensitive work. Surprisingly, the controversy received quite limited publicity outside the Chicago metropolitan area, and nothing like the global soul-searching precipitated by later feuds over reputedly anti-Catholic works displayed at the Brooklyn Museum of Art (BMA).[12]

The Chicago incident sounds amazing in light of more recent disputes. Just why was the Chicago picture removed and the gallery cowed into submission, and all with so little reaction? If militant Catholics had acted similarly in one of the cases involving the BMA, we can only imagine the media outcry against Catholic bigotry and clerical fascism. The courts would have intervened to protect the artwork involved, regardless of any appeals to "higher moral law." The response in this case was different because the Chicago row involved not religion but political and racial issues. Specifically, art student David K. Nelson had produced the painting "Mirth and Girth," depicting the city's lately deceased black mayor Harold Washington in a ludicrous pose, wearing only women's underwear. Since Washington was so popular with Chicago's black community, the painting was seen as a deliberate racial slur, and the public response shows that in contemporary America, racial sensibilities far outweigh religious. Nelson himself remarked that while he respected Washington, "that doesn't mean he is a deity, that he can only be dealt with in a certain way." This comment is ironic, because if a deity had been mocked or insulted, rather than a black mayor, the outcome of any protest would have been very different.[13]

Other egregious instances of artistic censorship occurred about the same time, without any media outcry. In Miami in 1988, the small Cuban Museum held a fund-raising auction that included works by artists who either lived in Cuba or who had not severed their relationships with the Cuban regime. Protests from anti-Communist exiles were fierce. Extremists launched two bomb attacks, while city authorities tried several means to penalize the museum, including an eviction attempt. Though a federal court defeated the official actions against the museum, this did not prevent the institution being ostracized and, within a few years, forced out of existence. In this case, public pressures actually destroyed an artistic institution for favoring views deemed offensive to the mainstream. And, as in the Chicago case, few people outside the immediate geographical area expressed any real concern over the threat to artistic freedom.[14]

In other instances, museums and galleries have heartily acknowledged the need to respect specifically religious sensitivities, even to the point of self-censorship. This attitude is amply illustrated by the changing treatment of Native Americans. In years gone by, museums nonchalantly displayed Indian skeletons in a way that would be unconscionable for any community, but which was especially offensive for Native peoples, with their keen sensitivity to the treatment of the dead. In 1990, Congress passed the Native American Graves Protection and Repatriation Act (NAGPRA), which revolutionized the operation of American museums and galleries by requiring that all Indian remains and cultural artifacts be repatriated to their tribal owners. NAGPRA established a legal principle that artistic and historical interests must be subordinate to the religious and cultural sensibilities of minority communities. Under NAGPRA, anything that is considered a frontal insult to a cultural tradition (such as the old-time skeletal exhibits) is not only taboo but probably a violation of federal criminal law.

Even so, museums and cultural institutions have gone far beyond the letter of this strict law. They have systematically withdrawn or destroyed exhibits that might cause the slightest offense to Indian peoples, including such once-familiar displays as photographs of skeletons or grave goods. In southwestern museums today, one commonly sees such images replaced with apologetic signs, which explain gaps in the exhibits in terms of new cultural sensitivities. Usually, museums state simply that the authorities of a given tribe have objected to an exhibit because it considers it hurtful or embarrassing, without even giving the grounds for this opinion, yet that is enough to warrant removal. Where religious and cultural issues are concerned, one cannot be too considerate. Anthropological correctness also demands that Native American history be presented in certain ways, that specific terms and theories be excluded from scholarly discourse, and that where disputes arise, the viewpoint of the minority group must be treated as authoritative. In the context of NAGPRA and the other museum controversies, we can see that Catholics were by no means the only group demanding protection from offensive displays.

"Piss Christ"

In just the same years, several better-reported controversies seemed to set artistic freedom at odds with religion. During the late 1980s, the National Endowment for the Arts (NEA) was repeatedly criticized for sponsoring artistic exhibits and displays that were widely regarded as pornographic, especially those with homoerotic and sadomasochistic themes, such as the photographs of Robert Mapplethorpe. Some of the most controversial art of this type involved visual attacks on organized religion and specifically Catholicism, chiefly for its attitude toward homosexuality and AIDS. A centerpiece of the controversy was the "Piss Christ" of Andres Serrano. According to different interpretations, the image represented either a gross attack on formal religion or a symbol of Christ's suffering and humiliation. Even so, pressure to limit the use of public money in such controversial ways led Congress in 1990 to create a "decency test," requiring the NEA to "take into consideration general standards of decency and respect for the diverse beliefs and values of the American public." In 1998, the U.S. Supreme Court declared the test constitutional.[15]

The restrictions on the NEA were widely attacked, and liberals presented them as part of a rightist attack on self-expression, especially where sexual minorities were concerned. For major media outlets, the Serrano-NEA story was a simple battle between artistic freedom and the religious right, an episode in the culture wars. Undoubtedly, anti-NEA activism was led by familiar far right figures, including Senator Jesse Helms and the American Family Association. New York Republican Alfonse D'Amato personally tore up a copy of the "Piss Christ" photograph on the Senate floor.

Yet it is instructive to view anti-NEA protests in terms of other movements in these years that were also struggling to regulate hostile or provocative speech, yet which were classified as being on the political left. Through the late 1980s and early 1990s, feminist groups were campaigning for state and city ordinances that would suppress pornography as a form of hate speech, laws that in practice would have severely restricted erotic visual displays. (At least as implemented in Canada, such feminist-inspired hate speech laws have mainly served to restrict access to gay-oriented erotic materials.) In one celebrated case at a branch campus of Pennsylvania State University, a feminist professor demanded that a copy of Goya's famous painting "Maja Desnuda" be removed from her class-room, on the grounds that the display of female nudity created a chilly professional climate. The university swiftly moved the "disruptive" painting to a less visible location.[16]

This was also the time of intense activism on college campuses to establish draconian hate speech codes. In these debates, a major justification for suppressing speech or symbols was that they incited violence. This rationale would certainly seem to apply to items such as "Piss Christ." When this photograph was displayed in Melbourne, Australia, in 1997, it was the subject of two separate physical attacks, and it was severely damaged. If an object so offends members of a religious group that they are provoked to criminal violence, is the making or display of that object not an example of hate crime? The very different public reactions to the works of David Nelson and Andres Serrano suggest the existence of a fundamental double standard.

The issue of controversial religious art returned sporadically through the 1990s, sometimes with more justification than others. Penn State University was again the setting for a censorship controversy in 1996 when student Christine Enedy mounted an exhibit featuring twenty-five pairs of panties, each with a cross sewn over the crotch, symbolizing her twenty-five years of Catholic-induced chastity. Critics were irked to see the sacred symbol of the cross juxtaposed with an intimate sexual symbol, so that Catholicism was associated with self-repression. As in the Serrano case, we can debate at length whether the art in question was anti-Catholic. A viewer might just as well see the display as the artist's wry commentary on her own life, on the conflicting impulses of sexual desire and religious restraint. Yet the affair kept alive the controversy over art and blasphemy, especially when public funding was involved.[17]

Other artworks did not lend themselves so easily to benevolent interpretations. In 1997, the Los Angeles Museum of Contemporary Art was attacked following the debut of a chapel-like installation by Robert Gober in which a concrete figure of the Virgin Mary was pierced by a drainage pipe. Gober himself reported being troubled by "using a beloved icon, putting her on a grate, opening her up and piercing her with a pipe." Some observers were appalled, terming Gober's work "obscene," "garbage," "a twisted misrepresentation of art," and an example of "licentiousness and sacrilege." Yet the media were overwhelmingly sympathetic to the exhibit and showed little concern for Catholic sensibilities. Art critics were extravagant in their praise: the *Los Angeles Times* found the exhibit "quietly beautiful ... an unabashedly romantic grotto of sacred and profane love."[18]

Overtly anti-Catholic and anti-religious art displays proliferated in the late 1990s. In 1998, a Seattle gallery displayed two paintings by Leigh Thompson that can best be described as collages of anti-Catholic stereotypes. One was described as follows: "Hanging from a crudely designed crucifix made of intersecting penises is a Jesus Christ–like figure receiving oral sex from a veiled figure. Below the cross, two nuns lie on their backs with the ends of a coat hanger between their legs. Pages of the Bible are scrawled with the Satanic figure, 666." There is also a "painted depiction of a priest receiving oral sex from a small child." Equally startling was an exhibition at COPIA: The American Center for Wine, Food and the Arts, in Napa, California, which featured depictions of the Pope and nuns defecating. As with Gober's work, the obvious question might be: if these displays were not anti-Catholic, then what would be? Yet the media never presented stories on what appeared to be a rash of anti-Catholic hatred in the nation's art museums.[19]

Sensations

In 1999 and 2001, the Brooklyn Museum of Art mounted two exhibits that attracted worldwide controversy. Media coverage of these affairs not only displayed powerful anti-Catholic bias, but arguably showed that this bias was being deliberately exploited in order to generate publicity. Both the organizers and supporters of these controversial exhibits seem to have gone out of their way to show items that would offend religious believers and especially Catholics. In the ensuing free-speech fight, the media would demonstrate their Pavlovian tendency to depict critics of adventurous art as hidebound philistines. The more Catholics protest, the more the media place artists in a heroic role.

The first of these exhibits, in 1999, formed part of the exhibit "Sensation: Young British Artists from the Saatchi Collection."[20] Several pieces in this show were attacked for obscene or violent content, and animal rights activists were appalled by a display of sliced animal parts floating in glass tanks of formaldehyde. Another disturbing item was a portrait of British serial child killer Myra Hindley. Still, the controversy rapidly turned into a religious debate, focusing on one object in particular. This was "The Holy Virgin Mary" by the Nigerian artist Chris Ofili, a painted and collaged figure showing a black Virgin adorned by lumps of elephant dung and cutouts of female sex organs from pornographic magazines. Like "Piss Christ," this work too was attacked by an irate museum-goer, who smeared paint over it.

Catholic groups protested immediately against Ofili's Virgin, and they won the support of New York city authorities. Mayor Rudolph Giuliani termed the work "disgusting" and "sick stuff," and sparked a legal battle by threatening to cut the museum's funding. The battle was complicated by charges that the museum was improperly working with the owners of the collection, and with Christie's auction house, in order to boost the value of the artworks prior to possible sale. Several parties had a financial interest in generating controversy. Whatever the motives, the exhibit did attract enormous interest, and some two hundred thousand people attended the show, an amazing figure for a display of avant-garde art. Ultimately, too, the art museum emerged victorious in its legal conflict, as a court asserted the importance of artistic freedom and ordered the city not to penalize the museum then or in the future. As the magazine *Art in America* observed, "Irreverent toward artistic conventions, Ofili's feisty, dung-bedecked black Virgin became an icon of faith—in the First Amendment."[21]

Scarcely had this battle died down when in 2001 the BMA was once more attacked for mounting the Renee Cox photograph showing herself nude at the Last Supper. She was surrounded by twelve black apostles in what was entitled "Yo Mama's Last Supper." Like the "Sensation" affair, the Cox exhibit attracted charges of sacrilege, with Mayor Giuliani and William Donohue among the leading critics.

| Defenses?

Several different defenses could be mounted of the various articles under attack, with varying degrees of plausibility. Ofili's Virgin was defended as an example of religious inculturation. Over the last century, as an ever larger proportion of the world's Christians are located outside Europe and North America, believers in Africa and Asia have struggled to create new indigenous art forms that make sense in those cultures. Ofili identifies himself as a Catholic and derives from Nigeria's heavily Catholic Igbo people. In many African cultures, elephant dung has connotations of power, strength, and fertility, and surrounding the Virgin with this material has nothing like the debasing implications that a Westerner would find in smearing excrement. The notion of fertility is reinforced by the pornographic imagery. At least in its intent, the figure could perhaps be seen as a legitimate venture in religious art. European artists traditionally painted the Virgin's robe blue, because that is the color of the sky, and therefore of heaven; using a quite different cultural analogy, an African might use elephant dung.[22]

More generally, art writer Eleanor Heartney has argued that the various controversies are simply misguided. In her view, critics fail to understand the nature of a Catholic religious sensibility that is shared by all the artists who have been criticized and who are either Catholic themselves or come from Catholic backgrounds. Because of their sacramental theology and the notion of the redemption of matter, Catholics have always employed material and bodily images in their religious art and literature. Through history, we can find "startlingly sexy images which are enlisted in the service of spiritual teachings": Bernini's orgasmic figure of St. Teresa offers a prime example. Because of this theology of the redeemed body, even bodily fluids find a place in Catholic and especially Latin art. There is just "something about the Catholic perspective that pushes certain artists toward the corporeal and the transgressive."[23] This background offers a rather different perspective on recent controversies, including (argues Heartney) the debates over former Catholic Robert Mapplethorpe. The presentation of Gober's impaled Virgin involves "a complex meditation on the realms of spirit, matter, life, death and grace," while Ofili offers a "rather joyous female icon."

Heartney's arguments carry some weight, but she ignores how these material Catholic symbols can be deliberately used as weapons of attack and outrage. As one critic of her work wrote, "By her lights, a black mass would qualify as Christian, even Catholic, because it involves Christian emblems—e.g., the inverted cross—and is often performed by individuals born to the faith."[24]

Also, scholarly discussions of the sacramental nature of art rather miss the strongly political nature of the decision to display some of the recent objects. It is incredible that an artist or gallery would not expect the appalled reaction that would come from juxtaposing an image of the Virgin with both excrement and pornographic pictures. Nobody is that naive. And for all the claims that Renee Cox's identification of herself with Christ represented a mystical or religious image, nobody could have failed to predict that the nude image was going to offend. Following the previous year's battle over "Sensation," we must be skeptical about the comment of one of the curators who chose the Cox photograph: "We just thought these were great images. Nobody thought this was controversial!" In many such incidents, it looks very much as if the artists and the galleries concerned were deliberately seeking a *succès de scandale*. Explaining the wave of controversies, Giuliani argued that the galleries "do it on purpose; they do it to get more attention." Even *Salon*, which strongly supported Cox, said that "the whole brouhaha seems like an engineered controversy on the part of [the BMA]." Exhibit organizers have a vested interest in displaying and publicizing controversial art, and would stand to lose if religious groups ignored provocation. The *New York Times* commented that, "as in the real estate business, location is everything. There is no better spot to get noticed if you are taking aim at the Roman Catholic Church these days than the once attention-starved Brooklyn Museum."[25]

The Media and Anti-Catholic Art

On occasion, conservative groups probably have erred in their all-too-predictable outrage over controversial religious art. Though art exhibits can sometimes be seen as frontal attacks on a religion, in many cases they should be seen in a more nuanced manner. Yet while the critics erred in their way, the media and the art establishment were just as unsubtle in their defenses of the controversial displays. Though the twin Battles of Brooklyn raised complex issues about artistic freedom and religious sensitivity, the media presented the conflicts in more simplistic terms. The tabloid press largely accepted the Giuliani administration's position that the BMA was showing junk rather than art, and wasting public money in the process. More prestigious media outlets, however, depicted a simple confrontation between art and philistinism, Ku Klux Kriticism, and acknowledged no legitimate grounds on which any of the various works could be assailed—not "Piss Christ," not Ofili's Virgin.

The quality media all presented controversies such as the Brooklyn Museum affairs as the product of right-wing political agitation, pure and simple. The various artists under attack had been "demonized by the Christian Right." Eleanor Heartney wrote of the public controversies that they were "*initiated* by right-wing politicians" (my emphasis)—though in fairness, the debates were surely "initiated" when the galleries hung highly provocative artworks.[26] The controversies were presented as a phase in the ongoing war between freedom and repression; in attacking the exhibits, religious critics were threatening basic liberties of expression. The *Atlanta Journal-Constitution* published a column on the controversy headlined "Demagoguery Threatens Arts," which led off with the weary sentence "Here we go again." "The 'culture wars' have escalated to a frightening new level."[27]

Throughout the news coverage, too, the critics of the controversial art were analyzed purely in terms of their political motives. Rudolph Giuliani, for instance, was "pandering to upstate conservative voters … Giuliani has also been accused of going after the BMA because of his personal and political ties to the Catholic establishment." *Salon* wrote of "the 'Sensation' sensation (manufactured by a mayor and candidate for the Senate, Rudy Giuliani, in an obvious play to Catholic voters)."[28] Of course, in New York City as much as anywhere, political figures surely were paying close attention to their constituencies, but the media only discussed these factors in the context of conservative critics, not that of the galleries or their defenders. The implication was that critics were cynically seeking political advantage, while the defenders were selfless servants of art.

Media coverage of the art wars showed no sense that the critics might have any worthwhile arguments on their side, still less that significant civil rights issues were involved. The media regularly used puns and jokes to indicate the trivial nature of the objects under discussion. The *Village Voice* reported the Brooklyn affair under the headline "Dung Jury." The question then was why the critics became so upset about such minor provocations, and in these discussions journalists indulged in predictable stereotypes about Catholic ignorance and repression. *Salon*, for instance, noted that the Brooklyn protests "carry more than a whiff of condescension toward the very people they're designed to 'protect.' The point of such protests ... is that art that questions or challenges sacred beliefs is unacceptable. The message is that Catholics require a kind of cultural baby-sitting as if they were, to use one of the more common Christian metaphors, merely sheep."[29]

The suggestion was that Catholics screamed about "Catholic-bashing" at the merest hint of a challenge to the strictest doctrinal orthodoxy. As *Salon* argued, "It's become increasingly common for those who resent criticism of Christianity and the Catholic Church to play the victim ... anyone who dares to proffer a variation on the officially sanctioned imagery of the Christian canon is likely to find herself peppered with such missives from the faithful. ... Pretending that vulnerable citizens instead of religious ideas are being targeted isn't quite lying, but somehow I doubt it's something Jesus would do." Another *Salon* writer noted how "Giuliani unleashed his Torquemada imitation over 'Sensation.'" The lessons are clear. When Catholics protest that images are anti-Catholic, their objections prove that Catholics are "sheep," their leaders heresy hunters, and their clergy lying hypocrites; moreover, anti-Catholicism does not exist.[30]

Whether or not the controversial art displays in Brooklyn and elsewhere were anti-Catholic, their defenders often were. A common rhetorical device was to suggest that Catholic and other religious protesters were in fact responding not to perceived blasphemy, but rather to other issues, which placed critics in a very unflattering light. The debates over the Cox display in particular gave the media rich opportunities to denounce Catholic misogyny, as if the exhibit's chief sin was in elevating a woman to sacred status. The *New York Times* headlined its story "Female Jesus Draws Brooklyn Museum into Art Storm," concurring that the main objection was not the nudity but the elevation of women. Did the newspaper really believe that the exhibit would have attracted any controversy whatever if the central figure had been female but clothed? Cox was quoted favorably for her view that her work constituted a statement about the priestly ordination of women. Her photo was "a critique on how the Catholic Church has treated African-Americans and women." Katha Pollitt wrote, "A church that has a 2,000-year tradition of disdain for women's bodies ... and that still bars women from the priesthood because Jesus was a man can't really be surprised if a twenty-first-century woman wonders what would be different if Jesus had been female, and flaunts that female body."[31]

A subsidiary argument suggested that Catholic objections to the various shows reflected racism. Pollitt argued that critics were automatically finding "blasphemy" in the mere fact of Ofili's "Africanized Madonna." (In fact, Catholic and other Christian churches have often used black or Asian figures for Christ and the Virgin.) The Cox photograph raised racial issues because it was part of a major display by black photographers. Cox herself stressed the racism angle almost as much as the misogyny: "It also comes from research that I did—about the Catholic Church and how affairs were handled around slavery and Catholicism" Dismissing Catholic protests, she commented, "Maybe because it's a black female body . . . The hoopla and the fury are because I'm a black female. It's ironic that Chris Ofili and I are both of African descent." In an interview for the *New York Daily News*, she claimed a special expertise in Catholic racial politics: "I grew up Catholic. Being a Catholic—they are about business. Money. I don't believe in all the philosophy and how it's set up. ... Catholics had no interest in the abolition of slavery." [32]

| Mirroring Evil

The polemical quality of such attacks is evident when we think of art that stirs comparably strong emotions in other religions or racial groups. As the liberal Catholic writer Margaret Steinfels pointed out, "Elephant dung smeared on a church, synagogue or mosque would get the perpetrator arrested."[33]

This point about disparity of treatment is illustrated by another artistic controversy that occurred in 2002, which raised shades of the Brooklyn conflict. New York's prestigious Jewish Museum mounted its exhibit "Mirroring Evil: Nazi Imagery/Recent Art," a collection of art objects that interpreted the grimmest Holocaust imagery through the lens of contemporary popular culture. One jarring item was "Lego Concentration Camp Set." "It's the Real Thing" featured a computer image of artist Alan Schechner holding a can of diet Coke, apparently standing among starving inmates of the Buchenwald concentration camp. "Giftgas Giftset" showed Zyklon-B poison gas canisters packaged under designer labels such as Hermès and Chanel. The exhibit naturally provoked public protests and editorial outrage for apparently scoffing at the memory of the dead and violating a historical event that has acquired sacred status.[34]

Yet the differences between this and the Catholic controversies are sharply evident. The irreproachably Jewish setting of "Mirroring Evil" was critical in defusing charges of anti-Semitism, and it is unthinkable that a secular gallery such as the BMA would have dared mount such a show. More important, though, media coverage of the controversy always represented it as a real controversy, a conflict between representatives of competing opinions, both of whom had good arguments on their side. There never was a suggestion that the critics of "Mirroring Evil" were hidebound bigots, fanatics trying to strangle artistic freedom. Their real concerns and fears were presented as quite legitimate, and their views were reported respectfully. The issues raised were not dismissed as bogus on the grounds that the artists themselves were Jewish and could not therefore be accused of flouting Jewish beliefs. Nor did the media attribute the activism of Jewish political leaders to cynical electoral ambitions.

Nobody denied that the exhibit might cause real emotional pain. The museum itself acknowledged the depth of feeling by adding a special exit that allows visitors to leave before viewing the show's most controversial works, which were marked by warning signs. Neither the BMA nor the Los Angeles Museum of Contemporary Art offered such a merciful escape route from their exhibits. While supporting in principle the museum's right to present the "Mirroring Evil" show, some liberal writers in newspapers like the *New York Times* showed little respect for the artistic theories that motivated it or for the organizers. The show should go on, "no matter how stupid or unpleasant that may be." No newspaper or television commentators tried to tell Holocaust survivors or their protesting families to "[g]et over it."[35]

In all the media coverage of the protests over Serrano, Ofili, and Cox, we look in vain for any indication of what would constitute legitimate grounds for Catholic protests against works of art or literature, no matter how scurrilous. The media was arguing in effect for an unrestricted right to shock or offend the sensibilities of Christians and Catholics. This hatred of censorship might be admirable if there were not an equal recognition that definite limits did exist when dealing with the sensibilities of other groups. One does not make light of black heroes and martyrs, of AIDS or gay-bashing, yet when dealing with Catholics, no subject is off-limits. In this view, the concept of sacrilege applies only to secular icons.

7

"The Perp Walk of Sacramental Perverts"

The Pedophile Priest Crisis

The medieval Roman Catholic Church sold indulgences to sinners who thought cash could purchase exoneration in heaven. Today it's the church that is handing out money in hopes of buying forgiveness for itself.

— Johanna McGeary, *Time*, March 25, 2002

If the Catholic Church in America does not fit the definition of organized crime, then Americans seriously need to examine their concept of justice.

— Arthur Austin

Long-standing media hostility to the Catholic Church was expressed in singularly frank terms in 2002, during what was commonly (and misleadingly) called the nation's "pedophile priest" crisis. Even reputable news outlets presented a picture of a Catholic priesthood heavily infiltrated by perverts and child molesters, whose activities were treated so mildly by their superiors that the bishops themselves were virtually accomplices. This awful picture gave the opportunity for the widespread public expression of grotesquely anti-Catholic and anti-clerical sentiments and the revival of every ancient stereotype—even the sale of indulgences. News stories and cartoons revived and even exceeded the nineteenth-century propaganda of Nast and the rest. We recall that

Nast's famous "American River Ganges" depicted the miters of Catholic bishops morphing into crocodilian heads, which threatened to devour children. In 2002, a cartoon in an Alabama newspaper showed a bishop's miter with vicious jaws and teeth, and on the miter is written the word pedophilia: the cartoon is captioned "Shark." Historical reenactment is normally a harmless pastime, but the scandals of 2002 took us back 150 years into some of the grimmer moments of American history.[1]

Undeniably, some Catholic authorities had responded poorly to abuse problems in bygone years, sometimes callously or irresponsibly, and on occasion worse than that. Yet the disproportionate reaction to the clergy abuse issue, the suggestions of pervasive criminality, cannot be understood except as a reflection of accumulated political grievances over other issues, often involving sexuality and gender. Every interest group with an axe to grind now used the "pedophile crisis" as the grounds for unrestrained frontal attacks on the clergy, but also on fundamental aspects of Catholic belief. To appreciate the degree of hostility that now became evident, we can cite the placards carried by protesters outside Boston's Holy Cross Cathedral at Easter 2002, during a service presided over by Cardinal Law. One banner proclaimed "Let us prey"; another warned "Hold on to your children"; another labeled Law's cathedral a "house of rape." In a subsequent protest, placards declared that Law was "wanted for crimes against humanity." One lawyer suing the archdiocese proclaimed that the Church was "purportedly the most moral institution in the world, but they're evil. They're nothing but evil."[2]

In modern American history, no mainstream denomination has ever been treated so consistently, so publicly, with such venom. To find parallels, we would have to look at the media response to fringe groups and cults, such as the Mormons of the mid-nineteenth century, the Jehovah's Witnesses of the 1940s, or the controversial cults of the 1970s. That such a campaign was waged against the nation's largest religious grouping is remarkable. The only justification would have been if in fact the institutional Church had been guilty of the abuses alleged and the media were doing no more than reporting the sober truth—or at least they had solid grounds for their charges. Since in most cases they did not, it is reasonable to cite this affair as a gross efflorescence of anti-Catholic rhetoric.

The Geoghan Affair

The problem of sexual abuse by clergy first came to public attention during the mid-1980s, when the issue was commonly identified as that of "pedophile priests"—that is, an overwhelmingly Catholic problem. (Though clergy in some other denominations use the title "priest," in common parlance the word usually indicates a Roman Catholic setting.) As we have seen, for most of the past century, the media refused to examine sexual abuse by clergy of any denomination, but beginning in the early 1980s the volume of reporting grew enormously. One wave of scandals crested in 1992–93, when the clergy abuse problem was presented as a far-reaching crisis that threatened the moral foundations of the churches. These concerns subsided by about 1994, partly as a result of public revulsion at blatantly false charges brought against Chicago's Cardinal Bernardin. Still, litigation arising from abuse cases percolated through the decade and kept the issue in the public consciousness.[3]

The latest wave of scandals was launched by a Boston case that seemed to involve all the very worst stereotypes of clerical misbehavior and Church connivance. Through 2001, the case against former Father John Geoghan revealed the career of an all too genuine "pedophile priest," with a horrifying record of molestation. From his earliest days in the priesthood in the 1960s, he was repeatedly involved in scandals involving the molestation or improper touching of small children, in some cases as young as four. By the time he was finally defrocked (expelled from the priesthood) in 1998, he may have molested hundreds of children. Reportedly, he deliberately targeted the children of poor single-parent families, who were more likely to be open to an approach from a sympathetic authority figure and who would be less credible if they ever complained. This case attracted close attention in the Boston media, and at the start of 2002, an investigation by the *Boston Globe* demonstrated how directly Cardinal Law and other senior clerics had been involved in the mismanagement of this case through the years. This scandal was soon picked up by the national news media.[4]

The Geoghan story was troubling enough in its own right, but the story also gave a damning picture of Church attitudes. Geoghan's misdeeds came to the attention of Church authorities, but time and again, his superiors sent him for ineffective courses of treatment before placing him in a new parish. Obviously, parishioners were not warned of their pastor's previous record, and not surprisingly, the troubles began afresh. When this record came to light, the public was appalled to hear that Catholic authorities could so cynically have put children at risk. Some of those involved in making dubious decisions in the Geoghan case had themselves gone on to high Church office, so several bishops were indirectly implicated in the affair. Meanwhile, the investigation produced evidence of other cases almost as egregious, and the Geoghan scandal segued into the Paquin scandal, which merged into the Father Shanley affair, and so on. Charges of administrative incompetence by Church authorities escalated into accusations of high-level cover-ups.

To understand just why the Boston authorities drew such widespread condemnation, we can also look at the case of Father Paul Shanley. Shanley was ordained in 1960. Over the next three decades, he would often be accused of sexual molestation of young boys, in their teens or younger. He spent several years as a street priest ostensibly ministering to alienated youth, but he made no secret of his advocacy of sexual ethics radically at odds with those of the Church. While in regular contact with young people, he declared publicly that pedophilia was not deviant or immoral. In such cases, he said, "the adult is not the seducer—the 'kid' is the seducer, and further the kid is not traumatized by the act *per se*, the kid is traumatized when the police and authorities drag the kid in for questioning." He was reportedly active in the formation of the highly controversial advocacy group NAMBLA, the North American Man-Boy Love Association. Nor did he make any secret of his homosexuality. While ostensibly on sick leave in California, he ran a gay bed-and-breakfast with a highly charged sexual ambience.

Despite his very curious background, Boston archdiocesan authorities saw no obstacle to placing Shanley in parishes or to assuring other dioceses that his record was clean and he would cause them no problems. Two successive Boston cardinals went along with these deceptive policies. In 1996, Cardinal Law wrote to Shanley, saying that the priest had "an impressive record, and all of us are truly grateful for your priestly care and ministry to all whom you have served during those years." If there is a benevolent interpretation of this record of Church misbehavior, it does not immediately come to mind. The *Boston Globe* has asked outright whether Father Shanley was blackmailing the Boston archdiocese under threat of exposing other cases of abuse. Contemplating such a story, even those inclined to give Church authorities the benefit of the doubt had to be asking themselves: what was the archdiocese thinking?[5]

Going National

Pressure from the news media and from lawyers now forced dioceses across the country to turn over the names of other priests who had drawn complaints of abuse or misconduct through the years. Some complaints had been investigated internally, while others had resulted in lawsuits, but repeatedly, Church authorities had insisted on keeping these scandals from the public. Though very few other cases involved anything like the depravity of the Geoghan case—or of Father Porter before him—this emphasis on silence and secrecy gave a conspiratorial air to

Church actions. Almost daily in New England, one could count on reading headlines such as "Church Allowed Abuse by Priest for Years," "Former Priest Convicted in Sex Assault Case," "Papers in Pedophile Case Show Church Effort to Avert Scandal," "DAs Given Names of 49 More Priests," or "Hundreds Now Claim Priest Abuse." The *Boston Globe* printed phone numbers for those wishing to raise new complaints: "If you have information on child abuse by priests ... leave a confidential message at this number."[6]

Through the first half of 2002, the Boston crisis was replicated in many other states and cities. In Arizona, one could read "Church Hid Abuse, Victims Say"; in Florida, the headlines blared "Church Money Silenced Sex Claims." In the Florida diocese of Palm Beach, Bishop Anthony J. O'Connell was forced to step down after admitting sexual relations with seminary students years before; the bishop whom O'Connell had replaced three years before had himself been forced to resign in similar circumstances. Even Cardinal Roger Mahony of Los Angeles was the target of an abuse complaint, though the charge was strenuously denied and authorities dismissed it as implausible. In the first half of 2002, three hundred American priests either resigned or were removed from duty following charges of misconduct with minors. Time and again, the headlines were linking words such as church and priest with abuse, pedophile, and cover-up. Typically, the tabloid *New York Daily News* offered a sensational investigation under the banner headline "Predator Priest." Partly to give the media fresh material, lawyers indulged in sensational tactics such as attempting to sue the Vatican for complicity or threatening the hierarchy with a RICO suit, an attempt to label them as members of a "racketeer-influenced and corrupt organization."[7]

Media commentators generalized their criticism to the whole Catholic Church for its alleged softness on pedophilia, a point that emerged forcibly in op-ed pieces and cartoons. One widely syndicated cartoon originally published in the *Palm Beach Post* depicted a woman complaining about the Church's expectations: "For women, sexual conduct is always closely monitored—the Catholic Church tells me what I can or cannot do with my body. Truly unforgiving. Absolutely no compromises." And then the punch line: "Unless, of course, you're a pedophile." The message is obvious: as the Church knows all too well, Catholic priests can safely be presumed to be molesters.[8]

Such stories and images naturally had a dreadful effect on Catholics, lay and clerical. Anecdotal reports told of priests ceasing to wear the clerical collars that stigmatized them as potential molesters and exposed them to public insult. By March, the *New York Times* was reporting, accu-

rately enough, "As Scandal Keeps Growing, Church and Its Faithful Reel."
Without indulging in sensationalism, Catholic commentators of all political shades were describing the abuse crisis as one of the gravest moments in the long history of the Church in North America.[9]

Since I have been discussing the theme of media anti-Catholicism, I
should say that I certainly do not place the *Globe*'s coverage in this category: it was absolutely proper, tough, investigative journalism, which deserved all the praise it received. (Significantly, when evidence emerged
that some priests were being falsely accused, the *Globe* took the lead in
defending them.) Nor was it improper for other media to try to repro-
duce the *Globe*'s work in their respective regions. There were scandals to
uncover, and the press properly exposed them. Quickly, though, in trying
to contextualize the problem, sections of the media slid into much more
dubious attacks on the Church as a whole, and anti-Catholic imagery
soon surfaced. Some used the crisis to demand a revolutionary transformation of the American Church in ways that would eliminate much of
what had traditionally defined it as Catholic.

How Many Priests?

If the Geoghan and Shanley cases so precisely fulfilled the worst stereotypes of priestly misdeeds and Church misconduct, how can anyone
possibly claim that the media coverage indulged in anti-Catholic stereotypes, or indeed that the "pedophile priest" is anything other than fact?
How can anyone offer a defense of Church behavior? Yet on closer examination, the problem was, and is, rather different from what was perceived by the media, and at every stage familiar stereotypes break down.
Crucially, there is no evidence that Catholic priests are especially likely to
be abusers, still less to be pedophiles. If that point is accepted, then much
of the media coverage of the clergy abuse affair must be seen in quite a
different light. A casual observer relying on the mass media would form
the overwhelming impression of a Church institution awash in perversion, conspiracy, and criminality. That is very far from the truth.

Widespread media reports suggest that the pedophile priest represents
a very common type. Based on their misinterpretations of some expert
observation, the media presented the figure that 5 or 6 percent of all
priests were "pedophiles," a terrifying statistic that suggested perhaps
three thousand predatory individuals like Father Geoghan were active at
any given time. If we add to these figures for clerical pedophiles those
priests involved sexually with older teenagers, then a very large proportion of priests would be grave abusers, perhaps a quarter or a half. Often,
however, the media was relying uncritically on claims made by activists

and victims' groups. One activist in this field is David Clohessy of SNAP, the Survivor Network for Those Abused by Priests, who cites figures "that of the 53,000 Catholic priests in America, between 2 percent and 10 percent may be pedophiles—1,000 to 5,000 priests." Another survivor group, the Linkup, offers the following mind-boggling statistics: "Estimates of pedophile priests = 3,000 (6.1%) to 8,000 (16.3%) ... Current experts claim a pedophile could abuse 200–265 children in a lifetime. ...188 Bishops are responsible for the pain of at least 601,600 direct victims and as many as 9,475,200 indirect victims—a total of as many as 10,076,800 people. Clearly, something is wrong."[10]

In fact, something is very wrong indeed; such figures are wildly exaggerated. Insofar as it has a source, the popular 6 percent statistic claims to derive from the well-known work of Dr. Richard Sipe, though the statistic misrepresents his findings. The figure is misleading because it is based on studies of clergy who were already undergoing treatment for psychiatric or psychological disorders, a group among which we would naturally expect to see a far higher proportion of personality problems than in the mainstream priestly population. As such, the figure cannot be generalized. If any studies of the *general* population of Catholic clergy have ever indicated such outrageously high proportions of abusers and pedophiles, it would be helpful to know what they are. And if such studies do exist, why were they not cited during the national furor over abuse by clergy?

Yet we can form a sound judgment about the actual scale of the problem. Perhaps the most reliable source available is the Chicago study commissioned by Cardinal Bernardin during the previous national wave of abuse crises in the early 1990s. A committee of experts examined the personnel files of all men who had been priests in the Archdiocese of Chicago between 1951 and 1991, or 2,252 individuals. That number should be stressed, since it represents the kind of large sample that social scientists usually insist on, so that results can be applied to wider populations. Also, these priests were not pre-selected in a way that made them either more or less likely to have engaged in misbehavior, unlike a sample that only uses men undergoing treatment.

Between 1963 and 1991, fifty-seven of these priests had been the subject of allegations of sexual abuse, in addition to two visiting clerics. The commission reviewed all charges, not by the standard of criminal cases, which insists on proof beyond a reasonable doubt, but on the civil criterion of the preponderance of evidence. In addition, evidence was used that would not have been acceptable in a court of law, including hearsay testimony. Where there was doubt about a case, the commission decided to err on the side of the accuser rather than the priest involved. By these standards, the charges in eighteen cases were judged not to involve sexual misconduct—at most, they might have involved "inappropriate and immature behavior." Removing these eighteen cases left valid charges against thirty-nine priests in the archdiocese and the two externs.[11]

In short, 2.6 percent of Chicago's archdiocesan clergy were the subject of complaints, and charges against 1.7 percent of priests were probably true. As the Cardinal's commission was under intense public pressure to examine the records thoroughly and frankly, we can be reasonably confident about the validity of these figures. Some confirmation of this figure comes from more recent events in Philadelphia where, facing a comparable clamor for openness, the archdiocese released information on all the priests who had been the subjects of "credible" abuse complaints in the previous half century. The number of offenders was 35, out of some 2,100 priests who had served in the archdiocese since 1950. Again, this represents a proportion of around 1.7 percent.[12]

The figure that around 2 percent of priests might be involved in misconduct is a useful guideline, though we cannot insist on its absolute value. Obviously, unknown or unreported offenses are not included, and these represent what sociologists call a "dark figure" of unknowable offenses. Yet having said this, we must be struck by the relatively minor nature of many of the cases that people were reporting to Church authorities and which the committee did not count as abuse—behavior such as inappropriate speech or horseplay with teenagers. If people were prepared to report these misdeeds, it is not likely that they were too intimidated to speak out against the clergy on weightier matters. Although parents would have been very reluctant to denounce priests to police or social workers, they were clearly prepared to bring their suspicions to the Church, from which they expected a sympathetic hearing.

Perhaps the real figure for clergy abusers is 1 percent, perhaps it is 4 or 5 percent, but we should be suspicious of any figures far outside this ballpark. Also, we have to realize that this study is now somewhat dated, and the rate of misconduct may have changed in later years. Arguably, the contemporary figure should be rather lower, since awareness of the abuse issue has been so much greater since the late 1980s, and over the past decade diocesan policies have become much stricter than in bygone years. Put another way: if these figures are correct, 97 or 98 percent of Catholic priests are not involved with minors.

Having said this, a 2 percent offense rate is bad enough in its own right, and the problem requires action. As was often pointed out in 2002, the Church needed tough policies to ensure that complaints would be investigated thoroughly, that accused clergy would be kept from any further involvement with children, and so on. In fact, most dioceses implemented exactly these policies during the previous wave of abuse cases in 1993, and they have been observing them ever since. Contrary to the impression one might obtain from the media, most dioceses have in recent years done a respectable job of acknowledging the clerical abuse problem and responding to it.

Moreover, although 2 or 3 percent of Catholic priests might have offended sexually, this does not mean that they are pedophiles, namely, adults sexually interested in pre-pubescent children. (I will have more to say about why this distinction matters so much.) In the Chicago study, only a single priest out of over 2,200 fell into this pedophile category: one priest, not 1 percent of priests. All the other offenders were active with young people in their mid- or late teens. Even if we assume that the activities of pedophile priests are massively underreported, such individuals might account for at most one priest in several hundred. According to one of the most careful studies, "[i]t is rare to find a true pedophile in the priesthood or religious life." That fact is important for the number of victims affected by a given offender and the far-out claims made by activist groups such as the Linkup. Some rare serial pedophiles might indeed claim hundreds of victims, but the vast majority of clergy active with older teenagers are likely to be involved with just one or two individuals.

These numbers are radically different from the impression we normally find in the media and in public discourse. Though the notion that around 6 percent of priests are pedophiles has been discredited for a decade, it still appears in print. As recently as 2001, John Cornwell wrote that "the percentage of pedophile priests is said to be seven percent in the United States, and the numbers are probably typical for Europe as a whole." This is nonsense. Even worse errors occurred in the news media during the height of the crisis following the Boston revelations. One Los Angeles radio talk show aired the allegation that "[t]en percent of priests are pedophiles and the other 90 percent are equally as guilty [sic] because they don't do anything about it. I have always heard that men have a calling to the priesthood. Now we know that the calling is in his pants."[13]

A Catholic Problem?

Also contradicting conventional wisdom, there is strikingly little evidence that clergy of any kind are any more or less likely to abuse than non-clerical groups who have close contact with children, for instance, teachers, Scoutmasters, or supervisors in residential homes and summer camps. And though a sizable number of clergy have been implicated in this kind of abuse, no evidence indicates that Catholic or celibate clergy are more (or less) involved than their non-celibate counterparts. Some of the worst cases of persistent serial abuse by clergy have involved Baptist or Pentecostal ministers, rather than Catholic priests. Every denomination and faith tradition has had its trail of disasters: in addition to Catholics, this nightmare has affected Protestants, Jews, Mormons, Jehovah's Witnesses, Buddhists, even Hare Krishna devotees. A study of seventy-five priests and ministers convicted of criminal sex abuse between 1985 and 2002 found that thirty-eight were Catholic priests, while most of the rest were from Protestant denominations.[14]

Sexual misconduct appears to be spread fairly evenly across denominations, though I stress the word appears. Astonishingly, Catholic priests are literally the only profession in the country for whom we have relatively good figures for the incidence of child abuse and molestation. For these other groups, we have to depend on the volume of news stories and largely impressionistic evidence, but based on this, there do not appear to be significant differences in the amount of misconduct. If someone wants to claim that the Catholic priesthood is more prone to abusive behavior than other groups, then the burden of proof is upon that person: it is not possible to prove a negative. In order to establish a case proving priestly depravity, we would need to compare like samples of clergy from different denominations, with comparable systems of processing complaints and keeping records. No such studies have ever been attempted. As a result, the Catholic connection to abuse or pedophilia remains no more than an unproven assumption, or rather a prejudice.

As reported cases of priestly abuse proliferated during 2002, the media became increasingly intolerant of protests that the Catholic angle of the affair was being exaggerated. If that's so, they demanded, why is it we only hear about Catholic molestation stories? Actually, there are several answers to this question, which reflect the intertwined workings of the media and the courts.

One obvious point is that there are a great many Catholic priests and religious, and the media do not usually draw much distinction between abuse by priests and that by other clergy, such as monks and friars. If, say, 2 or 3 percent of this number might be sexually involved with minors, even that small proportion would yield a great number of investigations and lawsuits. Moreover, many of the cases revealed recently took place many years ago, often in the 1960s or 1970s, so we should really be looking at the total number of men who had been Catholic clergy since about 1960. Currently, there are rather less than 50,000 Catholic priests, but if we take all the current and former priests and religious who served at any

point in time since 1960, we are probably talking of at least 120,000 individuals. If we assume that 2 or 3 percent of that population have offended sexually, that represents perhaps 3,000 abusive clergy, a far larger
number of cases than have actually come to light to date. As of mid-2002,
the number of accused priests was around 1,500, and of course, not
all those charges would be substantiated. A large absolute number of
Catholic abuse cases does not necessarily reflect a high rate of priestly
misbehavior.[15]

Structural and bureaucratic reasons also help explain the number of
Catholic cases that appear in the news. Much of the evidence comes from
civil lawsuits involving priests and their dioceses. The proliferation of
specifically Catholic lawsuits does not mean that priests are more likely
to have offended, but rather that a centralized church with good record
keeping and extensive property holdings is a much more valuable legal
target than a small decentralized congregation. Catholic clergy lead the
list of known abuse cases because they are relatively easy to sue and because civil lawsuits produce a wealth of internal church documents.
Political probing and legal threats in the Geoghan case induced the
Boston archdiocese to hand over the names of eighty priests suspected of
sexual misconduct, a litigator's dream. In the diocese of Portland, Maine,
prosecutors asked Church authorities to hand over any records of abuse
allegations against priests within the past seventy-five years, that is, dating back to 1927. How many other agencies or denominations might
conceivably be expected to have records dating back anything like that so
far? Yet with the Catholic Church, such a fishing expedition might well
produce a rich haul.[16]

To some extent, the media concentration on Catholic abuse cases represents a kind of self-fulfilling expectation. Because priests are considered likely to offend, any cases that come to light can be fitted into a
prepared package of images and issues: the media has a lot of experts
handy and know what questions to ask, and those all deal with Catholic
themes. If a non-Catholic case comes to light (as it often does), it is usually treated as an isolated case of individual depravity, rather than an institutional problem. If a Presbyterian minister tries to seduce a young
boy met on the Internet, it is reported as the story of an evil or depraved
man, not of a troubled church. If a priest is caught in the same circumstances, then this event is contextualized with other tales of "pedophile
priests." The media knows what questions to ask about the institutional
crisis of the Catholic Church, the failures of celibacy, the abuse of episcopal power, the culture of secrecy, and so on. And the media know the answers they wish to obtain. Journalists find writing stories much easier

when they know from the start exactly what the finished product is going to look like. The more Catholic cases are treated in this way, the more the accumulation of sensational cases confirms the media expectation about the Catholic nature of the problem.

So Why Are We Always Hearing About Priests?

This issue of expectation is critical. Let us imagine a hypothetical series of events in which some other group might be labeled similarly as real or potential abusers. Just for argument, take public school teachers. (I am assuming the rate of sexual misconduct among teachers is not significantly higher than that for the population at large). Quite frequently, cases come to light of teachers involved in sexual misconduct or online seduction, trading child pornography, and so on. We generally see these cases as isolated examples of individual deviance. But the stories are surprisingly abundant, and newspapers and magazines have published exposés suggesting a widespread underlying problem. A 1998 survey of newspaper archives nationwide by the non-sensationalist magazine *Education Week* found 244 reported cases involving teacher-student relationships in a six-month period, with behaviors varying from "unwanted touching to sexual relationships and serial rape." That represents an average of over nine cases a week.

Of course, these are only the reported cases, and some activists feel that many other incidents remain undetected or unreported. The Web site of the advocacy group Survivors of Educator Sexual Abuse and Misconduct Emerge (SESAME) claims, "The best estimate is that 15 percent of students will be sexually abused by a member of the school staff during their school career." The organization's president complains, "Schools don't report rumors. Schools don't report allegations. Schools don't report teacher resignations under suspicious circumstances." No central clearinghouse collects and analyses such incidents. As a result, there are scandalous cases of teachers who have run into trouble in one school system moving to a new area, where they resume their abusive careers. One investigative study is titled "'Passing the Trash' by School Districts Frees Sexual Predators to Hunt Again." It all sounds very much like the worst image of priestly abuse before the recent upsurge of clerical scandals, though at the time of writing, abusive teachers rarely register on the popular consciousness. To use a social science term, they represent an unconstructed social problem.[17]

But let us imagine that civil lawsuits started exposing cases not just of actual criminality among teachers, but of internal complaints and disciplinary proceedings. Obviously, the number of cases that came to public attention would then increase dramatically. At that stage, the media might focus on an emerging social problem, which would be painted in the most sinister terms. Cases involving teachers and older teenagers would be reported alongside stories of child pornography and molestation, and presented as part of a single social menace. Media reports would tend to lump together minor acts of harassment with consensual affairs between teachers and students, and even forcible rape. Perhaps the issue would be framed in terms of memorable phrases— "peducators," for example. Since teachers are so numerous, even a tiny proportion of offenders would produce an impressive-sounding absolute number of cases, probably far higher than for priests or other clergy.

With the image of the pedophile teacher firmly established in the public mind, there would be a sizable incentive for further litigation, which would generate ever larger numbers of known and suspected cases. The news media and talk shows would give the issue daily coverage; the matter would become the subject of jokes on comedy shows, a theme in television dramas. Sensing the new public mood, individuals would be encouraged to come forward and report instances of victimization, often from the distant past. Reporting would encourage further reporting, litigation would stir more litigation, in a spiral that has no logical ending. Numbers beget numbers. With so many cases surfacing, experts would debate the circumstances that created such a dysfunctional culture in the schools and the teaching profession. The scale and seriousness of the problem would be so obvious a part of everyday discourse that any attempt to challenge public perceptions would be viewed as callous or self-serving.

If you expect a group to be villainous, you will generally find ample confirmation of that view. And once a problem becomes established, once it becomes a social fact, not much fire is needed to generate a very large amount of dense smoke.

Pedophiles and Homosexuals

During the 1980s, the media had to find a way of understanding a large number of misconduct cases involving clergy, and a number of different interpretations were open to them. For various reasons, though, the media had largely decided by mid-decade that clergy abuse was above all a Catholic problem. Once that decision was made, all future cases were fitted into a particular stereotype. The problem was that of the "pedophile priest." The popularity of the term served to channel and constrain discussion of the abuse issue by focusing entirely on (Catholic) priests and stressing the misleading angle of pedophilia. The use of this term, with all its connotations of predation and molestation, was clearly aimed at presenting the misconduct issue in the gravest and most repulsive terms.

As we have seen, the whole image of the "pedophile" is open to debate. Father Geoghan was indeed a pedophile, yet such individuals account for only a tiny minority of sexual misconduct cases involving clergy. If there is a "typical" clergy abuse case, then it involves a cleric sexually active with a young person between fifteen and seventeen, more commonly a boy than a girl. The act may be criminal as well as immoral, and it usually involves a disastrous violation of trust, but it is not pedophilia. In some instances, it is not even criminal: in many states, the age of consent is sixteen.

I thus draw a crucial distinction between pedophile activity and sexual misconduct with older teenagers—basically, pedophilia occurs when the younger party is seven or eight rather than seventeen or eighteen. Though the difference seems self-evident, some Church critics angrily reject any discussion of priestly misdeeds that denies the "pedophilia" of offenders. For Garry Wills, for instance, all sex between adults and young people below the age of consent must be classified as pedophilia, pure and simple. As Wills writes, this is a matter of "boy-sex (pedophilia)— the same thing that the inventers of the term meant by it and that society at large has always meant by it (despite the few psychiatrists who change its meaning to apply to child-sex)." By that standard, all the offending clergy in the recent U.S. cases are indeed "pedophile priests."[18]

The problem is that on this issue, Wills just has his facts wrong: at no point does his statement correspond with historical or linguistic reality. In my book *Moral Panic*, I traced the changing terminology used over the centuries to characterize child abuse, drawing on both professional medical literature and popular-culture accounts. Based on this extensive evidence, we can say quite certainly that ever since the word pedophilia emerged in psychiatric circles in the 1890s, it has never meant anything in medical usage other than sex with prepubescent children, regardless of their gender. This is what the "inventers" intended. Just how Wills decided that the word specifically refers to "boy-sex" is mysterious, unless he is confusing the word with the older term pederast. When the word pedophile entered American popular parlance in the 1930s and 1940s, it always referred to sex with small children, usually coercive in nature, and never referred to misconduct with older teenagers. This amply documented stress on prepubescent children (both male and female) was standardized in the diagnostic manuals of the psychiatric profession. This has for decades been the standard view of the whole profession, rather than the perverse opinion of "a few psychiatrists," presumably (as Wills implies) libertine outlaws. Though some recent writers use the term pedophile in an expanded sense, referring to sex with adolescents, this usage reflects simple ignorance of the word's accepted definition, or else a rhetorical desire to exacerbate the conduct described.

So if it is not pedophilia, exactly what is the misconduct of which most errant priests are guilty? In the psychiatric literature, an adult sexually interested in a teenager is technically described as an "ephebophile," but that word is of limited usefulness because it is so obscure. But perhaps we do not actually need a formal medical label at all. When an adult man has consensual sex with a sixteen- or seventeen-year-old girl, we do not normally describe that act in terms of a psychiatric condition, but would rather speak of a heterosexual relationship (though we might well think that the age difference makes the affair inadvisable or dangerous). Equally, when a man has sex with a boy who is sixteen or seventeen, we refer to the act as homosexuality rather than pedophilia or child abuse.

In the reporting of clergy cases, however, we always hear of molestation, abuse, and victimization. In one Cleveland case, the *New York Times* told the story of a clergyman involved in "sexually abusing a 16-year-old boy." In one of the more notorious such affairs in California in recent years, a diocese paid over $5 million in a case in which a priest had allegedly had sex with a seventeen-year-old boy pupil in a Catholic high school. (The priest in question denied this and other related charges.) News stories generally spoke freely of the act as "molestation" and the youth as a "victim." The *Los Angeles Times* reported "a payout to an alleged victim of sexual abuse by a well-known priest." In general discussion, even that case is wrongly categorized together with instances of "priestly pedophilia." When *Newsweek* devoted its front-page story to the theme "Sex, Shame and the Catholic Church," a subheading told, questionably, of "Eighty Priests Accused of Child Abuse in Boston." On further examination, though, it is unlikely that many of these cases involved "children" in any conventional sense of the term. One egregious example of this distortion of language occurred when, in 2002, Milwaukee archbishop Rembert Weakland admitted that many years before, he had had a homosexual encounter with a man then in his early thirties. Consistently, the media spoke of this event as an "abuse" scandal. The *Los Angeles Times* headlined "Former Archbishop Accused of Abuse Apologizes for Scandal." *Newsweek* reported how Weakland "had used ... church money to silence a man who accused him of sexual abuse 22 years ago." The language of abuse and victimization is used just as loosely in cases of heterosexual misconduct. When in 2002 a group of women convened a panel to discuss their abuse by Catholic priests, some of the victims were reporting sexual advances made to them when they were eighteen or older, and in some cases, consensual sexual relationships continued through their twenties and thirties. The priestly behavior was reprehensible, but it meets no standard definition of child abuse, still less pedophilia. Nevertheless, the media reported these events in terms of the "female victims of priests."[19]

To stress that many instances of clerical misconduct involve what should properly be called homosexuality is not to minimize or excuse the activities. It is difficult to speak of full consent when there is such a grotesque imbalance of power and authority between the partners, and the priest is certainly breaching an assumed bond of trust, in addition to his clerical vows. Even so, the media treat such relationships very differently than similar instances in which the older partner is a non-clerical authority figure, such as a teacher or coach. In recent years, novels about youth homosexuality and teens coming out have proliferated, usually treating the subject very sympathetically, and often portraying an intergenerational relationship as a kind of "initiation." Words like molestation and victim are never used, except by the novel's unsympathetic characters, the homophobic villains.

This take on the topic is reflected when the books are reviewed by mainstream media, which normally advocate zero tolerance for any such offense involving a priest. In one review, the *New York Times* enthused about a "beautifully acted film about an introspective 18-year-old boy's homosexual initiation." Another reviewer in the same paper responds to Sylvia Brownrigg's book *Pages for You*, which tells the story of a relationship between a seventeen-year-old girl and a woman teacher. This is portrayed as an "age-old story of first love and sexual initiation," "a gay love affair" that must nevertheless be kept from outsiders. "Since Anne is a teacher and Flannery a student, the relationship is kept secret, but a certain amount of concealment suits Flannery's recessive, wary personality anyway." If anyone wrote in those genial terms of a relationship between a priest and a seventeen-year-old boy (or girl), the outcry would be enormous, and that proposition is not simply hypothetical. During the height of the clergy abuse crisis in 2002, Judith Levine's book *Harmful to Minors* attracted fierce protests, partly because she had suggested that a relationship between a priest and a youth "conceivably" could be positive for both parties.[20]

The benevolent interpretation of gay "initiation" is sometimes applied to people much younger than the sixteen- or seventeen-year-olds who commonly feature in clergy abuse cases. In 2000, the *Los Angeles Times* reviewed Gavin Lambert's *Mainly About Lindsay Anderson*, observing that "since [Lambert's] sexual initiation at age eleven with a teacher at his preparatory school, he has felt only 'gratitude' for realizing his homosexuality." In the *New York Times*, film critic Stanley Kauffmann relates in matter-of-fact terms how "[w]hen Lambert was a schoolboy of eleven, a teacher initiated him." The lack of critical comment in these instances is stunning, as is the failure to place quotation marks around initiation or initiated. Others would choose much harsher terms, such as molestation, pedophilia, or child rape. Even in such a grossly exploitative context, journalists feel a need to avoid condemning alternative forms of sexuality. The fact that Oscar Wilde had sexual relations with street boys as young as fourteen has not prevented him becoming a contemporary gay icon, a heroic martyr figure celebrated in films like *Wilde* (1997). When clergy are involved, though, the media adopt a stern moralism and are prepared to launch very traditional-sounding assaults on homosexuality and pederasty. It is incongruous to read media accounts of priestly "perversion," a word that has not been commonly applied to homosexual relations for many years.[21]

In short, the media are quite justified in denouncing the sexual exploitation of the young and vulnerable; but why do they only do so when the perpetrator is a cleric? Where is the consistency?

The Media and the Pedophile Priest

Despite the inaccuracy of the term, the pedophile theme has dominated news coverage since clergy abuse cases first hit the headlines in the mid-1980s, and has continued to do so long after the news media should have known better.(To its credit, the *Boston Globe* avoided using the pedophile label, preferring to write of "priest sex abuse.") In the new crisis of 2002, yet again the standard image was of a middle-aged priest as a potential molester targeting small children—usually boys—of seven or eight. This was the visual message of the countless cartoons generated by the continuing exposés. One example from the *Louisville Courier-Journal* showed a priest greeting a penitent with the words "I'm Father Smith. I'll be hearing your confession." On the other side of the screen sits a small boy accompanied by an adult. The boy is saying, "This is Mr. Smigglesworth. He'll be my chaperone." Another cartoon from the *Record*, in Bergen County, New Jersey, played off the color-coded threat alert system developed in response to terrorist dangers. Three small boys are explaining to a priest their "color-coded system to rate the likelihood of an attack"— the attack in question being molestation. The message is that terrorists, of their nature, attack cities; priests attack small boys. Both cartoons were extensively syndicated. A cartoon in the *New York Post* showed "a priest in the confessional smoking a cigarette, with a bottle of booze next to him and his pants down around his ankles. On the other side of the screen is a boy who asks, 'Anything yuh wanna confess to me?'" The figure in such images is always a small boy, never an older teenager.[22]

The sweeping expansion of the pedophile label was commonplace in some of the most popular media outlets. *Time* magazine published a major story on the theme "Catholicism in Crisis": "As charges of priestly pedophilia pour in from around the country, a church besieged by law and laity seems incapable of making amends—even to save itself." A related story presented the words of "an ex-priest and child molester": in the setting, the casual reader might well ask if that phrase was not a kind of tautology. On the cover of the same issue appeared the question "Can the Catholic Church Save Itself?" Examining the impact of financial settlements on the Church, another *Time* story spoke simplistically of "the pedophile drain on Catholic coffers." *Newsweek* remarked how "across the country, the faithful are starting to question a culture that for too long has excused wayward clergy who abuse the kids who look up to them most." One revealing presentation aired on *CNN Headline News*, in which breaking news is reported summarily in text at the bottom of the screen. A report at the height of the crisis read "Brooklyn Bishop Expresses Regret in Handling of Pedophile Cases," with the headline preceded by the mocking phrase "Uh-huh."[23]

To insist on the strict definition of pedophilia may seem like verbal sleight of hand, but it is critical in determining whether an offending minister should be returned to parish life—and therefore, the degree of the Church's guilt in mishandling the sensational cases. According to what was long psychiatric orthodoxy, a cleric who offended with an older teenager could be treated successfully with little risk of recurrence, so returning him to parish life was a reasonable decision, while such mercy was wholly inappropriate toward a true pedophile. The fact that the Boston archdiocese acted abominably in the Geoghan case does not mean that other dioceses acted foolishly or dishonestly when they returned other priests to parish service: sometimes they did, sometimes they didn't. It is not fair, though, to conclude that Catholic priests are especially likely to be abusers, that they are likely to be pedophiles, or that their superiors usually act irresponsibly. To that extent, the image offered by the cartoons and columns described above is indeed inaccurate, and anti-Catholic.

Equally dubious is the assumed linkage between clerical misdeeds and celibacy, yet this too was a very common theme in media reporting.

Again, cartoons are valuable indicators for attitudes and prejudices. In the *Philadelphia Daily News*, a priest is shown sitting behind bars, as the caption reads "Cell-ibate": celibacy promotes pedophilia. One baroque example by cartoonist Mike Ritter showed a priest labeled "Seminary" using a tiny padlock marked "Celibacy" to close a trunk on which he is sitting. He is saying confidently, "I'm counting on this keepin' a lock on things." The reader can see that in the trunk, struggling to burst forth, is a huge and dreadful monster with claws and tentacles, which is labeled "Personal Demons." The message is that celibacy is a thin disguise used by hypocritical Catholic priests to mask their appalling criminal urges. Some journalists used the scandals to mock the priesthood mercilessly. One writer in *Slate* entitled his analysis "Booty and the Priest: Does Abstinence Make the Church Grow Fondlers?"[24]

The media has to know just how distorted is the picture of the legion of pedophile priests shielded by an uncaring Church hierarchy. They know about cases involving other denominations, and they can see that the vast majority of clergy abuse stories involve older teenagers or young adults. They are also aware that a proportion of lawsuits against the Church are driven as much by a quest for multi-million-dollar damages as by any notion of justice, and that at least some charges are quite false: recall the allegations against Cardinal Bernardin. It is distressing to see how many of the accusations stem from victims whose charges are based on memories supposedly "recovered" many years after the event. Such recovery is all the more questionable when memories are assisted by therapy, a profoundly controversial procedure that has repeatedly produced suspect and simply fictitious claims. As media attacks on the Church reached new heights in the spring of 2002, the liberal Catholic journal *Commonweal* remarked: "Admittedly, perspective is hard to come by in the midst of a media barrage that is reminiscent of the day care sex abuse stories, now largely disproved, of the early nineties, or the lurid details of Bill Clinton's impeachment. All analogies limp, but it is hard not to be reminded of the din of accusation and conspiracy-mongering that characterized the anti-Communist witch hunts of the early 1950s."[25]

Fixing the Church

The pedophile stereotype is so popular because it meshes so well with ancient images of Catholic perversion and inversion, stories that once circulated in anti-Catholic tracts and which more recently were confined to vulgar jokes. But the image is also politically and rhetorically useful in any political disputes involving the Church, conflicts that so commonly revolve around questions of sex and morality. The Church claims to speak for morality, yet (according to the stereotype) it puts the interests of its own perverts above those of innocent children. The charge that thousands of clergy are reputedly involved in the sexual abuse of youngsters and small children makes nonsense of the Church's claims to moral authority or integrity. The legend of the pedophile priest is a powerful weapon for feminist groups in debates over abortion, for gay rights groups over proposed civil rights legislation, or anyone opposing the Church over matters affecting children or families. When the Catholic Church attacks controversial films or art exhibits, the obvious defense is to ask why the bishops are not setting their own house in order and protecting children, rather than worrying about naughty pictures. In one *Chicago Tribune* cartoon, a bishop is smugly lecturing to a terrified couple lying in bed about Church bans on grievous evils such as contraception, abortion, homosexuality, and "thinking about sex." When the man holds up a newspaper reporting on "pedophile priests," the bishop responds, "Hey! We'll do the lecturing about sex around here."[26]

Activists of various stripes attack the Church hierarchy, and these critiques are then echoed, uncritically, by the mass media. When the activists themselves claim Catholic credentials, this further erodes any restraint the media might have had about offering the most florid anti-clerical and anti-Catholic imagery. Catholic reformers themselves have enthusiastically accepted the pedophile priest motif. Since "everybody knows" that Catholic priests are so prone to perversion, internal critics of Church structures and policies can use that fact to add urgency to their calls for reform, which have been faithfully reported in most mainstream newspapers and television news outlets. Child abuse or pedophilia even become metaphors for systematic Church abuses. For Catholic psychologist Eugene Kennedy, "[t]he sexual abuse of children is the same pattern the church uses in relation to its own people."[27]

Celibacy is a natural target for anti-clerical reformers. Since the media never tell us about "pedophile pastors," the abuse problem must of necessity reflect the frustrations of men imprisoned by the Catholic Church's archaic rules, and abolishing celibacy would solve the problem. So would ordaining women, reducing the separate and privileged status of the clergy, or curbing the authority of the hierarchy. One of the most-cited experts on clerical abuse is Richard Sipe, who makes no secret of his sweeping reformist agenda. Since the early 1990s, he has spoken frequently of the role of the sexual "crisis" in detonating a "new Reformation," and he has told anti-abuse activists that they stand at "Wittenberg," recalling the site of Luther's movement against the Catholic orthodoxy of his day, the "celibate/sexual system." James Carroll argues that the crisis reveals the failures of "a corrupt, misogynist, self-protecting clerical elite. The Vatican's dishonesty on all matters concerned with sex—no birth control, no condoms for AIDS prevention, etc.—is now fully perceived by the Catholic people. Sexual totalitarianism will no longer succeed as an organizing principle of this institution." Longtime Church critic Terrance Sweeney has written, "If there were women priests and women bishops and married bishops, the likelihood of this [abuse crisis] happening in the first place would be close to nil." Clearly, Sweeney has not examined conditions in the U.S. Episcopal Church or its British Anglican counterpart.[28]

Feminists have been especially active in deploying the abuse crisis to support their goals, in presenting their analysis in the media—and in duly exaggerating the "pedophile" angle of the crisis. In *Newsweek*, Anna Quindlen wrote of the "new revelations of pedophile priests" and explained how celibacy made priests so warped, "so estranged from normal human intercourse that for some, the rapacious pursuit of altar boys passes for intimacy." Lisa Sowle Cahill, an academic at Boston College, has written that the "pedophile scandal exposes the weaknesses of a virtually all-male decision-making structure." In the *Nation*, Katha Pollitt attacked "[t]he bishops who presided over the priestly pedophilia in the Catholic Church's ever-expanding scandal," implying that the bishops themselves were accomplices in the molestation. How could they retain their moral authority in issues such as the use of condoms to prevent AIDS, or the restrictions imposed on abortion and contraception in Catholic hospitals?[29]

Through the height of the crisis in early 2002, some of the strongest (and often the oddest) invective came from *New York Times* columnist Maureen Dowd, for whom the "pedophilia" scandals resulted from the abuse of specifically masculine priestly power. As she writes, "We have turned a light on these cloistered, arrogant fraternities and they can no longer justify themselves. Their indulgences, conducted in secret, have hurt the welfare of their most vulnerable charges." "It is glaringly clear that mandatory celibacy—stifling God-given urges—draws a disproportionate number of men fleeing confusion about their sexuality." Dowd mocks the naivete of Church leaders, and she imagines Cardinal Law saying, "Who knew that priests' dating eleven-year-olds was wrong? We need to commission a major study. Is it all right when they're twelve?" The U.S. Catholic Church was overwhelmed by the deadly sins: "Lust ran unchecked—in a tortured, destructive form—in the Catholic priesthood. ... Greed ... prompted Catholic prelates to defame victims rather than face civil fines and depleted contributions." The hierarchy "know-ingly put children in harm's way because they did not want the priests they should have punished to divulge the church's hypocrisy."[30]

Sometimes Dowd goes still further, to present Church abuses as on a par with outrageous acts of violence, terrorism, and corporate crime. In these instances, anti-clerical sentiments certainly venture into openly anti-Catholic territory. In one column, she brought under a single rhetorical umbrella "the church subsidizing pedophilia; the Afghan war-lords' resumption of pedophilia; the Taliban obliteration of women; the brotherhood of Al Qaeda and Mohamed Atta's misogynistic funeral instructions; the implosion of the macho Enron Ponzi scheme." Analogies to Islamist fanaticism recurred frequently in Dowd's tirades during these months. In another piece, after condemning Islamist extremism, she noted that "the pedophilia scandal" in the Catholic Church "also provides evidence of the damage that dogmatic faith can do ... A little like some of the institutions of Islam, Rome is in a defensive crouch, protecting criminals in its midst instead of telling the truth and searching its soul." Such tirades give cranks a bad name.[31]

Any liberal nostrum can be claimed as a means of reducing clerical pedophilia, and for the mainstream media, the linkage seems so self-evident that it is baffling why the Church authorities do not concede the point forthwith. As the *San Francisco Chronicle* commented about the Church's treatment of abuse cases, "Why it took so long for reality to dawn upon the ultimate stewards of the church—Pope John Paul II and his men in the Vatican—is a thorny issue being argued in many Catholic circles. Theories range from the insistence on celibate priests to this pope's near-totalitarian style of governance." For Maureen Dowd, the issue proves the un-American quality of the Church, a basic tenet of anti-Catholicism: "The Vatican's cavalier attitude will only intensify the collision between the open, modernizing spirit of America and the deeply anti-democratic spirit of the church." Un-American and totalitarian themes were much in evidence in anti-Church attacks during 2002. In the *New York Times*, Bill Keller offered an extended analogy between the modern Church and discredited Soviet-era Communism—and, of course, all Catholic evils are presented as the personal responsibility of the demonized John Paul II. This Pope "has replicated something very like the old Communist Party in his church," with his *apparat* of cynical bureaucrats, ruling through the "corrosive rain of hypocrisy." He has also "carefully constructed a Kremlin that will be inhospitable to a reformer. He has strengthened the Vatican equivalent of the party Central Committee, called the Curia, and populated it with reactionaries." The more

bishops and priests oppose liberal reforms, the more they can be condemned for obscurantism and self-interest, or worse—are they perhaps
pedophiles themselves?[32]

The New Reformation

Many activists are currently speaking in terms of the abuse crisis launch-
ing a "new Reformation," and perhaps their expectations are not too
wide of the mark—though their historical knowledge is at best patchy.
They are generally working with a common myth of the sixteenth-
century Reformation that goes something like this. By 1500 or so, the
Church was awash with corruption; ordinary lay people were appalled by
their corrupt, depraved, and ignorant clergy, and they demanded a radical change, which resulted in the establishment of new Protestant
churches. To quote Victorian rationalist J. W. Draper, "It wanted nothing
more than the voice of Luther to bring men throughout the north of Europe to the determination that the worship of the Virgin Mary, the invocation of saints, the working of miracles, supernatural cures of the sick,
the purchase of indulgences for the perpetration of sin, and all other evil
practices, lucrative to their abettors, which had been fastened on Christianity, but which were no part of it, should come to an end. Catholicism,
as a system for promoting the well-being of man, had plainly failed in
justifying its alleged origin."[33]

That is one way of looking at things, but for some years, mainstream
historians have favored a much less simplistic approach. Many modern
accounts of pre-Reformation religion stress how wholeheartedly the
Church's role was accepted, how widely popular were Catholic beliefs
and rituals, and how well the clergy fitted into their society. Generally,
the clergy were respectable and pious, did their best in difficult economic
circumstances, and were open to the idea of reasonable reforms. There
were scandals, to be sure, but the Church was accepted as a fundamental
part of life. What lay grievances existed were limited and specific, and in
no sense demanded a revolutionary reform. Popular though the idea
may be today, European people did not overnight convert to Luther's
complex theological notions as soon as he nailed them on the church
door in Wittenberg.[34]

However, the sixteenth-century Church came under increasing attack
from vehement anti-clericals, who exaggerated and often invented tales
about corrupt and predatory clergy. Some Church critics authentically
wanted a systematic religious change, but many were demagogues or
time servers who used the mass media available to them at the time, including scabrous cartoons and visual imagery. The attack on the Church

succeeded in many countries because governments resented Church independence and its resistance to the new nationalism. When Church authority collapsed, governments ensured that the new religious establishments were totally docile. Other beneficiaries of religious "reform" included lay elites such as the lawyers, who enriched themselves through the massive legalized plunder of Church property. The main casualties of the reform were the ordinary lay believers, who saw their cherished religious practices prohibited and mocked by the new elites in the Church and in society. The parallels to contemporary realities are too numerous to detail here, but most obvious is the gulf that separates the popular allegations made against clergy from any kind of objective reality.

Many of the most damaging attacks against the Church derived from internal sources rather than external critics: Dowd, Carroll, Quindlen, Kennedy, Wills, and Sipe would all describe themselves as faithful Catholics. Yet their rhetoric deploys an often ferocious range of anti-Church arguments, which are readily adopted and amplified by the most fervent anti-Catholics. In this view, the Church is of its nature un-American, abusive, and totalitarian; clergy are closeted perverts. The effects of the clergy abuse crisis, what Dowd calls the "perp walk of sacramental perverts," have been far-reaching.[35] Over the last fifteen years, we have seen the massive revival of an ancient anti-clerical and anti-Catholic image that had largely been excluded from respectable discourse. Today, though, the priestly caricature has returned to the social mainstream. It remains to be seen whether the anti-clerical assault will have consequences anything like those of Luther's time.

8 | Catholics in Movies and Television

I love Jesus. I don't need an institution between him and me. You see. Just God and man. No priests, no churches. The first words in Jesus' gospel are "The kingdom of God is inside you and all around you."

— *Stigmata*

Since entertainment companies are often part of the same corporate networks that control the news, it is not surprising that Catholicism also receives quite hostile treatment in movies and television. What is remarkable, perhaps, is that the torrent of anti-Catholic imagery stirs so little comment. Because film has been such a powerful cultural force over the past century, many academics have turned their attention to the medium. In historical studies of the cinema, one powerful theme has been that of stereotypes and how American films in particular have dealt with various groups that have been viewed as unpopular or suspect. We now have shelves of studies on the treatment of blacks, Jews, Latinos, Native Americans, Asian-Americans, homosexuals, and so on.[1] Catholics, though, have been little studied in their role as targets of prejudice, which is odd when we consider how many films over the past twenty years or so have offered such very unflattering or hostile images. In these years, several films have treated the Church's leadership as a band of cynical, violent conspirators little different from a stereotypical organized crime family. Several more have portrayed priests and clergy as hypocrites who routinely betray their vows of celibacy, sometimes as ruthless sexual exploiters of young people. A film such as *Stigmata* portrays the whole of Catholicism as a cynical lie that survives only by deceit and violence. Catholics are not quite the only targets of systematic media calumny— evangelical and Pentecostal ministers are also harshly treated—but at least since the 1980s, Catholics and specifically Catholic clergy have been much the most consistent media villains.

| The Age of Spencer Tracy

The treatment of Catholics in American films has changed enormously since the mid-twentieth century, when the Catholic Church played a major role in shaping the standards under which Hollywood operated. From the early 1930s through the 1950s, American cinema obeyed censorship codes that were in large measure a response to Church pressure, and even films that passed these stringent tests might still be attacked by Catholic organizations such as the Legion of Decency. If Church authorities ordered the faithful not to view a particular film, that boycott could be commercially disastrous. Nor were financial pressures the only reason filmmakers were so anxious to avoid offending Catholic interests. Given the widespread anti-Semitism of the 1930s and 1940s, Jewish studio managements were terrified that a moralistic attack against the movies could be transformed into a racial campaign. As a result, Hollywood filmmaking became a peculiarly American hybrid, "an industry largely financed by Protestant bankers, operated by Jewish studio executives, and policed by Catholic bureaucrats." There were also formal legal sanctions: not until 1952 did the U.S. Supreme Court strike down a New York state law against showing "sacrilegious" films (*Burstyn v. Wilson*).[2]

The need to accommodate Catholic pressures affected many aspects of American cinema in this period, in terms of the presentation of sexuality and family life, violence, politics, and, necessarily, religion. Any presentation of the clergy or particularly the Catholic Church had to be handled with kid gloves, which explains the generally heroic and saintly images of Catholic priests. Think of classic priest films such as *The Keys of the Kingdom, Going My Way, Boys Town, The Bells of St Mary's,* and *Angels with Dirty Faces,* all made between 1938 and 1944. Uniformly, priests were played by admired actors such as Bing Crosby, Gregory Peck, Spencer Tracy, or Barry Fitzgerald. This genre of priest films culminated in 1947 with John Ford's *The Fugitive*, in which the appearance of the priest is usually accompanied by streams of light and angelic music. *The Fugitive* was an adaptation of Graham Greene's novel *The Power and the Glory*, which had shown how a very unheroic alcoholic priest became a saint and martyr. Needless to say, the film omitted all these negative features, presenting an uncomplicated Catholic superman. *I Confess* (1953) featured a thoroughly heroic priest wrongly suspected of murder because he cannot breach the secrecy of the confessional: his own trial (on false charges, naturally) includes obvious visual references to the condemnation of Jesus. *On the Waterfront* depicted a heroic priest struggling against labor racketeers.

In such a political setting, no studio could have made an anti-Catholic or anti-clerical film, nor even one that might offend the most sensitive members of the Church hierarchy. The United States produced nothing vaguely close to the vigorous European traditions of anti-clerical and anti-Catholic film (consider the work of directors such as Buñuel, Fellini, and Pasolini), and the American Church was determined to preserve the transatlantic contrast.[3] Even during the 1960s, as American censorship rules were collapsing and the Catholic faithful were liberalizing politically, studios still showed little desire to tackle controversial religious themes. Besides their residual fear of boycotts, politically liberal filmmakers had no wish to be accused of the ugly anti-Catholicism that had surfaced in the 1960 election. Moreover, the Church and its clergy were overwhelmingly on the approved side in the political issues of the day, such as civil rights. Even when a Catholic priest was portrayed in the aggressively left-wing film *M*A*S*H* (1970), the unit's chaplain is at worst an amiable fool, and is not one of the demonized warmongers; the role of religious hypocrite is left to a Bible-thumping Protestant fundamentalist.

In television too, the threat of Church pressure on corporate sponsors ensured that the networks exercised restraint in their treatment of Catholic themes. In a notorious 1973 censorship debate, Catholic groups tried to suppress an episode of the show *Maude*, in which the lead character had an abortion. Though the show was aired, many stations refused to carry it, no corporate sponsor bought airtime, and thousands of protest letters were received.

The Thaw

Not until the late 1970s did the media begin to offer more daring treatments of Catholic themes. A departure from old standards was signaled by the 1976 British film *Nasty Habits,* which satirized the Watergate affair by transforming the whole sordid drama into a conflict for control of a convent. This was not too sensational in itself, but when the film was publicized in the United States the following year, advertising posters used a mildly suggestive picture of a nun showing a stockinged leg. The world was changing.[4]

The number of once-unthinkable treatments grew rapidly between 1978 and 1983, a period that I have hitherto described as critical in the emergence of the new liberal anti-Catholicism. This trend owed much to the speculations surrounding the twin 1978 papal elections and the ensuing scandals. On television, it was in 1978 that *Saturday Night Live* allowed Don Novello to introduce his character Father Guido Sarducci, allegedly "gossip columnist and rock critic for the Vatican newspaper *L'Osservatore Romano.*"[5]

Encouraged by the success of Andrew Greeley's novel *The Cardinal Sins,* the media now experimented with other once-forbidden topics, and illicit clerical sexuality was the subject of the films *Monsignor* (1982) and *Agnes of God* (1985). Both films dabbled in other familiar anti-clerical themes, exploring the far-reaching hypocrisy that was said to lurk behind the mask of saintliness. Drawing on the conspiracy theories of the late 1970s, *Monsignor* presented a cardinal allied to the Mafia and involved with financial fraud, who thus recalls the nightmarish Vatican conspirators of Protestant mythology. *Agnes* offered another familiar Protestant icon, namely, the sexually deranged nun who has murdered the baby she has mysteriously delivered. Adding to the shades of *Maria Monk,* the tale even takes place in a Quebec convent. Even so, *Agnes* is nothing like the simplistic anti-papist tract that it initially promises, and indeed the woman investigating the death is thoroughly disappointed not to find the web of ecclesiastical corruption that she confidently expects.

Neither of these films enjoyed widespread popularity, but both demonstrated that highly critical treatments of the Church were now possible. In 1982, we find dark observations of Catholic *realpolitik* in films like *The Verdict* and *True Confessions.* In 1983, the new freedom to explore Catholic issues reached television with the mini-series of Colleen McCullough's novel *The Thorn Birds* (1977), which covered a sexual liaison between a prominent Catholic cleric and a laywoman. Though the series was scarcely controversial by the standards of later productions, it was attacked by Catholic leaders, particularly because it was broadcast during the Easter season. By 1988, the theme of clerical sexuality had become so nearly commonplace as to attract little protest when it was treated in the highly forgettable film *Last Rites.*

A new willingness to tackle religious controversy was also demon-strated by the British film *The Life of Brian* (1979). This film, by the Monty Python troupe, presented some outrageous satirical imagery not just of the Church, but of the world of Jesus. Its most famous image is probably the chorus of crucified men singing "Always look on the bright side of life." In 1983, the same team produced *The Meaning of Life*, with a sequence of outrageously anti-Catholic songs and sketches. In one spec-tacular song-and-dance number, Catholic attitudes toward sex and con-traception are ruthlessly parodied in the song "Every Sperm Is Sacred" ("Every sperm is sacred / Every sperm is great / If a sperm is wasted / God gets quite irate"). The dancers included figures dressed as Catholic clergy and nuns, who looked as though they had stepped out of a Communist anti-clerical skit of the 1920s or a Buñuel fantasy. By about 1983, it was clear that Catholicism was available as a legitimate subject of serious fic-tion, and a target for negative coverage.

The Wrong Targets?

Since the late 1980s, Catholics have denounced many films and televi-sion programs for their anti-religious and specifically anti-Catholic con-tent. In some cases, the charge is undoubtedly justified, while in others, it is more questionable. In deciding what is "offensive," much depends on the individual's capacity to take offense. People vary greatly in their sen-sitivity to religious matters, and for some, almost any deviation from the strictest and soberest orthodoxy is unacceptable. For many others who consider themselves religious believers or church members, there cer-tainly is room for humor or satire, especially when that satire raises im-portant questions or deflates extremist positions. Most Catholics are prepared to laugh at themselves, and many Catholic viewers found Fa-ther Sarducci hilarious in much the same way that Jews were prepared to laugh at the self-parodies of Woody Allen. When the good Father offered the post-mortem tariff list for sins committed during life, at least some Catholics probably saw a legitimate satirical comment on the way priests calculated the penances they issued during confession ("Stealing a hub cap is around $100. Masturbation is 35 cents—it doesn't seem like much, but it adds up"). One popular theater piece in recent years has been the improvisational *Late Nite Catechism*, which makes fun of generations of Catholic schooling, but is sufficiently good-natured that Catholic par-ishes use it for fund-raising. As G. K. Chesterton said, "It is the test of a good religion whether you can joke about it."[6]

Also, given the volume of news coverage given to disputes over contro-versial films such as *Dogma*, it is worth noting that by no means all post-

1980 films on the Catholic Church have been hostile. Some, in fact, have been remarkably positive, even pious. In 1999, the publicity for the film *The Third Miracle* made it look like a damning attack on the Church, with its theme of a priest who demolishes tales of fraudulent miracles and contemplates a sexual relationship with a woman. In the event, the film told of a heroic priest who finds himself investigating quite authentic miracles and the life of a genuine saint. It is a significant comment on the mood of the times that even such a relatively pious production had to be marketed as a steamy exposé of clerical sexuality. Hollywood films dealt intelligently with ecclesiastical politics (*True Confessions*) and the nature of sanctity (*Household Saints*). Steven Spielberg's film *Amistad* (1997), with its theme of slavery and racial injustice, offered a powerful portrait of the religious dilemma faced by a Catholic judge.

The Church was treated with respect when it was clearly on the liberal side of a public controversy, as it was during the Central American crises of the 1980s. Catholic clergy and Church leaders thus emerge very favorably from films such as *Romero* and *Salvador*. Both films in fact had strong elements of hagiography in their depictions of (respectively) Salvadoran archbishop Oscar Romero and the American churchwomen murdered by Salvadoran national guardsmen. We cannot speak of an unqualified attack on the Catholic tradition.

In looking at the media controversies of these years, the films and television shows that have been attacked as anti-Catholic or anti-Christian, we can arrange individual cases along a spectrum, from the mild and fairly well-intentioned to the genuinely malicious and sinister. As we saw in the context of controversial art exhibits, in some cases the critics' fury has been amply justified, while in other cases it has not. In the latter category, I would place the television series *Nothing Sacred*, which ran on ABC in 1997–98. The Catholic League protested repeatedly against the show's perceived hostility to established Church positions, with William Donohue describing it as "a depressing show about a dissident priest in a dysfunctional parish." Through 1997, a major portion of the league's activism was devoted to persuading corporate sponsors not to advertise during the show. The organization celebrated when the show was not renewed for the 1998 season: "In the end, the Catholic League succeeded in killing most of the sponsors with its boycott. We have since been credited with conducting the first successful boycott of a TV show by means of our website."[7]

Nothing Sacred made no excuse for its sympathies in the continuing partisan battles within the Church. The scripts were, after all, written by a Jesuit, under an assumed name. The clergy characters, the heroic priests and nuns, were all identified with liberal positions, in terms of both secular politics and ecclesiastical causes, such as the ordination of women. The parish priest consistently showed a distressing preference for feel-good New Age spirituality over most Catholic traditions. The show also demonstrated sympathy for abortion rights. Orthodox or traditionalist characters were portrayed less sympathetically, though the show was flexible enough to give them their positive moments. The only real villains were the faceless superiors at diocesan level, who only emerged to thwart the daring creativity of the admirable liberal clergy. The most telling criticisms of the series were artistic rather than religious or political: stereotypes ran rampant, and the characters were cardboard.

Yet it is difficult to find a moment in the show that could be described as anti-Catholic or even anti-clerical, and all the political positions that so irritated the Catholic League were well within the customary range of intra-Church debate. If this was a dysfunctional parish, then so are a large number of urban parishes across the United States. In fairness, the Catholic League did not charge explicit anti-Catholicism in this instance, but rather said "that the show fed an ugly stereotype: Catholics loyal to the Church were cold-hearted dupes, if not phonies, while those in dissent were enlightened, caring and noble."[8]

The show can be seen as a tragically lost opportunity. *Nothing Sacred* arguably offered the best pro-Catholic propaganda that had appeared in the U.S. media since the 1960s. Allowing for the general change in social values, the clergy of this "dysfunctional" parish emerged quite as heroically as the figures played by Gregory Peck or Spencer Tracy during the 1940s. In one episode, the nun attached to the parish has to announce to a Christmas congregation that the priests cannot celebrate mass because they have been arrested following a confrontation with the Immigration and Naturalization Service. Parishioners greet this news with neither anger nor astonishment, but rather as a natural event in parochial life. To a mainstream audience this suggests that modern Catholics expect their clergy to be in the forefront of struggles for social and racial justice, even at the risk of their own liberty. However much this interpretation might offend political conservatives, it is enormously attractive to liberals and moderates, and in the context of the mid-1990s, this representation provided a powerful antidote to the awful images of "pedophile priests" that had prevailed a year or two before. *Nothing Sacred* depicted Catholic clergy as tough, independent fighters for justice.

Other prominent Catholic League targets can also be defended on similar grounds. In 1995, the British film *Priest* depicted two Catholic priests, each of whom systematically violated his vows of celibacy, one by living in a stable relationship with a woman, the other being promiscuously homosexual. The Catholic League objected strongly, calling for a boycott of Disney, which had released the film through its Miramax subsidiary. The league stated, "We objected not because the film showed five dysfunctional priests, but because it suggested that their depravity was a function of their religion." But the film went beyond a simple intention to shock viewers by presenting clergy in sexual situations. The central theme of the film is the contrast between the older heterosexual priest and his young gay colleague, but the difference between them goes far beyond their sexual preference. The older man is a left-wing activist who preaches a social gospel, while his colleague believes in personal holiness and the centrality of individual sinfulness—in other words, the ideas of John Paul II, as opposed to liberation theology. The film argues for the futility of the individualist view and the necessity for a social (or socialist) approach to problems. Another plot line challenged the idea of the absolute confidentiality of the confessional, showing a young girl whose life is ruined because the priest will not violate the rule of secrecy in order to save her from sexual abuse.

There is no doubt that the film was intended to be critical of the contemporary Church and its hierarchy, who are denounced as "careerists," Pharisees, and hypocrites. As in the case of *Nothing Sacred*, though, many observers found in *Priest* a sympathetic representation of the human dilemmas of the priesthood. Whether we approve of the fact or not, some priests do carry on sexual relationships, heterosexual or homosexual. The film's political debates also gave a fair reflection of the kind of controversies that are familiar to Catholic circles across the globe. *Priest* dealt with important issues; moreover, its conclusion emphasized Christian themes of forgiveness and reconciliation.

It would be difficult to see this film as anti-Catholic. Nor should we use the term about another controversial production, *The Boys of Saint Vincent's*, which dramatized a devastating clergy sex abuse scandal in a Newfoundland orphanage. This film shows clergy and brothers engaged in a systematic conspiracy to abuse the boys in their care, a story so horrible that its depiction can be justified only by the fact that events really happened very much in this way and both Church and civil authorities did indeed make the grievous errors of judgment shown. While the resulting film offers neither comforting nor inspiring images of the Catholic clergy or religious, it offers a fine case study of how a culture of abuse can develop in any closed institution. Like *Priest*, the film raises disturbing questions about the Church, but it cannot fairly be described as hostile to any religious system.

Moving along the spectrum, we find other films that have been attacked for their stance on Catholicism and which once upon a time certainly would have been blacklisted by the Legion of Decency but which scarcely deserve their awful reputation. Prominent in this category was *Dogma*, which the Catholic League targeted as singularly iniquitous, as did conservative Protestant groups such as the American Family Association; even Cardinal O'Connor protested against it. Facing widespread criticism, the film was dropped by its original studio, Miramax, which had taken enough heat over *Priest*. *Dogma* was subsequently picked up by Lion's Gate, who released it widely in the fall of 1999. This timing contributed to the outrage it provoked, because it followed so closely upon the protests at the "Sensation" exhibit at the Brooklyn Museum of Art.[9]

Dogma certainly touches on some very sensitive points. Its leading figure is Bethany, who is chosen to play a prophetic role because of her biological descent from the family of Jesus. In a premise that aroused special ire among conservative critics, Bethany, the potential female messiah, is employed in an abortion clinic. God is also played by a woman, singer Alanis Morissette. The film offers a vicious caricature of a Catholic cardinal, Glick (played by George Carlin), who plans to raise money for the Church by reviving the sale of indulgences. Some critics detested the film's angle on religion, and William Donohue described it as "one of those Howard Stern insult toilet-humor attacks." Yet with the possible exception of the abortion theme, little of *Dogma* looks terribly offensive. Even the idea of Jesus's surviving kin should not be controversial: for decades after the crucifixion, Jesus's blood relatives continued to occupy a dominant role in the Palestinian church, and theoretically, their genes could still be found today. Oddly, given its conservative opposition, one of the film's main targets is the trendily mindless liberal Catholicism symbolized by Cardinal Glick, whose "Jesus, Wow!" campaign is symbolized by a ludicrously winking figure of "Buddy Jesus" giving a thumbs-up sign. If anyone should protest *Dogma*, it is the Church's liberals.[10]

Giving Offense

We can question whether films such as *Dogma* and *Priest* were even remotely as malicious as their critics claimed, but it is still remarkable that they were released in anything like their present form. Though Hollywood is sometimes attacked for permissiveness, in practice it operates under extremely stringent limitations as to the themes and issues that can be addressed, and over the years an ever larger range of interest groups has demanded that their sensitivities be respected. No studio would contemplate making a film that would be deemed offensive by (for example) blacks or Native Americans, and if a negative depiction is offered, it has to be framed by ostentatious disclaimers stating that the representation is not intended to be typical. According to many critics, the 1990 film version of *The Bonfire of the Vanities* failed so abjectly because it bent over backward to avoid giving offense to blacks and Latinos and thus failed to convey the sharp satire of Tom Wolfe's novel. In 1985, the television series *Our Family Honor* depicted an obviously Italian-American crime family, but the need to avoid ethnic stereotyping led them to christen these particular Mafiosi with the baffling non-Latin surname of Danzig. (*The Sopranos* needed no such ethnic disguise, but a cable television program does not face the kind of direct pressure from advertisers that can bedevil a network production.)

For most interest groups besides Catholics (and perhaps evangelicals), it is not scurrilous or hostile intent that makes a film unacceptable, but whether it causes offense, and Hollywood has in practice adopted that very low standard. True, religious objections led one company to abandon *Dogma*, but the film was still released by another company; a controversial project involving another group would probably not have seen the light of day.

Other groups have succeeded in making themselves heard and in placing themselves off-limits for critical treatment. In the mid-twentieth century, homosexuality could not openly be discussed in American films because the issue was considered so controversial. More recently, negative portrayals of homosexuals have become taboo, and films depicting gay killers or criminals have been vigorously protested. The campaigns against both *Cruising* (1980) and *Basic Instinct* (1992) taught the studios that self-censorship was prudent.[11]

As social or ethnic groups grow in number and influence, they make their public presence felt by gaining the right to be free from offense by the media. In the aftermath of the civil rights movement of the 1960s, Asian-Americans and Latinos made it clear that once-familiar stereotypes would no longer be tolerated, and newer communities have tried to send the same message. When, in 1998, the film *The Siege* offered a (prescient) tale of New York City under assault by Arab terrorists, the producers thought it politic to work closely with Arab-American and Muslim groups to minimize charges of stereotyping and negative portrayals. Activists thought that any film depicting how "Arab terrorists methodically lay waste to Manhattan" not only was clearly fantastic in its own right, but also "reinforces historically damaging stereotypes."[12] Hollywood had a public responsibility not to encourage such labeling.

Yet no such qualms affect the making of films or television series that might offend America's sixty million Catholics. Any suggestion that the makers of such films should consult with Catholic authorities or interest groups would be dismissed as promoting censorship and as grossly inappropriate religious interference with artistic self-expression. The fuss over a film like *Dogma* misses the point. The question is not why American studios bankroll films that will annoy and offend Catholics, but why they do not more regularly present subject matter that would be equally uncomfortable or objectionable to other traditions or interest groups. If they did, American films would be more interesting as well as more consistent. If works of art are to offend, they should do so on an equal-opportunity basis.

| The New Borgias

Perhaps because critics attacked innocuous productions such as *Nothing Sacred* and *Dogma* so ferociously, they failed to arouse public outrage when they protested against some genuinely offensive films and the stereotypes that they made so commonplace during the same years. The evil prelate or cardinal was a recurring image, vividly recalling the nativist cartoons of the nineteenth century and several hundred years of anti-papist imagery before that. Somewhere in the 1980s, Hollywood decided that senior Catholic clerics made reliable stock villains, as predictably evil as corporate executives or drug kingpins. In 1982, the courtroom drama *The Verdict* told the story of a heroic lawyer undertaking a quixotic lawsuit against a Catholic hospital, and thus, indirectly, against Boston's Catholic establishment. The clergy here feature only slightly, but we are left in no doubt that prelates lurk at the center of this lethal web.

Over the next decade, sinister cardinals and bishops became an ever-greater media staple, chiefly in consequence of the ongoing speculation about Vatican scandals. The theme surfaced in *Monsignor* and in the trivial 1991 comedy *The Pope Must Diet* (following protests, the last word of the title had been changed from *Die*), but it reached its widest audience in 1990, in the third film of the *Godfather* trilogy. Inevitably, given the subject matter, Catholic and clerical themes had run through the first two films and were used to make a strong point about the mentality of the Corleone family and their criminal subculture: however evil their deeds, they must still be seen as loyal sons and daughters of the Church. In the climax of the first *Godfather*, we flash back and forth between the pre–Vatican II splendors of a baptism ceremony taking place under the auspices of Don Michael Corleone and the grotesque series of assassinations that he has ordered.

The director himself, Francis Ford Coppola, is suffused in traditional Catholic imagery, its liturgy and architecture, and he is fully aware of how effectively Catholic themes can be deployed to make statements about the nature of good and evil.[13] In *The Godfather III*, though, the evils of the Church occupy center stage, and the baroque Catholic imagery acquires lethal overtones. Images of church and priesthood usually imply conspiracy and clandestine murder, while the nearest the film has to offer to heroes is the Corleone crime family. The New York Mafia might be psychotic thieves and killers, it is suggested, but at least they have more honor and decency than the higher ranks of the Catholic Church. The film begins with Michael Corleone receiving a papal knighthood at the hands of the evil archbishop Liam Francis Gilday, who heads the Vatican Bank. This is an especially sensitive reference, because the role must refer to the real-life Archbishop Marcinkus, who, despite some legal troubles, has never been convicted of anything like the career of murder and depravity indicated for Gilday. As in real life, the bank has been extensively looted, and its collapse can be prevented only by persuading Corleone to bail it out, at a cost of $600 million. In exchange, Corleone will acquire control of a giant European corporation dominated by the Church. However, the archbishop's Italian allies propose to defraud Corleone, too. In a bizarre alignment, the penitent don finds himself in alliance with the (strictly limited) forces of good in the Church, personified by Cardinal Lamberti, the good prelate who will become Pope John Paul I.

In this fictionalized version of real-life events, the conspirators succeed in killing the new Pope before he can purge the Church of their evil deeds. Even so (and this is wholly imaginary), Corleone's Mafiosi succeed in killing Archbishop Gilday, who had ordered the assassination of the good Pope. A climactic sequence of around twenty minutes offers what may be the most dazzling collage of anti-Catholic and anti-Latin images ever offered by an American film. As the intertwined stories of the various assassins seeking out their targets unfold, we see a battery of images of homicidal priests, including one variously armed with a sniper's rifle and a dagger. Meanwhile, Corleone assassins greet the fugitive Vatican banker they intend to kill by dropping a rosary on his face. The murder of Archbishop Gilday is an astonishingly potent image. He is killed in the Vatican while wearing papal robes, and his body plunges many stories from a staircase beneath the building's dome. The image is familiar to any historian conversant with Protestant fantasies of the collapse of the Roman Antichrist and the quite literal fall of the papacy. Meanwhile, we see Corleone himself watching the opera *Cavalleria*

Rusticana, with all its Catholic processions, bloody crucifixes, statues of the Virgin, and Klan-like hooded *penitentes*.

The Godfather III often looks like a Jacobean revenge tragedy four centuries out of its time. The Renaissance analogies are explicit: after one meeting with the Italian conspirators, a disgusted Michael Corleone emerges denouncing "the Borgias!" As Lamberti himself explains, Christianity has made little real impact in Europe, and so, we are meant to ask, what good can come of a foreign and European institution such as the Roman Catholic Church? Gilday says that wealth and property have irrevocably tainted the Church, and especially the papacy, beyond the hope of redemption. As a commentary on Catholicism, past and present, *The Godfather III* is about as restrained or respectful as the "Inquisition" dance number in Mel Brooks's *History of the World Part I*—but at least Brooks was trying to be funny. *The Godfather III* is so ludicrously over the top that it achieves the status of unintentional farce.

Church Conspiracies

Observers of Hollywood suggest that the studio's relationships with the Catholic Church reached an absolute nadir in the early 1990s, around the time of *The Godfather III*, but that matters improved following diplomatic moves by Los Angeles Cardinal Mahony.[14] Open warfare between the Church and the studios subsided, as did Church calls for censorship of gratuitous sex and violence. It is difficult, though, to see that this unofficial concordat produced any great improvement in cinematic treatments of Catholicism, since some of the most hostile films were yet to come.

Films during the 1990s offered still more nightmarish images of the Catholic Church and its hierarchy. One of the more remarkable examples of crudely anti-Catholic polemic was the 1996 film *Primal Fear*, which focused on cases of child sexual abuse by highly placed clergy. The film was based on a novel by William Diehl that appeared at the first peak of the clergy abuse scandals in 1992–93, when the most extravagant claims of priestly wrongdoing were commonplace. By 1996, film-makers evidently assumed that the truth of these charges could be taken for granted and that Catholic clergy were automatically to be viewed as villains.[15]

The title sequence of *Primal Fear* features a boys' choir performing at a Catholic charity gathering in Chicago. Over the next few minutes, we encounter the jovial and popular archbishop of Chicago, who is then foully murdered by a former altar boy. An hour or so into the film, we are scarcely shocked to learn that the archbishop was in fact a clandestine sexual pervert who was exploiting the teenage boys and girls under his charge and using them to make private pornographic videos. Worse, his predilections had long been known to law enforcement authorities, who failed to prosecute him because of his close business and political ties with city leaders. The film is singularly short of surprises because in the cultural environment of the mid-1990s, it is inconceivable that any Hollywood product could present an innocent or benevolent story featuring a senior Catholic cleric and choirboys. As in any number of films and television programs in these years, a happy or favorable depiction of a Catholic cleric is bound to be the preamble to a later exposé of dark inner secrets, probably of a sexual nature. Remarkably, the perverted villain of this film is Archbishop Rushman of Chicago. This is striking because some years before the film was made, the real-life archbishop of Chicago was Cardinal Bernardin, who was himself falsely accused of abuse. Given its assumptions about the perverted nature of the Catholic clergy and hierarchy, *Primal Fear* can be unhesitatingly described as an anti-Catholic film.

Anti-Catholic imagery also branded other films of these years. We have already seen Nathan Lane's depiction of the priest as predatory queen in the 1995 production of *Jeffrey*. Just as bizarre was *The Virgin Suicides* (2000), a strange obsessive study of five daughters growing up in a bizarre puritanical family, in which sexual repression ultimately drives all the girls to suicide. Though in most respects the destructive family seems to belong to a fringe fundamentalist faith, some scenes clearly indicate that they are traditionalist Catholics. One scene of an attempted suicide shows blood falling on an icon of the Virgin Mary decorated with rosary beads. The film was directed by Sofia Coppola, the daughter of Francis Ford Coppola, who had also starred in *The Godfather III*.

Perhaps the most sweeping indictment of Catholicism in the popular media in these years was the 1999 thriller *Stigmata*. Patricia Arquette plays a Pittsburgh hairdresser who develops the bloody wounds of Christ, a phenomenon first recorded of St. Francis of Assisi. Obviously this ordinary woman has been chosen for a prophetic role, channeling a divine message to the world, which emerges when she scrawls words that prove to be the Aramaic text of "the Jesus Gospel." This fictional text reports Jesus's words to his disciples at the Last Supper. It is identified as the one authentic gospel underlying the canonical texts of Matthew, Mark, Luke, and John, and thus "the most significant Christian relic ever found." This Jesus Gospel presents a Christianity very different from anything we know: according to this Jesus, God is a force within the individual believer, and thus church buildings and institutions are superfluous. If this was in fact authentic Christianity, then the historic churches would be based on a lie, or at best a fundamental error, and according to *Stigmata*, Church leaders know this very well. Though all Christians are equally misinformed, it is Roman Catholics who are selected as the most rigid and intolerant enemies of God's new revelation—a kind of back-handed compliment to Catholic insistence on theological orthodoxy.[16]

The plot revolves around the efforts of the Roman Catholic hierarchy to suppress this subversive gospel, through murder if necessary. Catholic biblical scholars are shown in whispered conversation about the hidden text, knowing that their lives are quite literally at risk if they dare to reveal the truth. Clearly, we are meant to assume, the Catholic Church could not survive for an hour if the authentic message of Jesus were known—the same idea that America's fundamentalists and other Protestants have been preaching ever since Plymouth Rock. Finally, the true gospel is revealed to the world through the heroism of a priest who defies his church, Father Andrew Kiernan (Gabriel Byrne). The film is replete with traditional anti-Catholic imagery, with Jonathan Pryce playing a thoroughly satanic cardinal who would have been quite at home dealing out poison in a Jacobean tragedy. Significantly, he is the clerical character whom we see engaged in traditional forms of Catholic piety, with a crucifix and a rosary. (Some enterprising film scholar could write a lengthy article on how modern Hollywood films came to regard the innocent rosary as such a symbol of moral turpitude.) Though Pryce is a wonderfully versatile actor, his portrayal of the evil cardinal had potent parallels to his recent role as a megalomaniacal super-villain in the James Bond film *Tomorrow Never Dies* (1997). Adding a modern touch, Pryce's evil prelate tries to suppress the divine truth that has been revealed by and through a liberated woman, again suggesting the misogyny so often attributed to the Church.

The message of *Stigmata* would have been aggressive enough if it had been presented entirely as fiction, but it was not. All the words quoted from the fictional Jesus Gospel were taken from the real-life *Gospel of Thomas*, a controversial text that some radical Bible scholars claim as an authentically ancient work that closely reflects the thought of the historic Jesus. An epilogue to the film records the discovery of the *Gospel of Thomas*, noting that the document was rejected by the Vatican even though scholars around the world acknowledge it as the "closest record we have of the words of the historical Jesus." (This is very tendentious: only a tiny handful of scholars claim anything of the sort.) The audience is meant to leave the cinema thinking that Christianity is founded on a lie, kept alive only by the power-hungry deceivers in the Vatican. There might be hope for individual believers, but only if they forsake the rotten structures of this evil church. By any reasonable definition, *Stigmata* is an overtly anti-Catholic film, all the more so because of the constant invocation of ancient stereotypes. To understand just how hostile the film was, how tainted its imagery, one would have to imagine a parallel production depicting evil Jewish financiers plotting to take over the United States.

| Television

When the Catholic League assembles its periodic lists of anti-Catholic portrayals, a rich crop is normally gleaned from television shows. In many of these cases, protests seem futile; no reasonable viewer expects anything like balanced treatment from shows such as *South Park* or *Politically Incorrect* any more than from performers such as Howard Stern or Marilyn Manson. All in their different ways use shock and bad taste as normal currency, though even so, some recent items have been remarkably violent. More disturbing is the presence of serious and pervasive anti-Catholic content in more mainstream productions, since these reach a still wider audience than the print media. The number and severity of such attacks have increased greatly over the last decade or so.

One curious example appeared in an episode of the series *The X Files*, which used the same theme of biblical conspiracy as *Stigmata*. Since this show regularly explored conspiracies by various governments and large institutions, it is not surprising that the Catholic Church was targeted for treatment, in an episode entitled "Hollywood AD." The story, written by David Duchovny himself, tells of the discovery of a hidden gospel that reveals a sexual relationship between Jesus and Mary Magdalene. The owner of the gospel is one Micah Hoffman, who is blackmailing a Catholic cardinal to keep it from the public. The cardinal is a key leader of the American Church, reputedly in line for the papacy. As in *Stigmata*, the Church is prepared to kill to achieve its goals, and the cardinal murders Hoffman, who proves to have forged the text, rather than discovered it. The cardinal then kills himself.

The story seems largely derived from *Stigmata* but has an interesting twist, namely, that the affair actually did happen, although with certain key differences. What we have here is a version of the story of Mark Hoffman, rather than Micah. Mark was a Utah-based documents dealer with a unique knack for finding (and forging) rare Mormon historical treasures. In the 1980s, he reported finding the "Salamander Letter," an early account of the revelations to Joseph Smith, which supposedly showed that Smith was far deeper into occult and magical practices than anyone had hitherto been able to prove. It was a forgery, but good enough to allow Hoffman to blackmail the church hierarchy of the Latter-Day Saints, who dreaded the exposure of such an embarrassing text. The real Mark Hoffman—like the fictional Micah—tried to cover his tracks by a series of bombings, which is what ultimately brought him to the attention of law enforcement. What the writers of *The X Files* have done is to transform a Mormon scandal into an anti-Catholic tract, complete with hypocritical prelates. The reason for the switch might just be that Catholics are more familiar to most viewers than Mormons, but other explanations come to mind. By the late 1990s, so many films and books had dealt with Catholic plotting and Vatican misdeeds that it simply seemed natural to present any tale of religious deceit in a Catholic context. This is what cardinals and bishops were presumed to do. And that belief constitutes a fundamentally anti-Catholic supposition, or rather prejudice.[17]

Other television shows in recent years have included the 1997 movie version of Tami Hoag's *Night Sins*, which included a sexually active priest and an obsessive homicidal deacon, the whole production lavishly illustrated by Catholic imagery and music. New series scheduled to appear in 2002–03 included *The Calling*, an ecclesiastical version of *The X Files*, in which the Catholic hierarchy is depicted as worldly, cynical, and dedicated to the suppression of any authentic spirituality.

Comedy shows have also become increasingly bold in using anti-Catholic and anti-clerical stereotypes. In 1998, an episode of *Mad TV* featured an Irish priest, "Father Fellatio," an alcoholic child molester, who was also bisexual: "his crucifix swings both ways." At times too, even a show like *South Park* has gone far beyond its usual level of all-encompassing vulgarity to target Catholics very specifically. In 1998, "Big Gay Al" warned, "Uh-oh, look out, it's the oppressors—Christians and Republicans and Nazis." Among the leaders of the homophobic crusade, we see a cross-bearing Catholic priest accompanying Hitler. In another episode in 2000, the children catch the local Catholic priest having sex with a parishioner in the confessional. The Pope is depicted as senile, and much of the show concerns the foolishness of belief in transubstantiation, "eating the crackers," as the one sure way of avoiding hell. At one point, the priest declares, "The Jews crucified our savior. If you don't go to hell for that, what the hell do you go to hell for?" During the sex abuse crisis of 2002, a *South Park* episode depicted a convention of U.S. Catholic priests discussing the ongoing furor. All but one of the priests believe the problem lies in persuading molested children not to report the incident, and only one thinks there is anything wrong with molestation as such. Appalled, the sole good priest goes to Rome, where he addresses a council of the world's senior cardinals and archbishops, all of whom believe that abuse by priests is justified by secret Vatican teachings. Ultimately, the Catholic Church literally collapses, and is replaced by a new religious structure that swears not to treat any religious scriptures or teachings as anything more than general guides to living a good life. In order to think of a parallel to such a sweeping denunciation, we would have to imagine a show in which all Muslims, men, women, and children, are portrayed as ipso facto suicide bombers.[18]

A recurrent bugbear of the Catholic League has been the Fox series *Ally McBeal*, in which themes of clerical sex and priest pedophilia have abounded. In one 1998 show, a Protestant minister is being prosecuted for having an affair with a church worker. He tells a lawyer, "I realize that doesn't make me an altar boy." The lawyer replies, "If you were an altar boy, you'd be with a priest." Another show deals with a sexually active nun, who declares, "A priest has sex with a boy, he gets transferred. ... At least my lover was of legal age." Ally McBeal herself remarks that "nuns are not supposed to have sex except with other nuns." In one story line, a priest videotapes confessions for the documentary *World's Naughtiest Confessions*. The plethora of genuinely offensive references should make us appreciate just how well-intentioned the show *Nothing Sacred* actually was. Speaking for the Los Angeles archdiocese, Father Gregory Coiro commented, reasonably enough, that "a person who would think this is not anti-Catholic would probably go to a minstrel show."[19]

Sister Mary as Hate Crime

These films and television shows all to different degrees raise significant issues about the public expression of prejudice, and the appropriate response. To illustrate these questions, we can look at Christopher Durang's 1979 play *Sister Mary Ignatius Explains It All to You*, which received national attention in 2001 when it was revived for the Showtime cable channel (as *Sister Mary Explains It All*).[20]

In the first half of *Sister Mary*'s single act, a nun lectures to Catholic families about her view of faith, the universe, and sin, which emerges as a broad and dismissive parody of every aspect of the Catholic religious framework. Catholicism, it is suggested, is for the stupid, the emotionally immature, the repressed, and the fanatical. As played by Diane Keaton in the Showtime special, Sister Mary herself is alternately a simpering moron and a brutal fanatic who neither understands nor tolerates the slightest questioning. She believes God errs far too much on the side of tolerance, and she cannot understand his failure to annihilate modern-day Sodoms such as New York, San Francisco, and Amsterdam—"well, basically anywhere where the population is over fifty thousand." Her moral sense also fails to make any distinctions between the gravity of offenses. She lists mortal sins, "the most serious kind of sin you can do—murder, sex outside of marriage, hijacking a plane, masturbation." Anti-Catholic stereotypes run rampant throughout: the sister's family includes twenty-three siblings, among them a gaggle of priests and nuns as well as several who are insane or mentally defective. Her mother "hated little children but they couldn't use birth control."

Matters turn even darker in the second part of the play, in which a group of adult former pupils return to re-enact the Nativity play they originally performed in the school twenty-five years earlier. The play is a broad anti-religious burlesque, which features, for example, the crucifixion of the doll used to represent the baby Jesus. The students have returned to denounce Sister Mary as a sadistic bully who ruined their lives. As she questions them, she finds that most have betrayed her ideas to some extent—one man is homosexual, a woman has had abortions, another is an unwed mother. Still, the play clearly implies that these sinners are far more ethical, far better people, than either Mary or her evil Church. The only one of them for whom she shows the slightest approval is a drunken wife-beater, whose character reflects her influence. Sister Mary eventually shoots and kills two of the alumni, justifying her acts as not really sinful, as she descends into grinning insanity, muttering stock phrases from the catechism.

Sister Mary is not just a play about a deranged individual. It is a denunciation of a religion and the people who take it seriously, and especially of its clergy. The audience is meant to understand that Catholicism leads to violence, abuse, fanaticism, and human misery, so there should be no dispute about the work's visceral anti-Catholicism. In terms of its stance toward the Church, it makes *Dogma* or *Priest* look like an official statement from the Vatican. Nevertheless, Durang's play has enjoyed much success. In 1981, it won a prestigious Obie award for off-Broadway productions, and it has been revived regularly: the Showtime production represented a definite stamp of approval and a new exposure to a mass audience. Reviews often comment dismissively on criticisms of the piece's religious content. *Variety* commented that "the material would undoubtedly still give the Catholic League fits," which suggests that the play would only offend the hyper-sensitive conservatives believed to populate that organization. Adrienne Onofri noted that "[t]he show is definitely not for people who are sensitive about Christianity or not amused by black comedy." In other words, though admittedly tasteless, the play should appeal to intelligent people with a sophisticated sense of humor. Why can't people just stop taking themselves so seriously and laugh at it?[21]

Sister Mary raises critical questions about the nature of censorship and hate speech, which can be understood if we imagine a comparably hostile or offensive work about some other group. As a hypothetical example, imagine a new farce about Matthew Shepard, whose death aroused national outrage over "gay-bashing." Imagine, also, that the play presented Shepard as a ludicrous comic character and his death as high comedy. The whole concept is loathsome and unacceptable in the highest degree, but it is scarcely more repulsive than some recent anti-Catholic treatments. In reality, the Shepard play would not be written, would not be produced, and would not survive the tidal wave of protests. Cable television companies would know better than to revive it. Reviews would assuredly not praise it while warning mildly that "the show is definitely not for people who are sensitive about hate crime." Nobody would remark cheerily that "the show will give gay righters fits!" In this instance, protesters would not be advised just to "lighten up," to "get over it." Any number of similar analogies could be suggested, each in its own way equally offensive to other groups. The only justification that might be advanced for Durang's work, as opposed to plays about hate crimes or lynchings, is that Catholicism is not like other religious or political systems because it is an oppressive weapon of the overmighty. That belief in itself represents anti-Catholic bigotry.

The play and film of *Sister Mary* encapsulate the arguments about hate speech in the media. If this particular work is tolerated, if the play is produced and the video is rented or sold, then no logical grounds exist for excluding or banning any literary works or films deemed offensive by other ethnic, religious, or social groups. Consistency demands that there should be no restrictions on racist, misogynistic, or anti-homosexual polemic. This conclusion is not troubling if one happens to be a First Amendment absolutist, who denies the right of government or institutions to restrict any speech or writing, but that is very much a minority stance. The case of *Sister Mary* provokes a simple question: why can Catholicism legitimately be attacked in such outrageous terms by the American media, while other racial, social, and religious traditions remain exempt?

9 | Black Legends

Rewriting Catholic History

*How can it be that [the Church's] overwhelming record
of anti-Semitic hatred and its obvious integral
relationship to the genesis of the Holocaust is often
denied?*

— Daniel J. Goldhagen

Spiritually, we are all Semites.

— Pope Pius XI

*For centuries, Jews have been unjustly treated
and despised. It is time they were treated with justice
and humanity. God wills it and the Church wills it.
St. Paul tells us that the Jews are our brothers.
They should also be welcomed as friends.*

— Pope Pius XII

Ever since the Reformation, historical writing has provided perhaps the most powerful weapon in the arsenal of anti-Catholic rhetoric. Accounts of alleged Catholic atrocities and distortions have been best-sellers, and works such as Foxe's *Book of Martyrs* were for centuries among the most popular titles in the English-speaking world. Usually, these books presented a predictable range of arguments and examples, to the extent that a standard anti-Catholic mythology has retained its broad general outlines from the sixteenth century onward. What is remarkable, though, is that such a mythology not only survives today, but is regarded as a respectable part of civilized discourse. Even popular films tap freely into these ideas: *The Godfather III* compares the modern Vatican to "the

Borgias," while *Stigmata* portrays the Church concealing the truths of the primitive gospel.

Most contemporary attacks on Catholicism or the Catholic Church draw heavily on history, or at least on a kind of mythic history that has become deeply embedded in popular thought. There are some historical facts that everyone knows, that are simply too obvious to need explanation. Richard Slotkin writes how social and political mythology is often encapsulated in highly charged phrases, such as "the frontier" or "Pearl Harbor" (and we might now add "September 11"). Slotkin describes how, over time, "the original mythic story is increasingly conventionalized and abstracted until it is reduced to a deeply encoded and resonant set of symbols, 'icons', 'keywords', or historical cliches. ... Each of these mythic icons is in effect a poetic construction of tremendous economy and compression, and a mnemonic device capable of evoking a complex system of historical associations by a single image or phrase."[1] When people refer to "Pearl Harbor," they are talking not only about a specific place or even a military event in 1941, but also a whole view of history, richly freighted with racial and political connotations. Equally, references to the Crusades, the Inquisition, the Borgias, Galileo, and Pius XII involve far more than the specific events or individuals. They draw on layers of collective memory that evoke deeply hostile imagery about Catholicism and, often, Christianity in general. To speak of "the Crusades" summons images of Catholic intolerance, fanaticism, greed, and subservience to cynical clergy. For centuries, European anti-Catholics made much use of the Black Legend, a mythologized account of Spanish greed and savagery during the conquest of the New World, and Church complicity in these actions.

When people evoke the alleged horrors of the Catholic past, they are not inspired solely by an interest in ecclesiastical history, but rather wish to make a polemical point that is strictly relevant to contemporary circumstances. When in the eighteenth century historian Edward Gibbon told horror stories about monkish superstition and Crusading brutality, he was trying to discredit the priests and aristocrats of his own time. Today, likewise, hyper-critical examinations of Catholic misdeeds are intended to support contemporary political positions, commonly in debates over morality and sexuality.

Sometimes the relevance of the historical examples cited seems contrived. During the "pedophile priest" crisis of the early 1990s, the book *A Gospel of Shame* described the reluctance of modern civil authorities to intervene in sexual scandals. The authors recall past eras of papal tyranny and oppression, when "popes sent Crusaders to deal with unruly civil leaders, when inquisitors led even the mighty to the torture chamber and the stake."[2] James Carroll draws an explicit parallel between acts of Catholic cowardice in various eras, between "the 'silence' of Pius XII before the Holocaust or the [modern-day] abuse of children by priests." This kind of historical analogy is surprisingly common today. Calling on the Catholic Church to support condom use, an editorial in the *Seattle Post-Intelligencer* recalled that "the hierarchy of the Roman Catholic Church declined to challenge Adolf Hitler as he ran amok through Europe ... the Vatican proved it wasn't part of the solution but the problem when it remained officially silent during the Holocaust." Describing HIV/AIDS as "a viral version of Hitler," the paper warned of "similar ignominy" if Catholicism failed to change its position. This desire to show contemporary relevance often gives modern historians and activists a powerful motivation to paint the picture as dark as possible, and generally darker than is deserved.[3]

While other familiar forms of bigotry are confined to the world of cranks and conspiracy theorists, anti-Church historical polemic makes money for major American publishing houses. Within the last decade, blue-ribbon publishers have produced such works as John Cornwell's *Hitler's Pope*, Garry Wills's *Papal Sin* and *Why I Am a Catholic*, James Carroll's *Constantine's Sword*, and Daniel J. Goldhagen's *A Moral Reckoning*. By 2002, readers had access to "a virtual book of the month club on institutional Catholicism, anti-Semitism and the Holocaust."[4] That is in addition to the widespread use of the anti-Catholic pseudo-history in many works on Catholic attitudes to sexuality and gender, on early Christianity, and on medieval history. Obviously, this run of anti-Church blockbusters does not mean that America's leading publishers are conspiring to destroy or calumniate Catholicism. The publishers act as they do because they believe that people will buy the books, and the success of authors such as Carroll and Cornwell indicates they are exactly right. Against the charge that the books are purely hostile attacks, the publishers can state, quite accurately, that in most cases the authors themselves claim to be loyal Catholics. Wills, Cornwell, and Carroll would all make such an assertion, and their insider status certainly helps to deflect criticism.

But whatever the publishers' motives, the total effect of such an outpouring of deeply hostile books is powerful. Imagine browsing the religion section of a major bookstore and finding Catholicism represented chiefly by these titles. The obvious lesson for the average reader is that the Catholic Church carries a huge burden of guilt for its historical atrocities, that it is a prime motivator of anti-Semitism and a collaborator with Nazism.

And though the books discussed here focus heavily on papal crimes, all to some degree serve to discredit the Church and its positions. Wills is the most explicit of the group in arguing that the record of papal misdeeds also taints many doctrinal positions that (he believes) were imposed by Vatican authority.

Of course, we have to draw a critical distinction between scholarship and polemic. Any number of serious studies of (say) medieval and early modern history paint an unflattering picture of the Church, illustrating it with examples of malicious and power-hungry prelates, deceitful and oppressive clergy. Many such books have been written by loyally Catholic authors, including clergy. Even the most naively triumphalist Catholic histories of decades past not only acknowledged the existence of "bad Popes," but admitted that some were truly dreadful individuals. When a historian such as David Kertzer itemizes well-documented examples of Catholic persecution of Jews in nineteenth-century Europe, he is doing no more than presenting sober truth, however painful it might be to Catholic or other Christian readers. He can be criticized on specific points, such as his failure to distinguish between religious anti-Judaism and racial anti-Semitism, but the broad outline is accurately told.[5]

A hostile account of Church misdeeds drifts into polemic, though, when it argues that these horrors are integral to the beliefs or value system of Catholicism or even Christianity, and suggests that Catholicism or Christianity is entirely based on error, malice, or violence. On occasion, Kertzer does lapse into what might be called this prosecutorial mode, and even into anti-Catholic rhetoric. His book's title, *The Popes Against the Jews*, is also inflammatory and deserves to be ranked alongside tendentious productions such as *Hitler's Pope*. Time and again, the anti-Jewish remarks he quotes derive not from "the Popes" or from any legitimate Church authority, but rather from individual Catholics or pressure groups, many of which were deeply disaffected from the papacy. Much recent historical writing on the Catholic Church can similarly be described as bitter anti-Catholic polemic—whatever the religious label claimed by its authors.[6]

| Getting Medieval

Binding together the various historical accusations against the Catholic Church is what might be termed a whole alternative history, or historical mythology. Though modern anti-Catholics rarely share the religious orientation of their nineteenth-century predecessors, they agree with the older critique that the Catholic Church betrayed the truths symbolized by Jesus and his earliest followers, replacing them with oppressive practices borrowed from the Roman Empire. Though feminists have been particularly active in seeking to rewrite early Church history for their ideological ends, this strategy has also been exploited by many liberals anxious to discredit contemporary Catholicism. Like earlier Protestants, modern critics of the Church claim to be recovering the pristine realities that lie submerged beneath layers of Catholic innovation. For both groups, as for the much-maligned proprietors of Bob Jones University, the core message is that the Catholic Church betrays Jesus.

The modern myth goes something like this. Once upon a time, there was a noble religious reformer called Jesus of Nazareth, who taught a simple message of love toward all, regardless of human distinctions. Following his tragic death, his ignorant followers increasingly distanced themselves from his message, which was submerged beneath crushing bureaucratic structures. Catholic power was at its height during the Middle Ages, which were accordingly a dismal low point of human civilization. In the popular mind, these were the "Dark Ages" (though serious historians despair when they hear this pejorative label applied to the whole medieval period). Until the Enlightenment, the chief goal of the Christian Church was to maintain its wealth and power by any means necessary. Any independent thinkers or dissidents were labeled heretics and sought out by the brutal mechanisms of the Inquisition. As a result, Christianity stifled any form of social or intellectual advancement for over a millennium, until heroic rebels overturned the Church's monopoly of power during the early modern period, the era of the Reformation, the Renaissance, and the scientific revolution. Overseas, the Church launched savage wars of aggression and religious brutality in the form of the Crusades. Putting these various charges together, little redeems either the medieval European Church or the Roman Catholic Church that is its obvious successor.[7]

The power of this lengthy indictment lies not in any single article, but rather in the cumulative picture of ecclesiastical misdeeds that emerges. And nobody can deny that there is enough truth in the story to make it plausible: there were inquisitions, Crusades did occur, fringe Christian groups were labeled as heretics and some of these minority sects were destroyed. In many ways, though, the commonly accepted picture is so inaccurate as to be almost worthless, and it would be acknowledged as such by most reputable historians.

To take the story at its foundations, there simply is no evidence that heretics kept alive an egalitarian and feminist version of primitive Christianity. As we have seen in the earlier discussion of the quest for the lost "women's church," this idea is based on bogus history. Nor is the memory of such a lost church preserved through mysterious hidden gospels—although this idea is reflected in much popular writing on the New Testament and emerges in films like *Stigmata*. As far as we can tell, a hierarchical church with a complex theology was in existence at least by early in the second century, and the four canonical gospels are much earlier than any of their heretical rivals. The idea of the lost early church, however, is an old one, since most later religious movements have tried to prove that they represent the authentic voice of Jesus's early followers.[8]

Another modern myth that has been much in the news recently concerns the origins of celibacy. Especially during the clergy abuse crisis of 2002, the media regularly reported the idea, found in many popular histories, that mandatory priestly celibacy was imposed only in the Middle Ages, in the eleventh or twelfth centuries. If this is true, modern Catholics are in effect insisting on a relatively modern innovation that has been around for less than half of the history of Christianity: Anna Quindlen writes of "the enforced celibacy of the male priesthood, an invention only of the faith's second millennium." In this view, the practice dates to the Middle Ages, the age of witch burning, the Inquisition, and the Crusades. When does anyone use the word medieval as a term of approval? Probably the best-known use of the word in recent popular culture occurs in the film *Pulp Fiction*, when a gangster refers to blood-curdling torture as "getting medieval on his ass." A "medieval" origin seems of itself to offer potent arguments against any practice, and critiques of celibacy normally stress the link to the despised Middle Ages. To quote journalist Chris Colbert: "The Vatican's insistence on imposing the medieval discipline of celibacy as a way of life on all homosexual people today rankles faithful gay Catholics like me." Worst of all, the reasons cited for the invention of celibacy are not even spiritual, but rather involve land rights and social power. According to a scholarly myth widely reflected in the mass media, the Church was just trying to ensure that the children of priests could not become legitimate heirs to Church land. Literally, according to this story, the modern Catholic Church is keeping alive a survival of feudal times.[9]

We do know that compulsory celibacy was not a practice of the earliest Church. St. Peter had a mother-in-law, the apostles traveled in the company of their wives, and some early Popes were, without causing scandal, the sons of other Popes. Yet beyond these facts, the commonly accepted idea of the roots of celibacy is just wrong. Mandatory celibacy goes much further back than medieval times, if not quite to the days of the apostles. Priestly celibacy was the usual expectation in western Europe by late Roman times, about the fourth century, and remained firmly in force for several centuries, from around 300 to 700. At that point, at least, fears of priests' families inheriting land played no part whatever in the decision to demand celibacy. Medieval statements on the subject were just reasserting discipline that had collapsed in times of war and social chaos. It is simply wrong to assert, as the contemporary media do so regularly, that "[p]riests were married for Christianity's first thousand years." Of course we can find married priests throughout the Middle Ages, just as we find priests committing molestation today, but that does not mean that, in either case, they were acting with Church approval.[10]

Priestly celibacy is a product of the very early Church. Indeed, celibate priests and monks helped make the final decisions about which books were going to make up the New Testament and which would be excluded. If, as most Christians believe, the ideas and practices of the early Church carry special authority, then we should certainly rank priestly celibacy among these truly ancient traditions.

Crusaders

There are other historical "facts" about the Middle Ages that we just "know," in the same way that we "know" that Columbus held his heroic belief that the world was round despite the opposition of the ignorant monks. We "know" that the Church supervised the brutal and superstitious means of criminal process known as the ordeal—whereas in reality, it was the Church that banned this absurd procedure, making way for trial by jury. Likewise, the Church is supposed to have favored governments that were absolutist tyrannies, though medieval regimes in fact formulated most of our contemporary ideas of representative government. The common popular view of the Middle Ages is a pseudo-history, which since the Enlightenment has been used to discredit Catholicism.

Another aspect of this flourishing Black Legend is the modern image of the Crusades. It seems odd to debate the events of eight or nine centuries ago in order to respond to anti-Catholic rhetoric of the early twenty-first century, yet such a resort to distant events is demanded precisely because critics of Catholicism themselves deploy these arguments so frequently. In the case of the Crusades, the Church's role appears nothing short of diabolical. During the eleventh century, we are told, the Catholic Church in western Europe suddenly decided to launch a war of aggression against the Muslim nations of the Middle East. Preaching hatred and extermination against all other faiths, the Church inspired Europeans to attack and invade the Levant, slaughtering countless Jews and Muslims in a racial war that foreshadowed both the worst features of European colonialism and the Holocaust of the 1940s. By demonizing non-

Catholics overseas, the Crusades justified the internal wars against deviants and dissidents within Europe itself, against heretics, Jews, and witches.

The Crusades were in the news once more following the terrorist attacks of September 2001, when many journalists referred to them as parallels and predecessors to modern Islamic fundamentalist terrorism. The suggestion is that Christianity has as grim and bloody a record as modern terrorism. Discussing the attacks, former president Clinton traced the conflict to the events of 1095 and the first Crusade, and stressed that "[t]hose of us from various European lineages are not blameless." These actions represented "[t]errorism—the killing of innocent people for political or religious or economic reasons." In this sense, Clinton was arguing, the crimes of Western Christians must be partially blamed for modern carnage in the Middle East. Ultimately, we started it—or rather, the Catholic Church started it.[11]

Such a damning picture of the Crusades is so familiar that it may be surprising that the events can be viewed in any other way. Undoubtedly, the Crusades were marked by horrific and unpardonable violence, notably the massacres of European Jews and the sack of Jerusalem itself. Speaking well of the Crusades sounds almost like trying to find a happier side of the Holocaust, an impossible and repellent venture. Yet the analogy is false. We have to see the Crusades as one chapter in a long and bloody series of wars between Islam and Christianity in which Islam normally held the upper hand. During these wars, Muslim conquerors annexed numerous lands that were then thoroughly Christian. On almost every occasion, the Muslims were the aggressors, and the Christians were fighting desperately for simple survival. By 1600, Muslims ruled much of the Balkans and Central Europe. During these struggles, there were two phases in which Christian nations gained the upper hand, the first in the Middle Ages (the Crusades) and the second beginning in the later seventeenth century. Not until the twentieth century was Muslim rule ended in most of the predominantly Christian lands of southeast Europe.

In these wars, both sides took territory by armed conquest, and both viciously repressed subject peoples of the other religion. This last point needs to be stressed in view of the popular myth that Muslim rulers practiced religious tolerance, in contrast to the fiendish Catholics. Some Muslim societies were tolerant, but others launched anti-Christian pogroms and imposed forced conversions. Muslims were not monsters, but contrary to legend, they did not rise above the prejudices of their age. The tendency in modern popular history to idealize Islam is the necessary corollary of the anti-Catholic myth.

Underlying the notion of the evils of the Crusades is the assumption that religious frontiers are somehow carved in stone and that the Muslim-ruled states of the Near East must always and infallibly have been destined to form part of the world of Islam. An equally good case can be made that the medieval Middle East was no more inevitably Muslim than other regions conquered by Islam and subsequently liberated, such as Spain, Hungary, and southern France. If, as some suggest, the West and the Church should apologize for the Crusades, should they also express regret for those successful reconquests, or for failing to let Muslim forces roll over Austria and Germany? Nor do Westerners suggest that Muslims apologize for the aggressive acts that gave them power over these various lands in the first place. If seizing Christian Syria and Palestine by the Muslim sword was acceptable in the seventh century, why was it so atrocious to try to reclaim them with the Christian lance four hundred years later? When we fail to take account of the larger historical context, of course we see the Crusades as the epitome of evil. It is almost as if we were to describe the D-Day landings of 1944 as an act of unprovoked Anglo-American aggression against a peaceful Continent.

From one perspective, the Crusades arguably do represent a betrayal of Christianity, on the grounds that the core Christian message can never be reconciled with warfare, or perhaps with any exercise of state power. Some Christians do hold this principled position, yet they are a small minority, and a more common view allows for Christian involvement in war under specified conditions. The Crusades were evil to the extent that any war is evil, and as brutal as any war was in the Middle Ages. But to present the Crusades as a singularly Western evil—or indeed a Catholic crime—is a perversion of historical fact. This interpretation is so persistent because it has become so invaluable a component of the critique of Catholic Christianity.

Inquisitors

A similar argument can be made when Catholics are tainted by their link to "the Inquisition," which is presented as a vast and bloody secret police apparatus that served as the true enforcer of the spurious gospel of love. While the popular image does draw on some authentic events, the real story is actually far more complex and less one-sided. There never was such a thing as a Church-wide inquisition, a terrifying monolith comparable to the NKVD or the Gestapo. It is more accurate to think of inquisitions that operated extensively in some areas in a highly decentralized way, although they notionally acted under papal authority. Inquisitions were important at certain times and places but never existed in other areas. Some inquisitions were highly repressive: the Spanish body of the early modern period is the most notorious, but the pioneering structure that rooted out the dualist heretics of thirteenth-century France may have been even more fearsome.

On occasion, then, the Catholic Church did indeed impose its beliefs through violence and what might be called secret-police tactics. Consistently, though, the number of "victims of the Inquisition" is absurdly exaggerated, quite as outrageously as the number of witches who supposedly perished during the Burning Times. While popular authors such as evangelical Dave Hunt imply that the Spanish Inquisition was guilty of hundreds of thousands of deaths, and others speak vaguely of millions killed, the real numbers are far smaller. The best estimate for the Spanish organization was three thousand to five thousand executions, spread over a period of 350 years.[12]

The main problem about speaking of "the Inquisition" is that it suggests that religious repression of this sort was a Catholic prerogative. In fact, before the Enlightenment, virtually all religious traditions on occasion acted similarly when they had the power to do so. And before the rise of modern humanitarian concerns about criminal justice, this meant that religious zealots employed the full range of secular means such as judicial tortures and capital and corporal punishments. Though the popular mind associates these horrors with ecclesiastical names like Torquemada, they were in fact the standard operating procedures of secular justice. This indictment of religious savagery and intolerance applies to Muslim societies and to all the Protestant nations, even relatively liberal ones such as England and the Netherlands. Protestants were, moreover, at least as enthusiastic about hunting witches as were Catholics. And the only reason that Protestant Elizabethan England has no record of anti-Jewish persecutions was because no Jews were legally allowed into the country.

In fairness, if we are to cite "the Inquisition" as a damning flaw of Catholicism, we should also hurl these bygone barbarities against Protestants of every stripe. Among the main targets should by rights be those now-liberal mainline denominations that claim descent from the state churches of early modern Europe, which pursued their religious debates with dissidents by means of hanging, beheading, burning, and disemboweling. Equally blameworthy would be Muslims, Hindus, and even Buddhists. After all, in the seventeenth century, when Catholic inquisitions were at their height, the Buddhist/Shinto nation of Japan was engaged in a ferocious attempt to stamp out the deviant faith of Christianity through torture and massacre. In just forty years, these

Japanese religious persecutions killed far more victims than the Spanish Inquisition would in all the centuries of its existence.

In these other cases, modern observers do not see the violence as an integral part of the religious system concerned. Instead, the repression is understood as incidental, sporadic, and as much a result of social and political tensions as of anything to do with the religion itself—which would be an excellent way of characterizing the role of inquisitions in the history of Catholic Christianity. In addition, anti-religious secularists have been responsible for far more murders than all the Catholic inquisitors in history combined. In practice, though, most popular awareness of past religious violence is encoded in the elegant if highly slanted term "Inquisition," and that linkage seems impossible to discredit. To paraphrase Mel Brooks, the Inquisition myth is here, and it's here to stay.

| Constantine's Sword

In modern times, the most potent charge against Catholicism is that the Church betrayed Jesus through its denial of his Jewishness and of Judaism as such. If true, the indictment of Christianity and specifically Catholic Christianity has had enduring consequences. According to this view, anti-Semitism is a central flaw of Western culture and reached its logical culmination in the Nazi genocide; anti-Semitism is a direct outgrowth of Christianity and of Christian hatred of Jews; Christian anti-Semitism has its roots in the text of scripture. As we will see, though, charges about Catholic anti-Semitism have been severely distorted, usually for polemical purposes.

The perceived chain of causation, this link between the New Testament and the death camps, has gained a mass audience through James Carroll's book *Constantine's Sword*. Put simply, Carroll argues that anti-Semitism is central to the making of Christianity—literally its original sin. Christian theology is founded upon anti-Semitism, and one cannot be a good Catholic without believing and teaching fundamentally anti-Semitic doctrines. From its foundations, Catholicism is built upon hateful error. Anti-Jewish mobs through history believed they were acting in the Christian cause, and the Church issued damning statements against Judaism and Jews (though the authorities almost invariably condemned violence). Only as late as 1959 did Pope John XXIII change the language of the ancient prayer in the Good Friday liturgy in which Roman Catholics prayed each year for the conversion of "the perfidious Jews." Anti-Semitism through history has drawn on Christian language and tradition, including texts in the New Testament itself that made Jews out to be "Christ-killers," literally deicides.[13]

Carroll believes that anti-Semites acted as they did because of ancient errors that lie at the heart of Christian theology. The central flaw in Christianity is simply "the full and awful truth of the cross," namely, the theology of atonement and redemptive suffering. In this view, sacrificial theology represents a fundamental distortion of the original teaching of Jesus, which was purely Jewish in character. Carroll suggests that as Jesus's followers became increasingly embroiled in conflicts with Jewish authorities during the first century, these hostilities deeply influenced the Gospel records that they were compiling in these years, which must not be read as historical in any modern sense. We must appreciate "the fear, envy, insecurity, despair, grief and finally, hatred, that corrupted the authors of the New Testament." This growing hatred can be seen in the text of the evangelist Matthew, who reports that the Jewish crowd cried, "His blood be upon us and on our children." The seeds of evil, already fully present in the New Testament, reached full fruition when the Church made its unholy alliance with Emperor Constantine in the fourth century. It was at this time, says Carroll, that the fascination with the relic of the True Cross helped to establish ideas of crucifixion and atonement at the heart of Christian theology. The cross and anti-Semitism both grew alongside "Constantinian imperial Catholicism." Ever since that time, the image of the cross of Jesus, the token of humility, has been irrevocably tainted by the bloody and arrogant symbol of the sword of Constantine. In its way, the argument harks back to Hobbes's view of the Church as "the ghost of the deceased Roman Empire."[14]

For Carroll, the linkage between Catholicism and anti-Semitism demands a total revision of the Christian faith, and especially of its Catholic aspects. As Carroll writes, "Auschwitz, when seen in the links of causality, reveals that hatred of Jews has been no incidental anomaly but a central action of Christian history, reaching to the core of Christian character. Jew-hatred's perversion of the Gospel message launched a history, in other words, that achieved its climax in the Holocaust, an epiphany presented so starkly it cannot be denied. Because the hatred of Jews had been made holy, it became lethal. The most sacred 'thinking and acting' of the Church as such must at last be called into question."[15]

The Apostles Against the Jews?

Carroll's interpretation can been disputed at countless points, but he is weakest on the critical era of the New Testament itself. He relies too heavily on the work of John Dominic Crossan and others of the Jesus Seminar group, who represent a radical fringe of New Testament scholarship. Repeatedly, for both Crossan and Carroll, a praiseworthy wish to purge possibly anti-Semitic elements leads them to reject the historicity of many incidents and passages that most mainstream scholars would accept as authentic. One article of faith among the Jesus Seminar group is the idea of Jesus as a simple religious reformer, whose life and death subsequently acquired mystical and mythological dimensions that were no part of the original story. Yet not even the most idiosyncratic member of that group suggests that the whole notion of the cross and the associated theology of redemptive suffering derived from any later than the mid-first century. Carroll is alone in his eccentric views about the role of the cross in early Christianity and his attempt to link these ideas to the time of Constantine. This notion is contradicted by any reading of Christian writings over the first three centuries.[16]

Though Carroll tells nightmarish stories of Christian anti-Semitism, he fails to link that tradition to the basic doctrines of the Christian faith—and his views on this issue find no support among the very large community of scholars of early Christianity, even those most sensitive to possible bigotry. Virtually all scholars regard anti-Semitic attitudes as founded on a vulgar misuse of the Christian tradition.

At this point, we need to stress the basic distinction between anti-Judaism (opposition to the Jewish religion) and anti-Semitism, hatred for the Jewish people. Writers critical of the Vatican denounce this distinction as a meaningless attempt by the Church to avoid the consequences of its crimes. In this view, when the Church admits to anti-Judaism, it is confessing only to an intellectual stance, while denying any kind of bigotry or political activism that would be suggested by the more modern term anti-Semitism. Unless we make such a distinction, though, we cannot understand what appear to be the anti-Jewish passages of the New Testament. In the Gospel of John, "the Jews" (*Ioudaioi*) appear as villains in almost every chapter, and on one occasion, Jesus tells the Jews, "You are of your father the devil, and your will is to do your father's desires." In response, "the Jews persecuted Jesus," "the Jews sought to kill him," "for fear of the Jews no one spoke openly of him." How can anyone claim that passages like these are not anti-Semitic? Some liberal clergy and scholars find them so embarrassing that they try to modify these passages (perhaps the word means Judeans rather than Jews?) or even to omit them altogether in public readings.[17]

Yet the one thing we can say with certainty about the author of these passages in John is that he (or she) was a Jew, who believed as an article of faith that "salvation is of the Jews." Almost certainly, this and every other so-called anti-Semitic passage in the New Testament was written by someone of impeccable Jewish descent, including the evangelists John and Matthew. The apostle Paul boasted that he and his followers "are Jews by birth and not Gentile sinners," yet Paul also preached supersessionism, the doctrine that the new faith of Jesus had replaced the old Jewish religion and made it unnecessary. All these writers were as thoroughly suffused with the Jewish learning of the day as were any of their rabbinic contemporaries.[18]

The authors denied the truth of the Jewish religion of their day, but insofar as they could have understood the later concept of anti-Semitism, they would have described it under a blanket term such as "the works of Satan" or "Antichrist." The passages are unquestionably anti-Judaic, but they are not anti-Semitic. This distinction becomes all the clearer when these passages are read alongside other ancient texts, such as the Dead Sea Scrolls, which were written by a group that hoped fervently for the extinction of the Gentile world. The language of the New Testament "is caressingly mild if compared with the vocabulary employed against fellow Jews by the authors of some of the Hebrew and Aramaic texts found at Qumran."[19] But it would be ludicrous to describe those texts as anti-Semitic, any more than the writings of Matthew or John.

Carroll is simply wrong about anti-Semitism being integral to Catholic Christianity: no direct historical highway leads from the evangelists to Auschwitz. Just as suspect, therefore, is Carroll's attempt to discredit traditional Christianity by contextualizing it together with the dreadful crimes of anti-Semitism. He is overpresenting his case in order to justify a "reform agenda" that amounts to a blueprint for the annihilation of the Catholic Church. Much of Carroll's book is devoted to his agenda for a proposed Third Vatican Council, which would cure the Catholic Church of the dreadful faults that have made it a "failed and sinful Church." For all its excellent intentions, its moral fervor, Carroll's book is a frontal attack on Catholic Christianity, and this agenda shapes its interpretations on every page.[20]

| Catholics and Muslims

A great many anti-Semitic acts through history have been undertaken by people who think of themselves as Christians and perhaps think that their actions are justified by their religion. In that sense, it might seem natural to take the anti-Semites at their word, to argue that their behavior is an integral part of their Christianity—or Catholicism. Yet this attitude certainly does not apply when other religious groups are involved.

Let us take the analogy of Islam. The Muslim scriptures clearly preach anti-Judaism, seeing the Jewish religion as an inadequate stepping-stone on the path to the true faith. Today, there is no question that anti-

Semitism is far more widespread among Muslims than Christians. Anti-Semitism is as normal and unexceptional in the Muslim world today as it was in the Europe of the 1920s. Copies of the *Protocols of the Elders of Zion* are as easily available in the contemporary Middle East as they were in Europe between the two world wars, and pseudo-learned volumes on the alleged Jewish practice of ritual murder are just as accessible. Across the Muslim world, even allegedly reputable news media peddle the lie that the September 11 massacres were the work of Jews, operating through the Israeli Mossad. Besides parlor bigotry, armed mobs call for direct action against Jews. The slogan "Kill the Jews!" (*itbah al-Yahud*) is commonplace among Middle Eastern radicals and Islamists and also in Arab immigrant communities across Europe. In 2002, Los Angeles schools withdrew a translation of the Quran from library shelves because of the violent anti-Jewish commentaries that accompanied the text.

At every point, Islam seems as fundamentally and pervasively anti-Jewish as Catholicism has ever been accused of being. Yet Western media and political leaders never condemn Islam as a religion, stressing repeatedly that outbreaks of hatred and violence must be seen as secular political phenomena that betray the true nature of a religion based on love and tolerance. People who charge otherwise, who claim that the violence and anti-Semitism are integral to the Muslim faith, are dismissed as racists and "Islamophobes." In 2002, Southern Baptist preacher Jerry Vines ignited a furious controversy when he drew a stark contrast between Islam and the Judeo-Christian traditions. "Allah is not Jehovah," he declared. "Jehovah's not going to turn you into a terrorist that will try to bomb people and take the lives of thousands and thousands of people." Vines was attacked by many Jewish and Christian leaders, who also denounced public figures who failed to condemn such remarks publicly. The president of the liberal pressure group People for the American Way specifically complained that President Bush "should not embrace leaders whose message is based on sowing intolerance." Yet this reluctance to condemn a religion for the failings of some of its members does not apply to Catholic Christianity. If only on grounds of consistency, Western media should depict the Catholic Church in colors no worse than those of Islam.

Hitler's Pope?

Whether or not orthodox Christianity is actually founded upon anti-Semitism, activists commonly portray a central Catholic role in fostering bigotry in later ages. In this view, Christianity has often preached and practiced strident anti-Semitism, and the Catholic Church's attitudes of the nineteenth and twentieth centuries effectively made Nazism possible. In recent years, anyone interested in investigating Christian anti-Semitism has had access to a number of well-publicized studies, the titles of which epitomize the whole argument. David Kertzer's *The Popes Against the Jews* is subtitled *The Vatican's Role in the Rise of Modern Anti-Semitism*; Cornwell's biography of Pope Pius XII (who reigned as Pope from 1939 to 1958) bore the loaded title of *Hitler's Pope*. Browsing the bookshelves produces other classic examples of guilt by association, such as *Unholy Trinity: The Vatican, the Nazis, and the Swiss Banks.*[21]

Responding to this scholarly outpouring, the *New Republic* in 2002 published a massive review essay by Daniel Goldhagen that painted the Vatican's record in the bleakest terms. Based on this study, *New Republic* editor Martin Peretz has described Pope Pius simply as "an evil man." (The points made in Goldhagen's essay are developed more fully in his book *A Moral Reckoning*.) While able defenses of the Vatican's role do exist, they are usually published by less mainstream presses and are not usually found so easily in the chain bookstores. Ronald Rychlak's *Hitler, the War, and the Pope* was published not by Penguin or Knopf but by the Catholic press Our Sunday Visitor. For the average reader, the lesson is that the sinister account of papal deeds in the 1940s is self-evidently that of mainstream scholarship, while any contrary opinion must be the work of self-serving Church apologists.[22]

For the authors of the anti-Pius books—and presumably for many of their readers—anti-Semitism is unquestionably a besetting sin of the Catholic Church, and this "fact" is being added to the store of "what everyone knows." "Pius XII" is fast becoming one of those evocative coded phrases like "the Crusades." This sinister linkage is especially effective in discrediting Catholic positions among American Jews and leading them to suspect the worst of the Catholic Church in other controversies.

Since the 1940s, the Vatican's attitudes toward dictatorships, and particularly toward Nazism, have been a controversial topic. Pius reigned at one of the most horrific moments of European history and was forced to confront the threats of both Hitler and Stalin. He spoke out forcibly against both and condemned atrocities, massacres, and mass deportations. Pius did not emerge from these events as a towering personal hero on the lines of some other Christian clerics, such as the leaders of the Bulgarian Orthodox Church, who cajoled and bullied that country's secular authorities into saving most Bulgarian Jews. For many years, though, the consensus was that Pius had done his best in an impossible situation, opposing the Axis as forcefully as circumstances would permit. We know that he supported internal German plots against Hitler, who in turn loathed the Pope. In 1943, the Nazis were planning to kidnap Pius and bring him to Germany.[23]

The Pope's opposition to the dictatorships—together with his undoubted personal piety—won him many admirers. As the *New York Times* wrote at Christmas 1941, "The voice of Pius XII is a lonely voice in the silence and darkness enveloping Europe this Christmas." Jews praised him highly. A leading figure in the Italian Jewish Assistance Committee remarked that "six million of my co-religionists have been murdered by the Nazis, but there could have been many more victims had it not been for the efficacious intervention of Pius XII." On his death, Israel's foreign minister, Golda Meir, recalled that "when fearful martyrdom came to our people in the decade of Nazi terror, the voice of the Pope was raised for the victims." Recognizing the overwhelmingly favorable public impression, even as deadly an enemy of the Church as Paul Blanshard could find nothing useful for his cause in Pius's record. Hating to say a good word of a Pope, Blanshard grudgingly admitted that "[t]he Roman Catholic record vis-à-vis Hitler is not as black as its record in Spain." Considering the source, that almost amounts to an endorsement. Catholics, naturally, found much more in Pius's record to be proud of. A movement for Pius's canonization has been under way for years, and gained ground rapidly under John Paul II.[24]

Some later writers, though, have painted a much uglier portrait of Pius, who is increasingly viewed as aggressively pro-fascist and viscerally anti-Jewish, effectively an ally and accomplice of the *Reich*. These charges were first popularized by Rolf Hochhuth's play *The Deputy* (1965), but in the past decade they have gained a still wider audience through the work of historians such as Cornwell, Carroll, Wills, and Goldhagen. Cornwell's book especially made a major impact in the media, and it was the basis of a sympathetic feature on television's *60 Minutes*.[25] If the anti-Pius charges are true, then any canonization would look like granting an official approval to anti-Semitism, and even a retroactive Church blessing of the Holocaust. The stakes in this debate are very high.

Pius as Nazi

The specific charges against Pius stress his personal reluctance to confront the Nazis. Pius never threatened to excommunicate the Nazis or their supporters in the way that he threatened Communists in the late 1940s. Hitler himself was never excommunicated. This meant that the Church took no serious action against clergy who accepted Nazi ideology wholesale, especially in Germany itself, or against Catholic allies of the Nazis in statelets such as Slovakia and Croatia. In these small regimes, it was not only Catholics but clergy and friars who undertook some of the worst atrocities against civilians, including Jews. (At the same time, some highly placed Catholic clergy spoke against the brutality, notably Archbishop Stepinac in Croatia.) Generally, it is fair to criticize the Vatican for the Church's limited role in suppressing these horrors. Here at least, Pius probably could have done more to intervene effectively.[26]

More sweeping, though, are the charges that Pius was in reality a supporter of the Nazi regime, in principle if not in detailed agreement with every one of its policies. Was Pius anti-Semitic? According to the critics, one strong piece of evidence against Pius involves a letter he wrote in 1919 at the time of the Bolshevik rising in Bavaria, in which he stresses that many of the Red activists were Jews, who are depicted according to familiar anti-Semitic stereotypes. For critics such as Goldhagen, this letter is decisive proof that the future Pius was "an anti-Semite" whose stereotypes were "of the kind that Julius Streicher would soon offer the German public in every issue of his notorious Nazi newspaper *Der Stürmer.*" When interviewed on *60 Minutes*, Cornwell drew an explicitly Hitlerian parallel. He said that the remarks were "the sort of expression that would—one would find in *Mein Kampf* during the same period." Interviewer Ed Bradley asked, "So you're saying that what Hitler wrote would have been similar to what Pius XII—the man who would become Pius XII—wrote?" Cornwell replied: "Absolutely."[27]

These statements are wrong on multiple counts. However ugly the words, what Pius wrote about Jews and Bolsheviks in 1919 could have come from any mainstream or liberal source anywhere in the United States or Europe that Red Year. To draw parallels between a couple of snide allusions and *Mein Kampf*—or the obsessive pornographic filth of *Der Stürmer*—is outrageous. Nor can we say that anyone who has ever uttered a racist or anti-Semitic remark suffers until the end of time from the incurable condition of racism or anti-Semitism, of which there are neither mild nor severe variations. It is absurd to claim that a person who on one occasion reflected the anti-Semitic platitudes of his day would automatically favor the fanatical policies of the Nazis.

To put this in perspective, let us imagine a comparable American situation. At some point between (say) 1920 and 1970, a great many white Americans in the media, in public life, and in organized religion used demeaning ethnic stereotypes to describe blacks, language that in retrospect appears deeply embarrassing. Some of them also used then-fashionable racial epithets (something that Pius never did about Jews). Though many of these American public figures today have the reputation of being liberals and radicals, by Cornwell's standard, every one of them must automatically have been a member of the Ku Klux Klan and probably led lynch mobs personally, and only a massive cover-up prevents us from seeing that fact. Cornwell's notion of Pius's anti-Semitic obsession really is that outlandish.

Much more significant is the question of whether the Vatican in Pius's time tried to save Jews from slaughter, a question on which historians differ quite bewilderingly. By some calculations, Vatican efforts saved large numbers from persecution and death, perhaps more than eight hundred thousand (the figure derives from the Israeli consul in postwar Italy). According to Goldhagen and the rest, though, the Vatican saved precisely none. In part, this question depends on issues of definition. In some instances, the people the Church was trying to save were of Jewish blood but had converted to Christianity, partly in an effort to save themselves from persecution. The act of conversion made no difference whatever to the Nazis, whose war was based on race, not religion, and they inflicted ruthless penalties on anyone who tried to help or defend these victims. Modern critics can argue that by strict definition, the Vatican was in many cases trying to help not Jews but Catholics. Yet even if we assume that all the refugees assisted by the Church fell into this category, then we can agree that the Vatican was making intense efforts—and running deadly risks—to prevent the Nazis from implementing their genocidal policies. Other historians go much further and praise the Vatican for its extensive use of Church-run safe houses to rescue Jews, that is, those who were Jewish by both birth and religion. The exact scale of Vatican rescue efforts is open to debate; the fact that such efforts were made is not.[28]

Unholy Silence

The other major charge against Pius involved his sin of silence, or near silence. This can be exaggerated. During the 1930s, Pius and the Vatican abused Nazism publicly in terms that we more often associate with Winston Churchill. In 1935, for instance, Pius (then Eugenio Pacelli) published an open letter describing the Nazis as "false prophets with the pride of Lucifer." In 1937 he named Germany as "that noble and powerful nation whom bad shepherds would lead astray into an ideology of race."[29] Vatican radio provided sympathetic and well-informed coverage of the plight of German Jews. As Vatican secretary of state in 1937, Pius must have had a role in drafting the strongly anti-Hitler encyclical *Mit Brennender Sorge*. At enormous risk to individual Catholics, copies of this work were smuggled into Germany to be read in churches, to the fury of the Nazi regime. This was silence? For any historian accustomed to the mealy-mouthed attitudes of the Western democracies in the 1930s, Pius must emerge as something of a hero. The Nazi press loathed this "Jew-loving cardinal."[30]

During the war years, the Vatican became more cautious, and while statements did condemn genocide and anti-Semitism, they did so in the guarded language of international diplomacy, rather than in prophetic tones. The degree of "silence" can be exaggerated: the Nazis knew precisely whom the Vatican was attacking on every available occasion. Most troubling in retrospect, though, the statements usually failed to single out Jews as victims of oppression. However incomprehensible this absence appears in retrospect, it is less odd in the context of the time. Pius himself feared that too direct an attack on the Nazis would provoke still worse atrocities against both Jews and particularly Jewish converts to Catholicism, and in some instances his fears were justified. The Nazis did indeed respond to Vatican criticisms by intensifying their persecutions. In hindsight, we know that the Nazis aimed for the total obliteration of the Jews, so that a respite of a year or two would have made precious little difference either way, but along with most of his contemporaries, Pius could not have known this. As respected historian W. D. Rubinstein asks, "Can it be that, with all its frustrations, inadequacies, and apparent failures, the policy of 'silence' pursued by Pacelli was actually the most effective possible, given Hitler's obsessive and overriding intention to kill every Jew in Europe?"[31]

Pius's "silence" was no worse than that of other parties deeply involved in trying to save Jews. His public statements did not focus consistently or single-mindedly on the anti-Jewish atrocities; but neither did the wartime declarations of the U.S. and British governments, most international organizations, or indeed most Jewish organizations. To take a specific example, Cornwell criticizes Pius for his delayed response to the transportation of Jews from Hungary in 1944. As Rubinstein remarks, though, "If the Pope's protest was 'too late,' even later were those of Franklin Roosevelt, the International Red Cross, King Gustaf of Sweden, and the Jewish Agency in Palestine (headed by David Ben-Gurion)."[32]

Nor, in the context of the time, was it fanciful to suggest that the Nazis could have been provoked to launch an explicitly anti-Christian or anti-Catholic persecution. The Holocaust is sometimes presented in terms of Christian persecution of Jews, and Bill Clinton has claimed that "Adolf Hitler preached a perverted form of Christianity," yet this understates the violent antipathy of the Nazis toward the churches. Rubinstein argues that Hitler's upbringing in Austria had left him with a loathing of Catholicism and the Catholic monarchy "only slightly less vicious than that which he shows to Jews and Communists." Hitler himself wrote, "You can be a Christian or a German. You cannot be both." According to Baldur von Schirach, leader of the Hitler Youth, "the destruction of Christianity was explicitly recognized as a purpose of the National Socialist movement." Josef Goebbels aspired to exterminate "after the last Jew, the last priest."[33] Through the late 1930s, Nazi persecution of the Catholic Church intensified, and priests and bishops were widely attacked for publicly reading papal statements critical of the regime. In occupied countries like Poland, Catholic clergy and laity were subjected to persecution and death. Pius's fears of a full-scale Nazi war against Catholics were thoroughly justified.

Finally, none of Pius's political actions can be understood except in the context of his view of the pressing danger of Communism. Unlike many of his contemporaries, Pius saw little to choose between the totalitarian dangers of Nazism and Communism, no serious difference between their capacity to inflict mass slaughter. In retrospect, few can deny that Pius was exactly right in his reading, far more so than (say) the Roosevelt administration in Washington, which romanticized Stalin throughout the war years. If Pius is criticized for failing to denounce Hitler, it would be useful to know whom he is being unfavorably compared with. Who were these far-sighted people who spoke out unequivocally against totalitarianism of both the left and the right? There were indeed many ardent anti-Nazis in the West during the 1930s, but a sizable majority of these were willfully blind to the comparable horrors being perpetrated by Stalin. With a handful of exceptions, such as Churchill, virtually no Western leader in these years succeeded in recognizing the full evil of both Nazis and Communists.

This analysis explains some of Pius's more controversial actions, such as negotiating a Church concordat with the Hitler regime soon after it came to power: Carroll describes this treaty as "Nazi-legitimizing." It is stretching matters to claim that an establishment of diplomatic relations represents a total acquiescence to the other state's policies.[34] To take another event at this exact time, did Franklin Roosevelt's establishment of relations with the USSR make him culpable for that nation's purges and massacres? Like almost every other serious political figure in the West at that time, Pius felt that bolstering Germany was a vital necessity for the whole of Europe, partly to prevent Communist expansion. And like the rest of the political world, he failed to predict just how maniacally savage the new German regime would become within a very few years.

| The Evils of the Church

Historians can differ on their assessment of Pius's career. After all the recent research, the worst charge that can be made about his wartime efforts was that his silence was arguably more harmful than earlier writers supposed, and that an earlier and more explicit defense of Jews might conceivably have saved more lives. Examining his careful diplomacy, Charles Morris concluded, "Instead of being pope, that is, Pius played the neutralist diplomat, which is not much to be proud of." At the same time, we have to consider that such a risky policy might have endangered the Vatican's genuinely effective rescue work, which saved hundreds of thousands of lives.[35]

Some criticisms of Pius do leave unanswered questions, but their limited nature should always be borne in mind when we read some of the recent attacks on the wartime Vatican. The critics write as if they have obviously proven Church complicity in Nazism and the Holocaust, an overwhelming assemblage of evidence demanding a guilty verdict. They seem to believe that they have turned up a smoking-gun letter from Pius to Hitler congratulating him on what the death camps are contributing to Western civilization. To the contrary, the case against Pius is extremely weak, and *Hitler's Pope* in particular is seriously flawed. Rubinstein has characterized the book as "a malign exercise in defamation and character assassination." In one of the most damning reviews, *Newsweek* columnist Kenneth Woodward described Cornwell's book as "a classic example of what happens when an ill-equipped journalist assumes the airs of sober scholarship ... Errors of fact and ignorance of context appear on almost every page. Cornwell questions [Pius's] every motive, but never doubts those who tell a different story. This is bogus scholarship."[36]

Cornwell's book suggests that the publishers wanted to sensationalize the attack on Pius, despite the absence of any serious evidence. The book's cover has a memorable photograph showing a smiling Eugenio Pacelli, leaving what has presumably been a friendly diplomatic meeting with German authorities, as he walks past German soldiers in their familiar coal-scuttle helmets. The casual reader is meant to infer that Pacelli is emerging from a cozy tête-à-tête with Hitler—perhaps they have been chatting about plans for a new extermination camp? Reading the fine print on the back cover reveals that the event depicted occurred in 1927, during the Weimar Republic, and Pacelli, then papal nuncio, had been paying a diplomatic call on the constitutionally elected president of Germany, von Hindenburg. Perhaps photographs do not lie, but this particular book cover—offered in the context it was, and under the title *Hitler's Pope*—comes close.

This book cover symbolizes the approach of many recent books on Catholic anti-Semitism. Having proved unable to demonstrate links between the Vatican and the Holocaust, sections of the media have nevertheless decided to proceed as if the case is proven and all that remains is to explore the implications of this awful historical fact. For all their evident flaws, most of the recent blockbuster exposés of Catholic evils have been reviewed as if they were triumphs of pathbreaking detective work. Just how well they have been received is evident from the laudatory reviews published by major news outlets. The *New York Times* gave the task of reviewing Kertzer's *The Pope Against the Jews* to Garry Wills, a knowledgeable historian, but one whose own recent works demonstrate a massive animus against the papacy. Not surprisingly, Wills not only praised the work highly, but turned it into a direct attack on his special bête noire, Pope John Paul II.[37]

Goldhagen's Antichrist

The leap from the actual evidence about Vatican anti-Semitism to the claims based on it can induce a vertiginous crisis of reality. Goldhagen demands "a systematic investigation of the Catholic Church's contribution to the German-led persecution and extermination of the Jews" and argues that this has been prevented only by the "many sleights of hand" engaged in by "the defenders of the church." Rhetorically, this absolutist approach is quite powerful because it places anyone who seeks to defend Pius in the position of an unconditional "defender of the church" and, by implication, a defender of anti-Semitism.[38]

For Goldhagen, as for Kertzer or Carroll, anti-Semitism is a core Catholic value. Nazi anti-Semitism was, in his eyes, a direct outcome of Church attitudes, and he scorns any attempts to erect "an iron curtain" between the two. He argues that the linkage is so glaringly obvious that it scarcely deserves further proof. It is "an indisputable fact" that "the Church's anti-Semitism was the trunk that never ceased nourishing the modern European anti-Semitism that had branched off from it." Pius's supposed anti-Semitism was only to be expected from one who rose through "the profoundly anti-Semitic establishment of the Church, an institutional culture centrally animated by the notion that all Jews were Christ-killers and responsible for many of the perceived evils of modernity."[39]

At times, Goldhagen's attack on the Church becomes apocalyptic, to the extent that one is forced to reread some passages to see if they are really as fantastic as they appear. Based on his flawed reading of the Vatican's relationship to Nazi Germany, he claims, "Any evaluation of the

Catholic Church as a moral institution must centrally take into account that in effect the Church was serving—because not to choose is to choose—the closest human analogue to the Antichrist. I mean Hitler; and that it tacitly and sometimes materially aided him in mass murder." Is he really saying that the Pope was serving the Antichrist? By this point, any kind of detailed refutation is futile, because the critics have abandoned the realm of historical debate and moved into a grotesque realm of anti-Catholic mythology.[40]

Goldhagen's essay stirred a ferocious response, and by no means only from predictable "church defenders." Liberal Catholic Andrew Sullivan wrote that he viewed any attempt to canonize Pius as "obscene," but he was nevertheless appalled by Goldhagen's overt anti-Catholicism. As for the "Antichrist" reference, he writes, "It is a staple of street bigots. . . . The anti-Christ, huh? The last time I heard that was when I was being jeered in my Protestant high school in England. The sources change. The smears remain the same. But now they call them scholarship." Catholic writer Michael Novak has responded, "The reason Goldhagen is quite guilty of the charge of anti-Catholicism lies in the breadth and passion of the smears he spreads across a broad history, the distortion and hysteria of his tone, the extremity of his rage, and the lack of proportion in his judgments—dwarfing Hitler and making Pius XII a giant of evil, and then diminishing Pius XII so as to indict the whole of Christian theology down the ages." Ronald Rychlak condemns Goldhagen's use of "selective sources, doctored quotations, sloppy inaccuracies, half truths and outright falsehoods." These Catholic critics are less damning than Jewish author Sam Schulman, who writes of Goldhagen's "lack of learning and his inability to think or sort out evidence." Schulman echoes Novak's charge of anti-Catholicism, remarking how Goldhagen "begins to throw charges about which are uncomfortably close to those which the Jewish people have suffered for centuries—not out of maliciousness, but from genuine dim-wittedness which shines through every awkward, goofy sentence he writes."[41]

| Guilt by Association

For Goldhagen, as for Carroll, Catholicism is an evil, tainted religion, and desperately needs salvaging. "What should be the future of this church that has not fully faced its anti-Semitic history, that still has anti-Semitic elements embedded in its doctrine and theology, and that still claims to be the exclusive path to salvation?"[42] The various authors are not shy about using the story of the wartime papacy as the basis for far-reaching efforts to reform the Catholic Church or, as others would say, to transform it so thoroughly that it would cease to exist in any recognizable form.

Critics use a familiar rhetorical tactic of guilt by association, suggesting that any aspect of Christianity that can be linked to anti-Semitism must of its nature be evil and worthy of change. The argument sounds plausible, but the linkages that are drawn are often wildly improbable. Typically, Cornwell writes, "Pacelli's failure to respond to the enormity of the Holocaust was more than a personal failure, it was a failure of the papal office itself and the prevailing culture of Catholicism. That failure was implicit in the rifts Catholicism created and sustained, between the sacred and the profane, the spiritual and the secular, the body and the soul, clergy and laity, the exclusive truth of Catholicism over all other confessions and faith. It was an essential feature of Pacelli's ideology of papal power, moreover, that Catholics should abdicate, as Catholics, their social and political responsibility for what happened in the world and turn their gaze upward to the Holy Father and, beyond, to eternity."[43]

The charges here are familiar—Catholicism is ritualistic and otherworldly, it is focused on dogma and hierarchy rather than ethical conduct, Catholics are sheep-like followers—though it is very difficult to see what any of this has to do with the Holocaust. Moreover, what is under attack here is not just Catholicism or even Christianity, but the whole concept of supernatural religion. *Hitler's Pope* cannot be understood except as a series of very low blows against the modern Catholic Church, and specifically the papacy of John Paul II. And whatever Cornwell's personal religious views, his rhetoric is unabashedly anti-Catholic.

| Structures of Deceit

Just as sweeping in its way is the book *Papal Sin*, by Garry Wills, who offers a catalog of tales in which the Popes and Vatican authorities allegedly behaved in a dishonorable or cowardly fashion. The title and subtitle (*Structures of Deceit*) make it clear that this is about the evils of the hierarchical Church, and specifically of the papacy. The book's cover reproduces a medieval painting showing Popes and prelates in the flames of hell. Among the "papal sins," Wills would certainly include the failure to condemn anti-Semitism in the 1930s. He also complains about the emphasis placed on Catholics martyred by the Nazis, including Edith Stein and Maximilian Kolbe, his argument being that the Vatican's approach to such figures represents a cynical attempt to de-Judaize the Holocaust. Naturally, Pius XII also emerges as a prime villain in his account. The papacy of John Paul II is presented as the logical outcome of centuries of contradictions, falsehoods, and "dishonesties," historical and doctrinal.

This is a book about "the papacy's stubborn resistance to the truth."[44]

Equally vehement is Wills's denunciation of papal horrors in *Why I Am a Catholic*, which summarizes the history of the papacy between 1815 and 1962 in two overheated chapters evocatively titled "War on Democracy" and "Reign of Terror." In this view, the second Vatican Council represented one brief shining moment of liberal enlightenment, but hellish darkness descended once more in the form of John Paul II, whom Wills depicts as a credulous megalomaniac. Time and again, the papacy—in its flawed, corrupted modern state—stands against the "people of God." A reviewer of *Why I Am a Catholic* in the *New York Times* comments that "the reader may be so bludgeoned by the book's exhaustive recital of a millennium and a half of papal horrors as to insert between the title's initial 'Why' and final 'a Catholic' the words 'On Earth Are You.'"[45]

Wills would certainly describe himself as a Catholic, but as with Carroll and Cornwell, his attacks on the Church are so basic as to raise questions about just what this term means. On one hand, he affirms a Christian faith rooted in basic institutions such as the New Testament, the sacraments, the creed, and the rosary, and he sees himself as a follower of such Catholic luminaries as St. Augustine and G. K. Chesterton. He is also on solid ground when he points out that the exact concept of papal authority has changed and developed over time: the idea of Petrine primacy has been manifested differently as social and political circumstances have altered. Perhaps a century or a millennium from now, the papal institution will indeed be structured differently from what it is presently, though without departing from that Petrine core.

Yet while Wills's Christian faith is explicit, it is frankly baffling why, apart from force of habit, he chooses to call himself Catholic. His concepts of the sacraments and of Marian devotion wander far from virtually all specifically Catholic interpretations. In both books, too, his argument for radical change goes far beyond any possible implications of the evils he exposes, to call for a wholesale revision of Catholicism, or rather, a revolutionary transformation. He calls for an end to the priesthood in anything like the sense in which it has been known for many centuries, as what he calls "magicians of the Eucharistic transformation."[46] In his ideal Church, women would be ordained, priestly celibacy would be abolished, papal supremacy would end, and no more would the Church make Mary "an empress." To quote a conservative critic of *Papal Sin*: "In the course of the book, he rejects the teaching authority of the Church if exercised without lay involvement and agreement, the concept of papal infallibility and any possibility of divine guidance to papal teaching, the ordained priesthood, the doctrine of the Real Presence in the Eucharist, and that the priest has the sacramental power alone to consecrate the Eucharist. Apostolic succession, the Immaculate Conception and Assumption, and Church teaching on homosexuality are dismissed as well. For the most part, the right for the Church to teach at all in the area of sexual morality is generally dismissed if it involves the actions of consenting adults." There is something deeply perverse about Wills's frequent references to the work of Chesterton, an author he clearly adores, inasmuch as Chesterton would have disagreed with him fundamentally on every issue of religious authority. Consistently, Chesterton's views on these matters place him much closer to the intellectual world of John Paul II than that of Garry Wills.[47]

After outlining his program for reform, Wills asks rhetorically, "But where can this church of the Spirit be found?" and he answers, fairly, that nothing like it currently exists among flawed human institutions. But in terms of the specific reforms he advocates, then many such institutions exist and survive, if they do not exactly flourish. They can be found among mainline Protestant denominations such as the Methodists, Episcopalians, and Lutherans. In these bodies, priesthood does not exist in anything like the Catholic sense of the term, women are ordained, Mary is not venerated, and Church authorities make little attempt to regulate the sexual lives of the faithful on the lines Wills objects to in his own church. We can unreservedly describe Wills's proposed church as a liberal Protestant body. One obvious difficulty with that proposed solution is that, as Wills must know, all the churches that exist on the lines he favors are hemorrhaging support and membership at an alarming rate, to the extent that their very existence is in question. (At least, that is the story in North America and Europe. The same churches are booming in the Third World—where, however, they are highly conservative in both theology and moral teachings.) Many observers would explain the crisis of American liberal Protestantism in terms of the lack of any distinctive values that distinguish the mainline churches from secular liberalism, and the absence of claims to authoritative teaching. His agenda for the Catholic Church is a call to institutional suicide.

Another problem with Wills's recent books is the question of whom he is actually attacking. Throughout their assaults on Church teaching, Wills, Carroll, and Cornwell all speak in terms of "the Popes" or "the Vatican" and the wrongs that these elevated authorities have committed. This is rhetorically necessary if they are to avoid an overt attack against the beliefs and practice of ordinary Catholics, an assault that would certainly appear as simple bigotry. Instead, they claim to be attacking papalism, Rome, or the Vatican, but not Catholicism as such. The impression given is that through the centuries, Catholicism has been shaped by orders from above, in which ordinary believers exercised only a passive role. In the modern context, it is almost as if mainstream Catholicism is a bizarre, cult-like heresy invented personally by John Paul II, and which nobody really believes in outside a narrow circle of sycophants. For Wills, Carroll, and the rest, authentic Catholicism is the skeptical liberal variety of Faith Lite favored by American elites. Seriously, they seem to ask, how could any sane person question current liberal orthodoxies about sexuality?

This implausible focus on "papal sin" creates serious logical difficulties for Wills in particular, who exalts what he believes to have been a long tradition of lay organization and popular consultation within the Church. He stresses that for much of its history, the Vatican did not play a large part in the ordinary lives of Catholics far beyond the confines of Italy. Yet he then proceeds to blame this distant and powerless Vatican for the imposition of beliefs and doctrines that he condemns within the Church, such as celibacy and the veneration of the Virgin Mary. And he has already shown that the movement for clerical celibacy arose from a surging mass movement supported by ordinary Christian faithful themselves, who demanded this standard of their clerical leaders. He can scarcely have it both ways. Though presented as a critique of the Vatican, his attacks are more commonly on what any reasonable person would think of as Catholic Christianity.[48]

The Cult of Mary

Reading these authors, we consistently find an odd disjuncture between the historical problems they describe—such as the alleged evils of Pius XII—and the solutions they recommend. The argument is that the Church has failed totally, needs thorough reconstruction, and specifically needs to change its policies on matters such as the nature of priesthood, the requirement for celibacy, and so on. This lack of connection between problem and solution is evident when critics of Catholic anti-Semitism devote a remarkable amount of space to attacking the Catholic devotion to one particular Jewish woman: the Virgin Mary.

While nobody has argued seriously that Catholic devotion to the Virgin Mary has any necessary link to anti-Semitism, Wills uses this supposed connection to attack a form of worship of which he does not approve. He is damning about what he calls the medieval notion of Mary as "this idol-goddess," a phrase that might come straight from a radical Protestant tract of a century ago—and which is all the more puzzling for someone who reports his own loyalty to the practice of the rosary (a quintessentially late-medieval devotion). His attack on Marianism may be stimulated by his knowledge of the particular devotion that Pope John Paul II has to the Virgin. After discussing the Marian apparitions of the nineteenth century, Wills notes, "No-one showed more devotion to these appearances than Pope Pius IX, whom we met earlier as the kidnapper of Edgardo Mortara." Now, the case of Edgardo Mortara was, indisputably, an appalling example of anti-Jewish behavior by the Catholic Church. Briefly, an Italian-Jewish child who seemed to be on the point of death was secretly baptized by a Catholic nursemaid. In the event, though, he survived. According to Church law at the time, a Christian child could not be raised by Jews, so in 1858 young Edgardo was removed from his home by papal police—kidnapped, in effect—and raised by a Catholic religious order, despite years of campaigning by Jewish and Protestant groups. Nothing in Wills's sentence about Pius and Mortara is actually false, but the association is deliberately inflammatory: what does this have to do with the cult of Mary? It is much like someone condemning vegetarianism on the grounds that this was Hitler's dietary preference.[49]

Cornwell uses a similar rhetorical tactic when he associates the veneration of Mary with the alleged megalomania and repressiveness of Pius XII. He writes, "The vacuum created by the suppression of creative, dynamic theology in the postwar period was thus filled by Marianism. ... Its central ecclesiastical features were papal exaltation and triumphalism." If Pius supported it, it must have been bad. Cornwell also uses the anti-Semitic canard as a means of attacking other Catholic peculiarities that he dislikes, such as celibacy. He scorns Pius XII's canonization of the young virgin Maria Goretti, killed while protecting her chastity. He comments, "In stark contrast to [Pius's] expectations for moral behavior in those guilty of participating in the mass killings of Jews during the war, he did not hesitate to counsel martyrdom for those whose sexual morality was being challenged."[50] In this instance, the linkage to anti-Semitism may be even more remote than the imaginary parallel with Hitler's vegetarianism.

During the long religious controversies between Protestants and Catholics, anti-Catholic polemicists made so much use of historical stereotypes that they became almost comic. At least by the end of the nineteenth century, few respectable controversialists would sink so low as to use images as clichéd as the Inquisition, Pope Joan, or the St. Bartholomew's Day massacre. These particular horrors may well have lost their credibility, but they have been replaced by a new series of clichés that are just as distorted, however widely they are believed. If only through frequent repetition, the legend of Catholic guilt for the Holocaust is achieving the status of social fact, despite all the evidence that can be mounted against it. The fact that this terrible indictment could become accepted so easily is in itself remarkable testimony to the expectations of large sections of the American public, which had become so conditioned to anti-Catholic canards. The Black Legend of Pius XII was believed because its time had come.

10 | The End of Prejudice?

Americans! You are sleeping on a volcano, and you do not suspect it! You are pressing on your bosom a viper which will bite you to death, and you do not know it.

— Charles Chiniquy

In this world we have seen the Roman Catholic power dying ... for many centuries. Many a time we have gotten all ready for the funeral and found it postponed again, on account of the weather or something. ... Apparently one of the most uncertain things in the world is the funeral of a religion.

— Mark Twain

Tracing the history of anti-Catholic prejudice in the United States is rather like watching one of those slasher films that were so popular during the 1980s. Even after the villain has been spectacularly killed at the end of one episode, even when you have seen him decapitated, you have no doubt that he will infallibly be back in action at the start of the inevitable sequel. Anti-Catholic prejudice is equally resilient and, seemingly, indestructible. Its strength lies in its flexibility, its capacity to adapt to almost any circumstances. Just when it ceases to be the preserve of the racist right, it is reinvented as a mainstay of the anti-racist left. When one band of anti-Catholics has finished denouncing the religion for its blatant effeminacy, another contingent is complaining of its quintessential patriarchy. This particular prejudice may simply be ineradicable—which is not to say that it might not in a few years change its characteristics yet again. Though futurology is always a risky business, some current trends may allow us to suggest when and how we may expect anti-Catholicism to flourish in future years.

The Politics of Fear

Nothing stirs prejudice so much as fear, whether or not that fear is justified. However implausible or even ludicrous the supposed threat, the bitterest anti-Semitism arises from fear that Jews are about to inflict dreadful harm upon their neighbors. Racist outbreaks likewise often arise from fear—fear of immediate physical harm, or of a broader threat to a cherished way of life. Anti-Catholicism is no exception to this rule. It thrives in eras when non-Catholics feel most vulnerable, when for instance they feel that an imminent political change is likely to expand Catholic power and aggression. Key examples would include the presidential elections of 1928 and 1960, or the era of intense gender conflict in the early 1990s, when liberals and feminists dreaded a legal and cultural counter-revolution.

At first sight, this should mean that explicitly political anti-Catholicism is likely to wane in coming years, since what have long been the critical hot-button issues simply no longer generate the kind of controversy they once did. Though the abortion question still generates powerful emotions, it is difficult to imagine any political circumstances under which either national party would seriously consider restricting or abolishing present rights. In the area of homosexuality too, the liberal position has largely established itself as part of the national consensus. No likely political realignment in 2004 or 2008 is going to result in any plausible threat to the legal status of these issues. And while AIDS is still a deadly menace, medical advances mean that the disease inspires nothing like the widespread social desperation it did in 1989. Politically, too, the moral authority of the Church stands at a very low ebb following the clergy abuse crisis. If anti-Catholicism is chiefly motivated by a sense that the Church is going to impose its policies on an unwilling American public, then it could be a long time before such fears again become a potent political force. The U.S. Catholic Church today may look less fearsome, less potentially intimidating, than at any point since before the mass immigration of the early nineteenth century.

Yet this lack of an obvious threat does not mean that anti-Catholic sentiments and activism are going to vanish anytime soon, since a host of new potential issues and grievances are already emerging. Anyone who hoped that anti-Catholicism might fade in the new political environment would be deeply disappointed by the remarkable anti-Church hostility demonstrated during the recent explosion of stories of sexual abuse by clergy. This affair indicates how dramatically the sources of modern anti-Catholicism differ from previous years. Today, the main concern is less that the Church will oppress outsiders than that the hierarchy exercises an unjust and insensitive rule over its own members. The principal force driving modern anti-Catholicism is divisions within the Church itself, and the ferocious anti-clericalism that has accumulated during decades of strife among Catholics. Nobody expects that these internal Church controversies will fade away, and reforming zeal has if anything been galvanized by the battering the hierarchy has recently received. Internal Church critics will continue to produce vigorous anti-clerical polemics, which will be adopted and magnified by external enemies.

Also, as we have seen, anti-Catholic assumptions have become deeply rooted among substantial sections of the public. Since the emergence of the new liberal anti-Catholicism in the late 1970s, a whole generation has grown up regarding these opinions as normal and customary, a familiar part of the social landscape for anyone born since about 1970. Of course bishops hate women and gays, priests molest children, and the Church supported the Holocaust: everybody knows that. These prejudices are particularly entrenched in the mass media, so powerfully that they are scarcely even recognized as prejudices. The ideas are in place, ready to be mobilized with very little provocation.

Future Moralities

Also, perhaps the politics of fear are not quite as extinct as they appear. Over time, we see substantial shifts in the politics of morality. As new issues emerge, it is likely that the Catholic Church will continue to be portrayed as the unreasoning enemy of progress and freedom, and demonized accordingly. As feminists and gay activists have both learned to their advantage in the last quarter-century, the more an issue can be portrayed in terms of secular freedom versus religious dogma, the easier it is to claim for oneself the political middle ground. To take a recent example, most Americans know little about the debate over research into embryonic stem cells. However, they are likely to favor such research if the political conflict is framed in terms of a conflict between irrational Catholic dogma and the health of the severely disabled. By making it seem that opposition to any policy is chiefly associated with Catholic bishops, activists of many stripes can place themselves in the position of advocates of progress, personal freedom, and the separation of church and state.

These moral shifts are especially obvious in matters of gay rights. While thirty years ago, the core issue was the legal status of homosexual behavior as such, in future years political divisions may well involve still more sensitive topics such as gay marriage and adoption. Issues involving homosexuality and children are likely to become central. Since the 1960s, a substantial majority of Americans has come to accept the libertarian view that homosexuality is a matter for consenting adults, whose freedom should not be impaired. Even so, many who hold liberal positions on this question are more dubious about possible relationships between gay adults and children, and are deeply suspicious of the concept of gay "initiation." Apart from traditional stereotypes linking homosexuality to child molestation, there are genuine concerns that contact with adult homosexuals may influence impressionable youngsters to adopt that sexual lifestyle. (An influential school of thought holds that homosexual identity is predetermined at birth, by genetics or other factors, but the question is far from settled.) Apart from the question of whether gays should be allowed to adopt, this nervousness generates widespread public concern about the role of homosexuals in such sensitive roles as teachers and scoutmasters.[1]

These child-related issues will be pivotal to future debates over discrimination laws and the broader question of gay rights. As the concept of fundamental legal rights escalates, we may expect intensified opposition to organized groups that criticize or threaten to reverse those rights, and that will mean, primarily, the Roman Catholic Church. As in the past, prejudice will be stimulated by fear—in this case, though, the fear of the loss of rights that hardly exist at present.

With some confidence, we can also predict the substance of future anti-Catholic campaigns, which will inevitably draw on the memory of recent scandals and canards. The rhetoric of prejudice is dynamic and cumulative. If, as seems likely, gay and feminist causes continue to stir anti-Catholic agitation, then almost certainly the Church will be attacked in terms of its alleged connivance at political tyranny (the shade of Pius XII), and especially its tolerance of pedophile priests. The two issues seem to be connected through the common themes of secrecy, cover-up, and conspiratorial Church elites. If indeed the major morality debates in coming years concern children and child protection, then liberals are likely to discredit Catholic positions by referring to the threatening image of the "pedophile priest." Already, we can envisage the rhetoric of political controversy: how can Bishop X say that gays are a threat to children when his priests are likely to be pedophiles themselves? First cast the beam from your own eye. We can confidently expect

continuing outbreaks of "priest pedophilia" stories, images and cartoons, all recycling the fundamental nativist notion of the perverted celibate priest. These stories will be kept alive by ongoing civil lawsuits,
which should continue for many years to come.

It would be surprising, too, if within the next few years the concern
about child protection did not lead to pressure on the traditional notion
of the secrecy of the confessional and the related question of clergy privilege. In many American states, child protection laws mandate the reporting of abuse by professionals, without acknowledging an exemption for
clergy. Technically, this could mean that a Catholic priest could be prosecuted for failing to report a crime discovered in the confessional, but no
jurisdiction hitherto has dared to enforce such a controversial law. This
may well change as legislators become more hostile to church authorities
and more suspicious that they are concealing abusers within their own
ranks. In the aftermath of the abuse scandals in the Boston archdiocese
in 2002, the Massachusetts legislature was discussing an extraordinary
law that would make employers criminally liable for negligence if their
employees carried out acts of child abuse. The obvious target was the
Catholic Church, which was believed to tolerate abuse by its priests.[2]

Meanwhile, the Massachusetts attorney general's office had decided that
the abuse problem was so rife in the church that it would have to be subjected to some kind of secular supervision. Under such a scheme, state
authorities would exercise "sweeping influence in the way the church re-
cruits, trains, and monitors priests." (Needless to say, such proposals were
immediately criticized for demolishing the walls separating church and
state.) It would not be too large a step from such proposals to an outright attack on the confidentiality of confession, and at that point we could expect a
major church-state conflict. Any Church resistance to expanding mandatory reporting would be presented as part of continuing clerical denial or
cover-up: why are the bishops trying to protect child molesters? In this
event, images of clerical sexual deviance would be rife in the mass media.[3]

| After the Third Vatican Council

The persistence of anti-Catholicism is not difficult to foresee. Can we,
though, imagine circumstances in which this tradition might vanish?
Since Catholicism is so dependent on events at its Roman heart, and so
much depends on the attitudes of any given Pope, we can hardly predict
the shape of the religion in ten or twenty years. By all present signs and
portents, the conservative cast brought to the church by Pope John Paul
II looks as if it will continue for a good many years to come, and so, presumably, will liberal resistance.

But for the sake of a thought exercise, let us imagine that a new Pope initiates a series of radical changes that eliminate the key cultural markers that currently distinguish American Catholics from non-Catholics. As a result of a hypothetical Third Vatican Council, the church permits married priests, ordains women, and ends its opposition to abortion, contraception, and homosexuality. The American church attains a high degree of independence from Roman authority, so that the Pope is demoted to a symbolic focus of unity rather than a monarch. In other words, the church substantially becomes a mainline Protestant denomination. Surely at that point anti-Catholicism would end, simply because nothing remains to oppose. Everyone would live happily ever after.

Even in such radically changed circumstances, though, the anti-Catholic tradition probably would not disappear, although it would be transformed, much as the changes of Vatican II altered the nature of prejudice in that generation without actually ending the phenomenon. Of course, conservatives and traditionalists would attack the new church quite fiercely, and might even use supernatural or apocalyptic imagery, portraying the church reformers in the guise of the Antichrist and the Whore of Babylon. Such rhetoric, though, would not have much impact in the secular mainstream.[4]

Much more significant in perpetuating religious prejudice would be continuing conflict in ethnic Catholic communities, a fact that should become ever more significant in coming decades. As the U.S. population diversifies rapidly, so we can expect religious divisions that currently exist in Latin America or Asia to become an ever more familiar part of religious controversy within this country.

As a consequence of mass immigration, the character of the American population is changing rapidly, and so, of necessity, are its religious foundations. As Martin Marty observed in the 1970s, ethnicity is the skeleton of American religion. By the mid-twenty-first century, a quarter of Americans could well claim Hispanic roots, and they will then constitute one of the world's largest Latino societies, more populous than any actual Hispanic nation with the exception of Mexico or Brazil. No less than one-eighth of all Americans will claim Mexican ancestry. A further 8 percent of Americans will be of Asian stock. California is already a "majority-minority" state, in which no single group represents an overall majority, and Texas will share this status within a couple of years. In both cases, Latino populations are growing very rapidly.[5]

The fastest-growing ethnic groups in the United States usually boast a Catholic heritage, including Latin Americans, of course, but also Asian groups such as Filipinos and Vietnamese. Yet for decades, this Catholicism has been under severe challenge from Protestant and Pentecostal churches, which have made significant inroads into Latino communities. This conflict for the hearts and souls of traditionally Catholic populations is likely to rage for decades to come, and regardless of the changes made by our hypothetical Third Vatican Council, the struggle will certainly involve forthright attacks on Catholic belief and institutions.

Already in much of Latin America, Protestant-Catholic conflicts often involve traditional religious anti-Catholicism of a sort that went out of fashion among Anglo-Americans half a century since. Pentecostals attack cherished symbols such as figures of the Virgin, and extremists shock the faithful by public attacks on images of Mary, both verbal insults and actual vandalism. In areas of Brazil, Peru, and Mexico, iconoclasm in the best medieval style still flourishes. This tactic is all the more powerful because Latino Catholicism retains a strong veneration for the Virgin of a sort that has largely gone out of favor among U.S. Anglos. In addition, Protestants and Pentecostals resort to that old standby, the Book of Revelation, to characterize the Roman Church, which is seen as a literal tool of Satan. Latinos also have their own distinctive traditions of anti-clerical imagery from which to draw. Recently, Latino Pentecostals in the United States have begun to deploy the "pedophile priest" charge against their Catholic neighbors, to demonstrate the evils of clericalism. As the United States becomes ever more diverse ethnically, these various religious wars cannot be dismissed solely as a matter for a Latino "fringe," when that fringe accounts for a quarter of the population—and a quarter of the electorate.[6]

Even if the Church were tomorrow to resolve all the grievances of Anglo liberals and feminists, anti-Catholicism would not vanish. Though the imaginary reform might end the organized dissidence from these liberal groups, the shifting ethnic balance within the church will presumably unleash new tensions as Latinos and Asians demand appropriate representation within the ranks of the senior clergy. Such ethnic conflict would be quite capable of generating the kind of internal feuds that spill over into the secular media and that justify the familiar stories about conspiratorial and repressive clergy. Recall parallel situations that have occurred with earlier waves of Catholic immigration, when Irish and German Catholics stood in opposition to each other, or when insurgent Italians and Slavs protested the Irish hold on the Church hierarchy.[7]

In addition, however liberalized it was in its sexual attitudes, an evermore Latinized U.S. church could well become a primary target of hostility from other ethnic groups. As we have seen, anti-Catholicism has often been closely related to ethnic and specifically anti-Latin prejudice. Already, the disastrous decline in the number of American priests has forced the hierarchy to seek desperate solutions, and this has led to a greater reliance on priests imported from other parts of the world in which vocations are still flourishing, including Latin America, Africa, and Southeast Asia. If this trend continues, the U.S. Catholic clergy will have a strongly foreign complexion, which will sustain old charges that the Church is fundamentally alien and un-American.

For many reasons, anti-Catholicism might well survive even "Vatican III."

A Kind of Solution

The endurance of this particular antagonism may suggest that there is something deeply flawed about Catholicism itself that it inevitably arouses so much opposition, both within its ranks and beyond. In fact, like other forms of prejudice, the hatred can persist however its target changes, or even if the target exists. Around the world, anti-Semitism rages in many countries where there are few or no Jews, including East Asian lands like Japan and South Korea, where Jews are known chiefly as literary figures. Anti-Semitism flourishes in these circumstances because it provides a useful demon figure, and often because it is associated with a particular style of stubborn militancy that some find attractive, even romantic. Only a decade or so ago, North America possessed a flourishing movement dedicated to fighting the nonexistent problems of cult Satanism and ritual child abuse.

With anti-Catholicism, similarly, the ideas and the rhetoric are so powerful that they can flourish even when they are not directed against specific living targets. Nativist political movements commonly flourished most heartily in areas where Catholics were known only by distant repute. In modern times, prejudice is often directed less at specific local individuals than against distant figures who are known only in highly stylized versions. Many of the harshest critics of Pope John Paul II or Cardinal O'Connor in the 1990s knew or cared little about the detailed views held by these luminaries, but rather chose to identify them as human symbols of religious repression and sexual hypocrisy. If the individuals had not existed, they would have been invented, and in a sense they were indeed invented—or at least transformed from anything like their real characters.

Demon figures are simply useful, if not essential. We might think of Constantine Cavafy's poem "Waiting for the Barbarians," which imagines an ancient city preparing for the arrival of fearsome barbarians, who will destroy the ancient way of life. Finally, though, the citizens are shocked to hear that the barbarians will not in fact be arriving, and may never have existed in the first place. This is appalling news: "What will become of us without barbarians? / At least those people were a kind of solution." Liberal, gay, and feminist politics in the last two decades would have been utterly different without their own barbarians, nightmare images of the "religious right" such as the Pope and the cardinal.[8]

The problem is that when vilification is heaped upon these stereotyped "barbarians," it is also, however unwittingly, directed against a large number of ordinary people whose religious faith is insulted and demeaned. Many of these people suffer real offense and either complain openly or, perhaps worse, simply assume that such abuse is the natural order of things, so protests are futile. Looking at recent controversies over issues such as art exhibits, it probably is true that protests are counter-productive, since they do not prevent the displays but do give the media rich opportunities for a new wave of vilification. The political lesson is deeply unsavory.

The liberal stereotyping of Catholicism is all the more unfortunate because the real, living people, lay and clerical, who make up the Catholic community are in many ways a natural constituency for so many of the basic beliefs shared by liberals and feminists. As we have seen, on most political issues the American Catholic Church stands clearly on the left-liberal end of the political spectrum. Traditionally, Catholicism has been sympathetic to communitarian values and suspicious of unchecked capitalism; the Church hierarchy tends to like activist government and is nervous about militarism. Even so, liberal politicians fail to exploit these potential alliances. To take a specific event from recent history, the Clinton administration might well have succeeded in establishing a national health care system in 1993–94 if it had been able to enlist the support of the Catholic bishops. The bishops were all in favor of the scheme, as long as it did not include provision for abortion, and so were leading Catholic politicians such as Pennsylvania's Governor Casey. Yet the Democratic commitment to the abortion issue was so strong, the fear of Catholic domination so vivid, that any compromise with the church was unthinkable. Health care reforms thus foundered. We can echo Peter Viereck's exhortation of half a century ago, when he urged American liberals to explore the values that they shared with Catholics in opposition to secular materialism and consumerism.[9]

Anti-Catholic sentiment may simply be too deeply entrenched to eliminate in a decade or a lifetime, but this does not mean that it should simply be ignored. The greatest single achievement might be to acknowledge its existence and to treat it as a form of prejudice quite as pernicious as any other. As Andrew Greeley wrote in 1977, "It is fashionable, almost *de rigueur* now, to articulate, objectify and expiate the racist, sexist and anti-Semitic feelings one might have had in the past; but there is rather little propensity to do the same thing on the subject of anti-Catholic Nativism."[10] The intervening years have made this remark even more apposite. In the news media especially, it would be wonderful if writers dealing with Catholic themes would examine their work just long enough to see if they were recycling ancient stereotypes, in much the same way they should if writing about Jews, blacks, or other once-despised groups. Otherwise, Catholics will continue to be subjected to a particularly blatant double standard.

Notes

Abbreviations

BG	*Boston Globe*
CT	*Christianity Today*
LAT	*Los Angeles Times*
NYT	*New York Times*
SFC	*San Francisco Chronicle*
USNWR	*U.S. News and World Report*
WP	*Washington Post*

Chapter 1

1. Daniel J. Goldhagen, "What Would Jesus Have Done?" *New Republic*, Jan. 21, 2002, 21–45; Tony Kushner, "Matthew's Passion," *The Nation*, Nov. 9, 1998, 24–27; Tony Kushner, "Reply," in "Impassioned Mail on Matthew," *The Nation*, Dec. 28, 1998, 22+. On the PBS news program *News Hour with Jim Lehrer*, a 1998 discussion of mandatory DNA testing for criminals discussed groups notoriously "at risk" for criminal behavior, namely, "teenagers, homeless people, Catholic priests." The remark went unchallenged, presumably because the show's producers felt it was self-evidently correct: http://www.pbs.org/newshour/bb/law/july-dec98/dna_7-10.html.

2. The director was Marshall Brickman. Rob Owen, "Hollywood Hypocrisy," *Pittsburgh Post-Gazette*, Jan. 20, 2001; Jack Shafer, "Don't Hate Andrew Sullivan Because He's Catholic," *Slate*, Mar. 13, 2000.

3. Kushner, "Reply"; Andrew Greeley, *An Ugly Little Secret* (Kansas City, MO: Sheed Andrews and McMeel, 1977), 1.

4. Robert Goss, *Jesus Acted Up* (San Francisco: HarperSanFrancisco, 1993), 147.

5. Mark Steyn, "Vandals in the Churchyard," *American Spectator*, May 2000, 52–54.

6. "Denver Radio Station Apologizes to Muslims," *The Christian Century*, Apr. 17, 1996, 424.

7. Peter Viereck, *Shame and Glory of the Intellectuals* (Boston: Beacon Press, 1953), 45.

8. Robert Royal, *Catholic Martyrs of the Twentieth Century* (New York: Crossroad / Herder and Herder, 2000).

9. Greeley, *An Ugly Little Secret*, 107.

10. George Weigel, "The New Anti-Catholicism," *Commentary*, June 1992, 25.

11. For the annulment controversy, see Robert H. Vasoli, *What God Has*

Joined Together (New York: Oxford University Press, 1998). Donohue is quoted from Michael Paulson, "Catholic Leaders Hit Coverage," *BG*, Apr. 20, 2002. For Voice of the Faithful, see Michael Paulson, "Lay Catholics Issue Call to Transform their Church," *BG*, July 21, 2002; Paulson, "Push is on to Quell Voice of Faithful," *BG*, August 17, 2002. The organization has a website at http://www.votf.org/.

12. Michelangelo Signorile, "The Gay-Bashing Pope," *New York Press*, Nov. 20, 2001; Signorile, "The Real American Taliban," *New York Press*, Jan. 1, 2002; Kimberly Blaker in *San Francisco Examiner*, Sept. 20, 2001, quoted in http://www.catholicleague.org/01press_releases/pr0301.htm.

13. "Sharon Schools Ignore Bashing of Catholics," *Massachusetts News*, Dec. 12, 2001.

14. Jose M. Sanchez, *Anticlericalism* (South Bend, IN: University of Notre Dame Press, 1972); Peter A. Dykema, and Heiko A. Oberman, eds., *Anti-clericalism in Late Medieval and Early Modern Europe* (Leiden: E. J. Brill, 1993); S. J. Barnett, *Idol Temples and Crafty Priests* (London: Macmillan, 1999).

15. Laura Miller, "The New Victimology," *Salon*, Feb. 17, 2001; Eleanor Heartney, "Postmodern Heretics," *Art in America*, Feb. 1997, 32–39.

16. Jeff Sharlet, "Battle Lines in the Jesus Wars," *Chronicle of Higher Education*, May 11, 2001.

17. Philip Jenkins, "Anti-Popery on the Welsh Marches in the Seventeenth Century," *Historical Journal* 23, 2 (1980): 275–93.

18. Rosemary Radford Ruether, "The Mantra of 'Anti-Catholicism,'" online at http://www.cath4choice.org/conscience/archived/AntiCatholicism.htm; Frances Kissling, "Bully in the Pulpit," *The Nation*, Mar. 12, 2001; Frank Owen, "The Myth of Catholic Bashing," *The Village Voice*, Oct. 26, 1999, 52–55.

19. James Carroll, *Constantine's Sword* (Boston: Houghton Mifflin, 2001): "the inhuman idea," 587; "The coming of Jesus," 585; "Christian proclamation," 567. Compare James Carroll, *Toward a New Catholic Church* (Boston: Houghton Mifflin, 2002).

20. Robert P. Lockwood, "Constantine's Sword: A Review Article," http://www.catholicleague.org/research/constantine.htm.

21. Donald A. Downs, *The New Politics of Pornography* (Chicago: University of Chicago Press, 1989); Catherine A. MacKinnon, *Only Words* (Cambridge: Harvard University Press, 1996).

22. This particular example is taken from the hate speech code at St. Edward's University, Austin, Texas, but it is quite representative: http://www.stedwards.edu/hum/drummond/hc5.html.

23. Deanna M. Garrett, "Silenced Voices: Hate Speech Codes on Campus," online at http://www.uvm.edu/~vtconn/journals/1999/garrett.htm.

24. *R.A.V. v. City of St. Paul* (90–7675), *505 U.S. 377* (1992).

25. Valerie Jenness and Ryken Grattet, *Making Hate a Crime* (New York: Russell Sage Foundation, 2001).

26. James B. Jacobs and Kimberly Potter, *Hate Crimes* (New York: Oxford University Press, 1998); Valerie Jenness and Kendal Broad, *Hate Crimes* (Haw-

thorne, NY: Aldine de Gruyter, 1997); Steyn, "Vandals in the Churchyard"; Kenneth Reich, "Man Held in Religious Hate Crimes," *LAT,* Nov. 7, 2001.

27. Steyn, "Vandals in the Churchyard."

28. David H. Bennett, *The Party of Fear,* 2d ed. (New York: Random House, 1995).

29. Joel Best, *Threatened Children* (University of Chicago Press, 1990); Philip Jenkins, *Intimate Enemies* (Hawthorne, NY: Aldine De Gruyter, 1992); Erich Goode and Nachman Ben-Yehuda, *Moral Panics* (Oxford: Blackwell, 1994); Philip Jenkins, *Using Murder* (Hawthorne, NY: Aldine De Gruyter, 1994); Joel Best, ed., *Images of Issues,* rev. ed. (Hawthorne, NY: Aldine de Gruyter, 1995); Patricia A. Adler and Peter Adler, *Constructions of Deviance,* 2d ed. (Belmont, CA: Wadsworth, 1997).

30. Rick Hinshaw, "Anti-Catholicism Today," *The Priest,* Feb. 2000, 14–22; James Martin, "The Last Acceptable Prejudice?" *America,* Mar. 25, 2000, 9; Mark S. Massa, "The New and Old Anti-Catholicism and the Analogical Imagination," *Theological Studies* 62, 3 (2001): 549–70.

31. Recognition of the problem seems to be stirring. In May 2002, New York City's Fordham University was the setting for an important conference on the theme of "Anti-Catholicism: The Last Acceptable Prejudice?"

Chapter 2

1. John Higham, *Strangers in the Land* (New Brunswick, NJ: Rutgers University Press, 1955); Ray Allen Billington, *The Protestant Crusade 1800–1860,* originally published 1938 (Gloucester, MA: Peter Smith, 1963); Michael Schwartz, *The Persistent Prejudice* (Huntington, IN: Our Sunday Visitor, 1984); Mark J. Hurley, *The Unholy Ghost* (Huntington, IN: Our Sunday Visitor, 1992); David H. Bennett, *The Party of Fear,* 2d ed. (New York: Random House, 1995); Robert P. Lockwood, ed., *Anti-Catholicism in American Culture* (Huntington, IN: Our Sunday Visitor, 2000).

2. *The Trial of the Pope of Rome: The Antichrist, or man of sin … for high treason against the son of God,* 2d Amer. ed. (Boston: Tappan and Dennet, 1844).

3. Karl Keating, *Catholicism and Fundamentalism* (San Francisco: Ignatius Press, 1988); Keating, *The Usual Suspects* (San Francisco: Ignatius Press, 2000). The Bob Jones quote is taken from "News Analysis: Bush and Bigotry," at http://uspolitics.about.com/library/weekly/aa040800a.htm. Compare http://www.bju.edu/faith/vol9num6/movement.html; Dave Hunt, *A Woman Rides the Beast* (Eugene, OR: Harvest House, 1994).

4. For the debate following the evangelical-Catholic concordat, see, for instance, http://www.fundamentalbiblechurch.org/Foundation/fbcecta2.htm; http://www.swrb.com/newslett/actualnls/0_Shipwr.htm; http://aomin.org/Evangelicals_and_Catholics_Together.html.

5. Denis G. Paz, *Popular Anti-Catholicism in Mid-Victorian England* (Stanford: Stanford University Press, 1992); Raymond D. Tumbleson, *Catholicism in the English Protestant Imagination* (Cambridge: Cambridge University Press,

1998); Frances E. Dolan, *Whores of Babylon* (Ithaca, NY: Cornell University Press, 1999).

6. Linda Colley, *Britons* (New Haven: Yale University Press, 1992); Marjule Anne Drury, "Anti-Catholicism in Germany, Britain, and the United States," *Church History* 70, 1 (2001): 98–131.

7. John Webster, *The Duchess of Malfi*, act 1, scene 2, line 70.

8. Norman Cohn, *Warrant for Genocide*, new ed. (London: Serif, 1996); Frances E. Dolan, "Ashes and the Archive," *Journal of Medieval and Early Modern Studies* 31 (2001): 379–408.

9. F. Tupper Saussy, *Rulers of Evil* (New York: HarperCollins, 2001); Mark Rotella, in *Publishers Weekly*, June 25, 2001, 66.

10. Nigel Aston and Matthew Cragoe, eds., *Anticlericalism in Britain c. 500–1914* (Phoenix Mill, UK: Sutton Publishing 2001); Thomas M. Brown, "The Image of the Beast: Anti-Papal Rhetoric in Colonial America," in Richard D. Curry and Thomas Brown, eds., *Conspiracy: The Fear of Subversion in American History* (New York: Holt, Rinehart and Winston, 1972), 1–20.

11. Samuel F. B. Morse, *Foreign Conspiracy Against the Liberties of the United States* (New York: Leavitt, Lord; Boston: Crocker and Brewster, 1835); William C. Brownlee, *Popery: An Enemy to Civil and Religious Liberty and Dangerous to Our Republic* (New York: John S. Taylor, 1836); Carleton Beals, *Brass-Knuckle Crusade* (New York: Hastings House, 1960). The Know-Nothing statement is quoted in Lawrence P. Creedon and William D. Falcon, *United for Separation* (Milwaukee, WI: Bruce, 1959), 23.

12. This cartoon can be found in Charles Morris, *American Catholic* (New York: Times Books, 1997), 66. For other visual images see David Morgan, *Protestants and Pictures* (New York: Oxford University Press, 1999), 93–107.

13. Roger Lane, *Policing the City* (New York: Atheneum, 1967); Jenny Franchot, *Roads to Rome* (Berkeley: University of California Press, 1994).

14. Stephen Jay Gould, *The Mismeasure of Man*, rev. ed. (New York: Norton, 1996); Noel Ignatiev, *How the Irish Became White* (New York: Routledge, 1995); Philip Jenkins, "Eugenics, Crime and Ideology," *Pennsylvania History* 51, 1 (1984): 64–78; William T. Root and G. T. Giardini, *A Psychological and Educational Survey of 1916 Prisoners in the Western Penitentiary of Pennsylvania* (Pittsburgh: Board of Trustees of the Western Penitentiary, 1927).

15. *Baltimore Catechism*, questions 514–15, online at http://bible.crosswalk.com/History/AD/CreedsandConfessions/Catechisms/bcc.cgi?lesson=11.

16. Philip Jenkins, *Hoods and Shirts* (Chapel Hill: University of North Carolina Press, 1997).

17. Lyman Beecher, *A Plea for the West* (Cincinnati, OH: Truman and Smith; New York: Leavitt, Lord, 1835), 60.

18. Philip Jenkins, *Mystics and Messiahs* (New York: Oxford University Press, 2000), 28–30; *Harvard Journal*, Apr. 16, 1934.

19. Morris, *American Catholic*, 99–111; Emmett McLoughlin, *American Culture and Catholic Schools* (New York: Lyle Stuart, 1960); Michael Zöller, *Washington and Rome* (South Bend, IN: University of Notre Dame Press, 1999).

20. "To make any boy wonder" is from Marcus Bach, *They Have Found a Faith* (Indianapolis, IN: Bobbs-Merrill, 1946), 14; Donald L. Kinzer, *An Episode in Anti-Catholicism* (Seattle: University of Washington Press, 1964); Mark Wahlgren Summers, *Rum, Romanism, and Rebellion* (Chapel Hill: University of North Carolina Press, 2000).

21. Harold Frederic, *The Damnation of Theron Ware* (New York: Penguin Classics, 1986), 49; Kevin Kenny, *Making Sense of the Molly Maguires* (New York: Oxford University Press, 1998).

22. Jenkins, *Hoods and Shirts*, 67–69, 80; Paul M. Winter, *What Price Tolerance?* (Hewlett, NY: All-American Book, Lecture and Research Bureau, 1928).

23. Edmund A. Moore, *A Catholic Runs for President* (New York: Ronald Press, 1956); Robert A. Slayton, *Empire Statesman* (New York: Free Press, 2001).

24. John T. McGreevy, "Thinking On One's Own," *Journal of American History* 84, 1 (1997): 97–131.

25. John William Draper, *History of the Conflict Between Religion and Science*, 5th ed. (New York: D. Appleton, 1875), preface; Jeffrey Burton Russell, *Inventing the Flat Earth* (Westport, CT: Praeger, 1991); Stephen Jay Gould, *Rocks of Ages* (New York: Ballantine, 1999).

26. David J. O'Brien, *American Catholics and Social Reform* (New York: Oxford University Press, 1968); George Q. Flynn, *American Catholics and the Roosevelt Presidency 1932–1936* (Lexington: University of Kentucky Press, 1968); Jenkins, *Hoods and Shirts*, 78; Kenneth J. Heineman, *A Catholic New Deal* (University Park: Pennsylvania State University Press, 1999); Douglas P. Seaton, *Catholics and Radicals* (Lewisburg, PA: Bucknell University Press, 1981).

27. Mark J. Hurley, *The Unholy Ghost* (Huntington, IN: Our Sunday Visitor, 1992).

28. Leonard Dinnerstein, *Anti-Semitism in America* (New York: Oxford University Press, 1994); Donald Warren, *Radio Priest* (New York: Free Press, 1996); Jenkins, *Hoods and Shirts*, 165–91; Egal Feldman, *Catholics and Jews in Twentieth-Century America* (Urbana: University of Illinois Press, 2001); Annette Thackwell Johnson, "The Christian Front in Pittsburgh," *Equality*, Nov. 1939, 30–31; John L. Spivak, *Shrine of the Silver Dollar* (New York: Modern Age Books, 1940). For Boston, see James M. O'Toole, *Militant and Triumphant* (South Bend, IN: University of Notre Dame Press, 1992), 247–48; John Gunther, *Inside USA*, rev. ed. (New York: Harper, 1951), 529–30. One of the best accounts of urban Coughlinite militancy in these years can be found in Norman Mailer's 1948 novel *The Naked and the Dead* (New York: Henry Holt, 1998).

29. George Seldes, *The Catholic Crisis* (New York: J. Messner, 1939); Seldes, *Lords of the Press* (New York: Blue Ribbon, 1941), 166–70; "Notable Events in the Church in America During 1938," *Catholic Standard and Times* (Philadelphia), Jan. 6, 1939, 5.

30. George Q. Flynn, *Roosevelt and Romanism* (Westport, CT: Greenwood, 1976); Jenkins, *Hoods and Shirts*, 192–207.

31. Morris, *American Catholic*, 195; Donald F. Crosby, *Battlefield Chaplains* (Lawrence: University Press of Kansas, 1994); Mark S. Massa, *Catholics and American Culture* (New York: Crossroad, 1999), 38–56; Christopher Owen Lynch, *Selling Catholicism* (Lexington: University Press of Kentucky, 1998); Thomas C. Reeves, *America's Bishop* (San Francisco: Encounter Books, 2001).

32. Peter Viereck, *Shame and Glory of the Intellectuals* (Boston: Beacon Press, 1953), 228.

33. Paul Blanshard, *American Freedom and Catholic Power* (originally published 1949), rev. ed. (Boston: Beacon, 1958): "on the Catholic public school," 125; "for the revival of anti-Catholic feeling," 79.

34. Blanshard, *American Freedom and Catholic Power*, 52; Paul Blanshard, *Personal and Controversial* (Boston: Beacon Press, 1973); Martin E. Marty, *Modern American Religion: Under God Indivisible 1941–1960* (Chicago: University of Chicago Press, 1996), 158–68.

35. Blanshard, *American Freedom and Catholic Power*, 212; see also Paul Blanshard, *The Right to Read* (Boston: Beacon Press, 1955).

36. Blanshard, *American Freedom and Catholic Power*: "Roman-controlled priests," 3; "an autocratic moral monarchy," 14; "The American Catholic problem," 325; "a colonial dependency," 341. See also Paul Blanshard, *Freedom and Catholic Power in Spain and Portugal* (Boston: Beacon Press, 1962); Blanshard, *The Irish and Catholic Power* (Boston: Beacon Press, 1953).

37. Blanshard, *American Freedom and Catholic Power*, 302–5.

38. Ibid., 346.

39. Ibid., 152–54.

40. Ibid., 70, 180–84, "monstrosities," 149.

41. Creedon and Falcon, *United for Separation*; Thomas Carty, "The Catholic Question," *Historian* 63, 3 (2001): 577.

42. The language of "Inquisition" in the context of Red-hunting somewhat predated McCarthy, but proliferated after his rise. See Dalton Trumbo, *The Time of the Toad: A Study of Inquisition in America by One of the Hollywood Ten* (Hollywood: Hollywood Ten, 1949); Alvah Bessie, *Inquisition in Eden* (New York: Macmillan, 1965); Cedric Belfrage, *The American Inquisition, 1945–1960* (Indianapolis: Bobbs-Merrill, 1973); Larry Ceplair and Steven Englund, *The Inquisition in Hollywood* (Garden City, NY : Anchor Press/ Doubleday, 1980); Stanley I. Kutler, *The American Inquisition* (New York: Hill and Wang, 1982); Athan G. Theoharis and John Stuart Cox, *The Boss: J. Edgar Hoover and the Great American Inquisition* (Philadelphia: Temple University Press, 1988); Griffin Fariello, *Red Scare: Memories of the American Inquisition* (New York: Norton, 1995); Donald F. Crosby, *God, Church, and Flag* (Chapel Hill: University of North Carolina Press, 1978); Paul Blanshard, *Communism, Democracy, and Catholic Power* (Boston: Beacon Press, 1951).

43. Philip Jenkins, *The Cold War at Home* (Chapel Hill: University of North Carolina Press, 1999), 181; Robert Moats Miller, *Bishop G. Bromley Oxnam— Paladin of Liberal Protestantism* (Nashville, TN: Abingdon Press, 1990); Francis Eugene Walter, *Chronicle of Treason: Committee on Un-American Activities,*

House of Representatives, 85th Congress, Second Session (Washington, DC: Government Printing Office, 1958).

44. James A. Michener, *Report of the County Chairman* (New York: Random House, 1961), 26–31; Mark Silk, *Spiritual Politics* (New York: Touchstone, 1988); Carty, "The Catholic Question."

45. Quoted by Carty, "The Catholic Question;" Blanshard, *American Freedom and Catholic Power*, 3.

46. Daniel Alfred Poling, *Mine Eyes Have Seen* (New York: McGraw-Hill, 1959); Francis B. Thornton, *Sea of Glory* (New York: Prentice Hall, 1953).

47. Mark S. Massa, *Catholics and American Culture* (New York: Crossroad, 1999), 3.

48. Michener, *Report of the County Chairman*, 61–62. Zöller, *Washington and Rome*; Thomas H. O'Connor, *Boston Catholics* (Boston: Northeastern University Press, 1998); Morris, *American Catholic*, 165–95; James M. O'Toole, *Militant and Triumphant* (South Bend, IN: University of Notre Dame Press, 1992); John Cooney, *The American Pope* (New York: Times Books, 1984); James F. Connally, ed., *The History of the Archdiocese of Philadelphia* (Philadelphia: Archdiocese of Philadelphia, 1976).

49. John Davis, "Catholic Envy," in David Morgan and Sally M. Promey, eds., *The Visual Culture of American Religions* (Berkeley: University of California Press, 2001), 105–28; Franchot, *It*, 120–26.

50. Mark Twain, *Letters from the Earth*, ed. Bernard DeVoto (New York: Perennial Library, 1974), 53; Charles Chiniquy, *Fifty Years in the Church of Rome* (Montreal: Drysdale, 1886).

51. David Brion Davis, "Some Themes of Counter-Subversion," in *From Homicide to Slavery* (New York: Oxford University Press, 1986), 137–54; Marie Anne Pagliarini, "The Pure American Woman and the Wicked Catholic Priest," *Religion and American Culture* 9, 1 (1999): 97–128; Tracy Fessenden, "The Convent, the Brothel, and the Protestant Woman's Sphere," *Signs* 25, 2 (2000): 451–78. For the role of Catholic defectors in exposing these alleged horrors, see David G. Bromley, ed., *The Politics of Religious Apostasy* (Westport, CT: Praeger, 1998).

52. *Awful Disclosures of Maria Monk* (Philadelphia: T.B. Peterson, n.d. [c. 1840]); Joseph McCabe, *The Truth About the Catholic Church* (Girard, KS: Haldeman Julius, 1926); for McCabe, see Bill Cooke, *A Rebel to His Last Breath* (Amherst, NY: Prometheus Books, 2001); Steven Marcus, *The Other Victorians* (London: Corgi, 1969), 62–63; Nancy L. Schultz, *Fire and Roses: The Burning of the Charlestown Convent, 1834* (New York: Free Press, 2000).

53. Lorraine Boettner, *Roman Catholicism*, 1st Brit. ed. (London: Banner of Truth Trust, 1966), 399; Emmett McLoughlin, *People's Padre* (Boston: Beacon, 1954); McLoughlin, *Crime and Immorality in the Catholic Church* (New York: Lyle Stuart, 1962).

54. Michener, *Report of the County Chairman*, 94.

Chapter 3

1. Andrew Greeley, *An Ugly Little Secret* (Kansas City, MO: Sheed Andrews and McMeel, 1977), 4.

2. Maurice Isserman, *The Other American* (New York: Public Affairs, 2000).

3. John C. Raines, ed., *Conspiracy* (New York: Harper and Row, 1974); Jack Nelson and Ronald J. Ostrow, *The FBI and the Berrigans* (New York: Coward, McCann and Geoghegan, 1972); William O'Rourke, *The Harrisburg Seven and the New Catholic Left* (New York: Crowell, 1972); John Cooney, *The American Pope* (New York: Times Books, 1984); William A. Au, *The Cross, the Flag, and the Bomb* (Westport, CT: Greenwood Press, 1985); Patrick J. McGeever, *Rev. Charles Owen Rice—Apostle of Contradiction* (Pittsburgh, PA: Duquesne University Press, 1989); Richard Hofstadter, *The Paranoid Style in American Politics* (Cambridge: Harvard University Press, 1996); Philip Berrigan, *Fighting the Lamb's War* (Monroe, ME: Common Courage Press, 1996); Peter Matthiessen, *Sal Si Puedes (Escape If You Can)* (Berkeley: University of California Press, 2000). For changing media coverage of religious news, see Benjamin J. Hubbard, ed., *Reporting Religion* (Sonoma, CA: Polebridge Press, 1990), particularly the essays by George W. Cornell, "The Evolution of the Religion Beat," 20–35, and Kenneth A. Briggs, "Why Editors Miss Important Religion Stories," 47–58; Judith M. Buddenbaum, *Reporting News About Religion* (Ames: Iowa State University Press, 1998). For changing media attitudes, see Mark Silk, *Unsecular Media* (Urbana: University of Illinois Press, 1995).

4. George A. Kelly, *The Battle for the American Church* (New York: Doubleday Image, 1981); Kelly, *The Battle for the American Church Revisited* (San Francisco: Ignatius Press, 1995).

5. John T. McGreevy, *Parish Boundaries* (Chicago: University of Chicago Press, 1998); Gerald H. Gamm, *Urban Exodus* (Cambridge: Harvard University Press, 2001); William L. O'Neill, *Coming Apart* (Chicago: Quadrangle Books, 1971); Jules Witcover, *The Year the Dream Died* (New York: Warner Books, 1998).

6. Dan T. Carter, *The Politics of Rage* (New York: Simon and Schuster, 1995); S. A. Paolantonio, *Frank Rizzo* (Philadelphia: Camino, 1993); Alan Wolfe, "Liberalism and Catholicism," *The American Prospect*, Jan. 31, 2000, 1116–21.

7. William B. Prendergast, *The Catholic Voter in American Politics* (Washington, DC: Georgetown University Press, 1999); Michael Zöller, *Washington and Rome* (South Bend, IN: University of Notre Dame Press, 1999).

8. Greeley, *An Ugly Little Secret*, 70.

9. Philip Jenkins, *Moral Panic* (New Haven: Yale University Press, 1998).

10. Patrick Allitt, *Catholic Intellectuals and Conservative Politics in America 1950–1985* (Ithaca, NY: Cornell University Press, 1993); Richard Viguerie, *The New Right* (Falls Church, VA: Viguerie, 1981).

11. Penny Lernoux, *Cry of the People* (Garden City, NY: Doubleday, 1980);

Au, *The Cross, the Flag, and the Bomb*; Anne Klejment and Nancy L. Roberts, ed., *American Catholic Pacifism* (Westport, CT: Praeger, 1996); Susan Bibler Coutin, *The Culture of Protest* (Boulder, CO: Westview Press, 1993); Wolfe, "Liberalism and Catholicism."

12. John Cornwell, *Breaking Faith* (New York: Viking, 2001); George Weigel, *The Final Revolution* (New York: Oxford University Press, 1992); Weigel, *Witness to Hope* (New York: Cliff Street Books, 1999); Gordon Urquhart, *The Pope's Armada* (Amherst, NY: Prometheus Books, 1999); Robert A. Hutchison, *Their Kingdom Come* (New York: St Martin's Press, 1999).

13. Gene Burns, *The Frontiers of Catholicism* (Berkeley: University of California Press, 1994); Edward Stourton, *Absolute Truth* (London: Penguin, 1999).

14. Bernard Goldberg, *Bias* (Washington, DC: Regnery Publishing, 2001).

15. John Cornwell, *A Thief in the Night* (New York: Penguin, 2001).

16. David Yallop, *In God's Name* (New York: Bantam, 1984); Nick Tosches, *Power on Earth* (New York: Arbor House, 1986); Richard Hammer, *The Vatican Connection* (New York: Holt, Rinehart and Winston, 1982).

17. Andrew Greeley, *The Cardinal Sins* (New York: Warner, 1981).

18. Kenneth A. Briggs, *Holy Siege* (San Francisco: Harper, 1992).

19. Jay P. Dolan, *In Search of an American Catholicism* (New York: Oxford University Press, 2002); Andrew Greeley, *The Catholic Imagination* (Berkeley: University of California Press, 2000); Robert Orsi, *Thank You, Saint Jude* (New Haven: Yale University Press, 1996).

20. Orsi, *Thank You, Saint Jude*; Timothy Kelly, "Our Lady of Perpetual Help, Gender Roles, and the Decline of Devotional Catholicism," *Journal of Social History* 32 (1998): 5–26.

21. Adrian Hastings, ed., *Modern Catholicism: Vatican II and After* (New York: Oxford University Press, 1991); Thomas Day, *Why Catholics Can't Sing* (New York: Crossroad, 1990). For a traditionalist analysis of the changes, see E. Michael Jones, *John Cardinal Krol and the Cultural Revolution* (South Bend, IN: Fidelity Press, 1995).

22. Kelly, "Our Lady of Perpetual Help." Even so, the decline of traditional devotions has not ended perceptions that Catholics are primitive idol-worshippers: a survey of non-Catholic Americans carried out in 2002 found that "83 percent said that instead of worshiping only God, Catholics also worship Mary and the saints, while 57 percent believed the statues and images in Catholic churches are idols." Alan Cooperman, "Anti-Catholic Views Common, Poll Shows," *WP*, May 24, 2002.

23. Gustav Niebuhr, "Getting Below Surface of U.S. Catholics' Beliefs," *NYT*, Apr. 13, 1996; Larry B. Stammer, "John Paul Encounters 2 Degrees of Faith," *LAT*, Jan. 26, 1999; Richard C. Dujardin, "Taken on Faith: Beliefs About the Eucharist Concern Catholic Church Leaders," Knight Ridder news service item, June 23, 2001; Peter Steinfels, "Many Young Catholics Stay with the Church Despite Disagreeing on Some Issues, a Study Finds," *NYT*, Aug. 25, 2001; Dean R. Hoge, William D. Dinges, Mary Johnson, and Juan L. Gonzales,

eds., *Young Adult Catholics* (South Bend, IN: University of Notre Dame Press, 2001).

24. Thomas Merton, *The Seven Storey Mountain* (New York: Harcourt, Brace, 1948); J. F. Powers, *The Stories of J. F. Powers* (New York: New York Review of Books, 2000).

25. David Rice, *Shattered Vows* (London: Michael Joseph, 1990); Tim Unsworth, *The Last Priests in America* (New York: Crossroad, 1991); Richard A. Schoenherr and Lawrence A. Young, *Full Pews and Empty Altars* (Madison: University of Wisconsin Press, 1994); Peter McDonough and Eugene C. Bianchi, *Passionate Uncertainty* (Berkeley: University of California Press, 2002); Helen Rose Fuchs Ebaugh, *Women in the Vanishing Cloister* (New Brunswick, NJ: Rutgers University Press, 1993); Lucy Kaylin, *For the Love of God* (New York: William Morrow, 2000).

26. David J. O'Brien, *From the Heart of the American Church* (Maryknoll, NY: Orbis Books, 1994); Philip Gleason, *Contending with Modernity* (New York: Oxford University Press, 1995); Kelly, *The Battle for the American Church*, 62–63.

27. Jim Bowman, *Bending the Rules* (New York: Crossroad, 1994); William V. D'Antonio, James D. Davidson, Dean R. Hoge, and Katherine Meyer, eds., *American Catholics: Gender, Generation, and Commitment* (Walnut Creek, CA: AltaMira Press, 2001).

28. William V. D'Antonio, James D. Davidson, Dean R. Hoge, and Ruth A. Wallace, eds., *Laity, American and Catholic* (Kansas City, MO: Sheed and Ward 1996); Thomas J. Ferraro, ed., *Catholic Lives, Contemporary America* (Durham, NC: Duke University Press, 1997); Michele Dillon, *Catholic Identity* (Cambridge: Cambridge University Press, 1999).

29. Mark S. Massa, *Catholics and American Culture* (New York: Crossroad, 1999) 174; Kelly, *The Battle for the American Church*; James Colaianni, *The Catholic Left* (Philadelphia: Chilton, 1968).

30. Anthony Kosnik et al., *Human Sexuality: New Directions in American Catholic Thought: A Study Commissioned by the Catholic Theological Society of America* (New York: Paulist Press, 1977), 214–15.

31. William W. May, ed, *Vatican Authority and American Catholic Dissent* (New York: Crossroad, 1987).

32. All the organizations listed here have an active presence on the Internet. See, for example, http://www.womensordination.org; http://www.futurechurch.org; http://www.women-churchconvergence.org; http://www.cta-usa.org (Call to Action); http://www.dignityusa.org; http://arcc-catholic-rights.org (Association for the Rights of Catholics in the Church).

33. Briggs, *Holy Siege*; Eugene C. Kennedy, *Tomorrow's Catholics / Yesterday's Church* (New York: Harper and Row, 1988); Mary Jo Leddy, Remi J. DeRoo, and Douglas Roche, *In the Eye of the Catholic Storm* (Toronto: HarperCollins, 1992); Terrance Sweeney, *A Church Divided* (Amherst, NY: Prometheus Books, 1992); Richard P. McBrien, *Report on the Church* (San Francisco: HarperSanFrancisco, 1992); Jim Naughton, *Catholics in Crisis* (New York: Penguin,

1997); Mary Jo Weaver, ed., *What's Left—Liberal American Catholics* (Bloomington: Indiana University Press, 1999); Joseph A. Varacalli, *Bright Promise, Failed Community* (Lanham, MD: Lexington Books, 2000).

34. Harry Sylvester, *Dearly Beloved* (New York: Duell, Sloan and Pearce, 1942); Harry Sylvester, *Dayspring* (New York and London: D. Appleton-Century, 1945); Harry Sylvester, *Moon Gaffney* (New York, H. Holt, 1947), "pietistic shysters," 210; "lacks both charity and humility," 263.

35. Paula M. Kane, *Separatism and Subculture* (Chapel Hill: University of North Carolina Press, 1994); Thomas H. O'Connor, *Boston Catholics* (Boston: Northeastern University Press, 1998); James T. Fisher, *The Catholic Counterculture in America, 1933–1962* (Chapel Hill: University of North Carolina Press, 1989).

36. James T. Farrell, *Studs Lonigan* (New York: Penguin Classics, 2001).

37. Paul Blanshard, *American Freedom and Catholic Power* (originally published 1949), rev. ed. (Boston: Beacon, 1958), 230.

38. Charles Morris, *American Catholic* (New York: Times Books, 1997), 177.

39. Philip Jenkins, *Pedophiles and Priests* (New York: Oxford University Press, 1996).

40. For a liberal response to the pedophile priest scandals, see Andrew Greeley, *Fall From Grace* (New York: G. P. Putnam, 1993); William D. Dinges and James Hitchcock, "Roman Catholic Traditionalism and Activist Conservatism in the United States," in Martin E. Marty and R. Scott Appleby, eds., *Fundamentalisms Observed* (Chicago: University of Chicago Press, 1994).

41. Andrew Sullivan, "The New Double Standard," *NYT Magazine*, Mar. 12, 2000, 28.

Chapter 4

1. Smeal is quoted from http://www.cath4choice.org/new/inthenews/032701 ProChoiceReligions.htm.

2. "Greeted with a Yawn," *The Advocate*, Sept. 21, 1993, 25; Joanna Manning, *Is the Pope Catholic?* (Toronto: Malcolm Lester Books, 1999; New York: Crossroad, 2000), 8.

3. Marina Warner, *Alone of All Her Sex* (New York: Vintage Books, 1983).

4. Philip Jenkins, *The Next Christendom* (New York: Oxford University Press, 2002).

5. Technically, the church only prohibits "artificial contraception," since it does permit the kind of birth regulation known as natural family planning. In this chapter, though, I will follow the common usage of "contraception," which includes the Pill as well as barrier devices. James Reed, *The Birth Control Movement and American Society: From Private Vice to Public Virtue* (Princeton: Princeton University Press, 1984); John T. Noonan Jr., *Contraception: A History of Its Treatment by the Catholic Theologians and Canonists* (Cambridge, MA: Belknap Press of Harvard University Press, 1986); Janet Farrell Brodie, *Contraception and Abortion in Nineteenth-Century America* (Ithaca, NY: Cornell University Press, 1994).

6. Paul Blanshard, *American Freedom and Catholic Power* (originally published 1949), rev. ed. (Boston: Beacon, 1958), 171; Ellen Chesler, *Woman of Valor* (New York: Simon and Schuster, 1992); Margaret Sanger, *My Fight for Birth Control* (New York: Farrar and Rinehart, 1931), 220; Cardinal Hayes is quoted from "Sanger, Censorship, and the Catholic Church," *Margaret Sanger Papers Project Newsletter 6*, winter 1993/94, at http://www.nyu.edu/projects/sanger/censor.htm.

7. Blanshard, *American Freedom and Catholic Power*: "important part of its sexual code," 164; "the greatest blunder in the history of the church," 169; "growing defiance," 170. The Greeley study is quoted in George A. Kelly, *The Battle for the American Church* (New York: Doubleday Image, 1981), 132–33.

8. Paul Ehrlich, *The Population Bomb* (New York: Ballantine Books, 1968); Donella H. Meadows et al., *The Limits to Growth* (New York: New American Library, 1974); Patrick Allitt, "American Catholics and the Environment, 1960–1995," *Catholic Historical Review* 84 (1998): 263–80.

9. Hans Lotstra, *Abortion: The Catholic Debate in America* (New York: Irvington, 1985); Flora Davis, *Moving the Mountain* (New York: Simon and Schuster, 1991); Marvin Olasky, *Abortion Rites* (Wheaton, IL: Crossways Books, 1992); Leslie J. Reagan, *When Abortion Was a Crime* (Berkeley: University of California Press, 1997); Rosemary Nossiff, *Before Roe* (Philadelphia: Temple University Press, 2001).

10. Mary Daly, "Abortion and Sexual Caste," *Commonweal*, Feb. 4, 1972, 415–419 (I owe this reference to Scott M. Williams); Mary Daly, *The Church and the Second Sex* (New York: Harper and Row, 1968); Daly, *Beyond God the Father* (Boston: Beacon, 1973).

11. James J. Diamond, "The Troubled Anti-Abortion Camp," *America*, Aug. 10, 1974, 52–54; Dallas A. Blanchard, *The Anti-Abortion Movement and the Rise of the Religious Right* (New York: Twayne Publishers 1994); Robert Booth Fowler and Allen D. Hertzke, *Religion and Politics in America* (Boulder, CO: Westview, 1995); Donald T. Critchlow, ed., *The Politics of Abortion and Birth Control in Historical Perspective* (University Park: Pennsylvania State University Press, 1996); Kerry N. Jacoby, *Souls, Bodies, Spirits* (Westport, CT: Praeger, 1998); Everett Carll Ladd and Karlyn H. Bowman, *Public Opinion About Abortion* (Washington, DC: AEI Press, 1997).

12. Cynthia L. Cooper, "Women's Services Cut as Catholic Hospitals Expand," at http://www.now.org/eNews/oct2000/102300catholic.html.

13. Kenneth L. Woodward, "Sex and the Church," *Newsweek*, Aug. 16, 1993, 38–41.

14. Toni Carabillo, Judith Meuli, and June Bundy Csida, *Feminist Chronicles, 1953–1993* (Los Angeles: Women's Graphics, 1993).

15. Ibid.

16. Ibid., for a chronology of protests. For the self-crowning, see "A Mouse That Roars Turns 25: An Interview with CFFC President Frances Kissling," http://www.cath4choice.org/spanish/aboutus2.htm. The California demonstrator is described by Don A. Schanche and Maura Dolan, "Pope Stresses

Varied Themes as He Moves Up the Coast," *LAT,* Sept. 18, 1987.

17. Lavinia Byrne, *Woman at the Altar* (New York: Continuum, 1999); Barbara Brown Zikmund, Adair T. Lummis, and Patricia M. Y. Chang, *Clergy Women* (Louisville, KY: Westminster John Knox Press, 1998); Mark Chaves, *Ordaining Women* (Cambridge: Harvard University Press, 1997); Paula D. Nesbitt, *Feminization of the Clergy in America* (New York: Oxford University Press, 1997); Catherine M. Prelinger, ed., *Episcopal Women* (New York: Oxford University Press, 1992); Mary Sudman Donovan, *Women Priests in the Episcopal Church* (Cincinnati, OH: Forward Movement, 1988).

18. Kelly, *Battle for the American Church,* 331. For ongoing debates about gender within American Catholicism, see for instance Paula Kane, Karen Kennelly, and James Kenneally, eds., *Gender Identities in American Catholicism* (Maryknoll, NY: Orbis Books, 2001); Kelley A. Raab, *When Women Become Priests* (New York: Columbia University Press, 2000); Byrne, *Woman at the Altar*; Jane Redmont, *Generous Lives* (New York: William Morrow, 1992); Ruth A. Wallace, *They Call Her Pastor* (Albany: State University of New York Press, 1992); Denise Lardner Carmody, *The Double Cross* (New York: Crossroad, 1986); Mary Jo Weaver, *New Catholic Women* (San Francisco: Harper, 1985); Andrew Greeley and Mary G. Durkin, *Angry Catholic Women* (Chicago: Thomas More Press, 1984).

19. Rosemary Radford Ruether, *Women-Church* (San Francisco: Harper, 1985); Donna Steichen, *Ungodly Rage* (San Francisco: Ignatius Press, 1991); Frances B. O'Connor and Becky S. Drury, *The Female Face in Patriarchy* (East Lansing: Michigan State University Press, 1999); http://www.women-churchconvergence.org.

20. Carabillo et al., *Feminist Chronicles.*

21. Ellen McCormack, *Cuomo vs. O'Connor* (Commack, NY: Dolores Press, 1985); Barbara Ferraro, Patricia Hussey, and Jane O'Reilly, *No Turning Back* (New York: Poseidon Press, 1990); Timothy A. Byrnes, *Catholic Bishops in American Politics* (Princeton, NJ: Princeton University Press, 1991). The *NYT* story is quoted from Mark J. Hurley, *The Unholy Ghost* (Huntington, IN: Our Sunday Visitor, 1992), 132.

22. Lawrence Lader, *Politics, Power and the Church* (New York: Macmillan 1987); George La Piana, John W. Swomley, and Herbert F. Vetter, eds., *Catholic Power vs. American Freedom* (Amherst, NY: Prometheus Books, 2002).

23. Ferraro et al., *No Turning Back.*

24. Philip Jenkins, "Fighting Terrorism as if Women Mattered," in Jeff Ferrell and Neil Websdale, eds, *Making Trouble* (Hawthorne, NY: Aldine De Gruyter, 1999), 319–46; Cynthia Gorney, *Articles of Faith* (New York: Simon and Schuster, 1998); Rickie Solinger, ed., *Abortion Wars* (Berkeley: University of California Press, 1998); Marian Faux, *Crusaders* (Secaucus, NJ: Birch Lane Press, 1990).

25. "Catholic League's 1995 Report on Anti-Catholicism," at http://www.catholicleague.org/1995report/activists95.htm.

26. These cartoons are discussed in Hurley, *Unholy Ghost.* Goodman is

quoted in George Weigel, "The New Anti-Catholicism," *Commentary*, June 1992, 25.

27. Robert P. Casey, *Fighting for Life* (Dallas: Word Publishing, 1996).

28. John Leo, "Here Come the Wild Creatures," *USNWR*, Oct. 19, 1992.

29. Susan Armstrong, "Sexual Abuse of Women and Girls by Clergy," *Canadian Women Studies 11*, 4 (1991); Angela Bonavoglia, "The Sacred Secret," *Ms.*, Mar.-Apr. 1992, 40–46; Paul Wilkes, "Priests Who Prey," *NYT*, Sept. 26, 1992; Cristine Clark, "Broken Vows," *Redbook*, Nov. 1992, 51–56; Elinor Burkett and Frank Bruni, *Gospel of Shame* (New York: Viking, 1993); Philip Jenkins, *Pedophiles and Priests* (New York: Oxford University Press, 1996). For Frank Bruni's more recent contributions, see, for instance, his article "U.S. Catholics See Priest Scandal as Testing Faith and the Vatican," *NYT*, Apr. 8, 2002.

30. Alan Light, "Sinead on a Tear," *SFC*, Nov. 1, 1992; Manning, *Is the Pope Catholic?*, 8.

31. *Population and Development: Programme of Action Adopted at the International Conference on Population and Development, Cairo, 5–13 Sept. 1994* (New York: United Nations, Dept. for Economic and Social Information and Policy Analysis, 1995). The hostile cartoons arising from the event can be sampled at http://www.catholicleague.org/1994report/94cartoons.htm and http://www.catholicleague.org/1995report/95cartoons.htm; see also Dale O'Leary, *The Gender Agenda* (Lafayette, LA: Vital Issues Press, 1997).

32. This cartoon was originally published in the *San Antonio Express News* and appeared in syndicated form on July 1, 1994.

33. Manning, *Is the Pope Catholic?* 154; John M. Swomley, "A League of the Pope's Own," at http://www.population-security.org/swom-98-01.htm.

34. "A Mouse That Roars Turns 25." The CFFC's website is at http://www.cath4choice.org.

35. For Kissling and her background, see Faux, *Crusaders*, 230–64; *Mother Jones*, May/June 1991, 11. The remark is widely quoted by conservative critics: see, for instance, http://www.nccbuscc.org/prolife/publicat/lifeissues/12222000.htm.

36. The "misogyny" remark is quoted from http://www.catholicleague.org/1994report/94activists.htm; "God, Women and Medicine." The *60 Minutes* broadcast occurred on Jan. 26, 2001.

37. Her remark about "intelligent, suave, sophisticated, tenacious" is from the *Financial Times*; it is quoted from http://www.cath4choice.org/nobandwidth/English/media/francis.htm.

38. The remark about Eurodisney, from a BBC television interview, is quoted from   http://www.cath4choice.org/nobandwidth/English/media/francis.htm. See also Laura Flanders, "Giving the Vatican the Boot," *Ms.*, Oct./Nov. 1999.

39. http://www.cath4choice.org.

40. http://www.cath4choice.org/portuguese/media/francis.htm.

41. http://www.cath4choice.org/nobandwidth/English/media/francis.htm.

42. Mary Daly, *Beyond God the Father* (Boston: Beacon Press, 1973); Carol P. Christ and Judith Plaskow, eds., *Womanspirit Rising* (San Francisco: Harper,

1979); Elisabeth Schüssler-Fiorenza, *In Memory of Her* (New York: Crossroad, 1984); Schüssler-Fiorenza, *Bread Not Stone* (Boston: Beacon Press, 1984); Schüssler-Fiorenza, *But She Said* (Boston: Beacon Press, 1992); Ursula King, *Women and Spirituality* (University Park: Pennsylvania State University Press, 1993); Cynthia Eller, *Living in the Lap of the Goddess* (New York: Crossroad, 1994).

43. Philip Jenkins, *Hidden Gospels* (New York: Oxford University Press, 2001).

44. Pagels is quoted from http://www.pbs.org/wgbh/pages/frontline/shows/religion/why; Elaine H. Pagels, *The Gnostic Gospels* (New York: Random House, 1979).

45. Rosemary Radford Ruether, "Women and Roman Catholic Christianity," http://www.cath4choice.org/PDF/_Ruether_report.pdf.

46. Alain Boureau, *The Myth of Pope Joan* (Chicago: University of Chicago Press, 2001); Lewis Lord, "The Lady Was a Pope," *USNWR*, July 24, 2000, 68–69. For the older debates, see Alexander Cooke, *Pope Joane. A Dialogue Betweene a Protestant and a Papist* (London, 1610).

47. Donna Woolfolk Cross, *Pope Joan* (New York: Ballantine, 1997); Peter Stanford, *The Legend of Pope Joan* (New York: Berkley, 2000); Mary T. Malone, *Women and Christianity*, vol. 1 (Maryknoll, NY: Orbis Books, 2001).

48. For Pope Joan, see http://www.dreamscape.com/morgana/popejoan.htm; http://www.ffrf.org/fttoday/may98/johnson.html; http://www.popejoan.com.

49. Marion Zimmer Bradley, *The Mists of Avalon* (New York: Knopf, 1982). For the idea of goddess worship as the religion of pre-Christian Europe, see Charlotte Allen, "The Scholars and the Goddess," *Atlantic Monthly*, Jan. 2001, 18–22; Philip G. Davis, *Goddess Unmasked* (Dallas, TX: Spence Publishing, 1998); Cynthia Eller, *Living in the Lap of the Goddess* (New York: Crossroad, 1994).

50. For the idea of the Burning Times, see *The Burning Times* (video, National Film Board of Canada, 1990); Loretta Orion, *Never Again: The Burning Times*, (Prospect Heights, IL: Waveland Press 1994); Jeanne Kalogridis, *The Burning Times: A Novel of Medieval France* (New York: Scribner, 2002); http://www.mi_Hlt19599864n_Hlt19599864dspring.com/~what/linda2.html; compare http://maxpages.com/acornerinsalem/The_Burning_Times). The term was apparently introduced by Starhawk, *The Spiral Dance* (San Francisco: Harper and Row, 1979).

51. Adam Ashforth, *Madumo* (Chicago: University of Chicago Press, 2000); Isak A. Niehaus, Eliazaar Mohlala, and Kally Shokane, *Witchcraft, Power and Politics* (London: Pluto Press, 2001). For a recent witch panic in the Democratic Republic of Congo, see Michael Dynes, "Frenzied Mob Hacks 300 'Witches' to Death," *Times* (London), July 4, 2001.

52. "Fallout Escalates over Goddess Sophia Worship," *CT*, Apr. 4, 1994, 72; James R. Edwards, "Earthquake in the Mainline," *CT*, Nov. 14, 1994, 40; Lynn Schofield Clark and Stewart M Hoover, "Controversy and Cultural Symbol-

ism," *Critical Studies in Mass Communication* 14 (1997): 310–31; Diane L. Knippers, "Sophia's Children," *Wall Street Journal*, May 8, 1998; Caitlin Matthews, *Sophia: Goddess of Wisdom* (San Francisco: HarperSanFrancisco, 1993). See also "The Re-Imagining Revival" at http://www.banneroftruth.co.uk/News/reimagining_revival.htm.

Chapter 5

1. Andrew Sullivan "The Fight Against Hate," *NYT Magazine*, Sept. 26, 1999.

2. John Boswell, *Same-Sex Unions in Premodern Europe* (New York: Villard Books, 1994).

3. Larry P. Gross, *Up from Invisibility* (New York: Columbia University Press, 2002); Suzanna Danuta Walters, *All the Rage* (Chicago: University of Chicago Press, 2001); Chris Bull and John Gallagher, *Perfect Enemies*, updated ed. (Lanham, MD: Madison Books, 2001); Edward Alwood, *Straight News* (New York: Columbia University Press, 1996).

4. Laura R. Olson and Wendy Cadge, "Talking About Homosexuality," *Journal for the Scientific Study of Religion* 41 (2002): 153–67; Larry B. Stammer, "Debating Faith and Sexuality," *LAT*, Feb. 22, 2000; Stammer, "A New Willingness to Listen," *LAT*, July 15, 2000. Gay-related debates have been especially fierce in the Episcopal Church. For the case of Bishop Walter Righter and his 1996 "heresy trial," see http://newark.rutgers.edu/~lcrew/scarletq.html. Compare http://www.integrityusa.org.

5. http://www.dignityusa.org; James L. Franklin and Ross Gelbspan, "Gay Catholics Find Sanctuary Outside Fold," *BG*, June 22, 1987; Shawn Zeller, "Dignity's Challenge," *Commonweal*, Jul. 14, 2000, 17–19.

6. John J. McNeill, *The Church and the Homosexual* (Kansas City, MO: Sheed Andrews and McMeel, 1976); Raymond C. Holtz, ed., *Listen to the Stories* (New York: Garland Publishing, 1991); Jeannine Gramick and Robert Nugent, *Building Bridges* (Mystic, CT: Twenty-Third Publications, 1992); Peter J. Liuzzi, *With Listening Hearts* (New York: Paulist Press, 2001).

7. Pastoral Letter, http://www.dignityusa.org/1993pastoral.html.

8. Robert Goss, *Jesus Acted Up* (San Francisco: HarperSanFrancisco, 1993), xiv; George Weigel, "The New Anti-Catholicism," *Commentary*, June 1992, 25. For controversies in other cities, see, for instance, Diego Ribadeneira, "Pilot Editorial on Gay Rights Draws Fire," *BG*, Nov. 9, 1987.

9. Nat Hentoff, *John Cardinal O'Connor* (New York: Scribner, 1988); *Time Out New York*, Jan. 4–11, 2001; "Sorry for Joy Over Dead Cardinal," *PlanetOut*, Jan. 4, 2001; http://www.tylerkelly.net/gaysatgrace/uploads/cardinal.html. For the St. Patrick's parade controversies in various cities, see William N. Eskridge Jr., "A Jurisprudence of Coming Out," *Yale Law Journal* 106, 8 (1997): 2411–74; Deirdre Hussey, "St. Patrick's Charade," *Village Voice*, Mar. 17, 1998, 11; Bull and Gallagher, *Perfect Enemies*.

10. "Greeted with a Yawn," *The Advocate*, Sept. 21, 1993, 25; Michelangelo Signorile, "Benevolent Hatemongers," at http://www.signorile.com/articles/advbhate.html; http://stopthepope.com.

11. http://www.thesisters.org; http://www.lasisters.org.

12. http://www.catholicleague.org/1999report/government1999.html.

13. Joanne H. Meehl, *The Recovering Catholic* (Amherst, NY: Prometheus Books, 1995).

14. Valerie Jenness and Kendal Broad, *Hate Crimes* (Hawthorne, NY: Aldine de Gruyter, 1997).

15. Michelangelo Signorile, "The Vatican's Closet," *New York Press*, at http://www.nypress.com/15/11/newsandcolumns/signorile.cfm; "Pope Backs Hate Crimes," *The Nation*, Aug. 17, 1992.

16. "Gay Protest at Mass—2 Arrested," *SFC*, July 24, 1989; Maria Newman, "Mahony Vows Not to Be Intimidated by Gays," *LAT*, Dec. 5, 1989; "AIDS, Abortion-Rights Groups Protest Near NY Cathedral," *WP*, Dec. 10, 1990; Carlos Sanchez, "AIDS Protest Disrupts Christmas Mass," *WP*, Dec. 26, 1990; John Leo, "The Gay Tide of Catholic Bashing," *USNWR*, Apr. 1, 1991; Don Aucoin, "Queer Nation at Center of Parade Debate," *BG*, Mar. 11, 1992; "Protest Outside Cathedral," *NYT*, Dec. 14, 1992. For ACT UP, see the websites of various local chapters at http://www.actupny.org; http://www.actupsf.com; http://www.actupdc.com. For continuing Stop the Church activities, see http://www.actupny.org/YELL/stopchurch99.html.

17. George Weigel, "The New Anti-Catholicism," *Commentary*, June 1992, 25. For the 1994 protest, see http://www.catholicleague.org/1994report/report94.htm; http://www.catholicleague.org/1995report/activists95.htm.

18. http://www.soulforce.org/dcaction.html.

19. For Petrelis, see http://www.actupny.org/YELL/stopchurch99.html; Goss, *Jesus Acted Up*, 148.

20. Sullivan, "The Fight Against Hate"; Randy Shilts, "AIDS Protests at Churches," *SFC*, Dec. 18, 1989; Alexander Cockburn, "Unchallenged, the Censors Will Prevail. People Are Too Intimidated by Charges of 'Anti-Catholicism,'" *LAT*, Sept. 20, 1991. See also Chris Bull, "Mass Action: A Raucous Disruption at St. Patrick's Cathedral Divides New York Gays," *Advocate*, Jan. 16, 1990, 6; M. Kent Jennings and Ellen Ann Andersen, "Support for Confrontational Tactics Among AIDS Activists," *American Journal of Political Science* 40, 2 (1996): 311.

21. "AIDS, Abortion-Rights Groups Protest Near NY Cathedral."

22. Michael Fumento, "A Church Arson Epidemic? It's Smoke and Mirrors," *Wall Street Journal*, July 8, 1996; Fumento, "Who's Fanning the Flames of Racism?" *Wall Street Journal*, June 16, 1997; Joe Holley, "Anatomy of a Story: Who Was Burning the Black Churches?" *Columbia Journalism Review* 35, 3 (1996): 26–27; Peter Steinfels, "Church Burnings Reveal a Larger Truth," *NYT*, Oct. 19, 1996. The NYT quote is from June 23, 1996.

23. Amy Kuebelbeck, "Under Fire? Is Anti-Catholic Sentiment Increasing?" *LAT*, Sept. 9, 1991; Gunther Freehill and Eliseo Acevedo Martinez, "Blasphemy, Lies, Videotape," *LAT*, Sept. 13, 1991; Scott Harris, "Gay Militancy—the Last Great Civil Rights Move?" *LAT*, Oct. 11, 1991; Larry B. Stammer, "The Messages That Bind," *LAT*, June 10, 2000.

24. The case has been the subject of several dramatized versions, including MTV's *Anatomy of a Hate Crime* (2001) and HBO's *The Laramie Project* (2002). See also the major related activity on the Internet: http://www.wiredstrategies.com/shepardx.html; http://www.matthewshepard.org; http://www.matthewsplace.com; Walters, *All the Rage*.

25. Tony Kushner, "Matthew's Passion," *The Nation*, Nov. 9, 1998, 24–27.

26. Tony Kushner, "Reply," in "Impassioned Mail on Matthew," *The Nation*, Dec. 28, 1998, 22+. Kushner's anti-Catholicism was attacked by Andrew Sullivan, "What's So Bad About Hate," *NYT Magazine*, Sept. 26, 1999.

27. Terrence McNally, *Corpus Christi* (New York: Grove Press, 1998), preface.

28. Robert Goss, *Jesus Acted Up* (San Francisco: HarperSanFrancisco, 1993), xiv, 147–50.

29. McNally, *Corpus Christi*.

30. "One or two scenes": Michael Feingold, "Texas Nativity," *Village Voice*, Oct. 20, 1998; David Patrick Stearns, "Corpus Christi a More Palatable Parable than Expected," *USA Today*, Oct. 14, 1998.

31. Paul Rudnick, *The Most Fabulous Story Ever Told* (New York: Dramatists Play Service, 1999), 9; Ben Brantley, "Cutting Icons Down To Clay Feet," *NYT*, July 25, 2002.

32. Byrne R. S. Fone, *Homophobia* (New York: Picador, 2001).

33. Mark D. Jordan, *The Silence of Sodom* (Chicago: University of Chicago Press, 2000). The quotation about "fiercely homophobic and intensely homoerotic" is from Mark D. Jordan, "9.5 Theses on Homosexuality in Modern Catholicism," at http://www.press.uchicago.edu/Misc/Chicago/410412.html; Michelangelo Signorile, "Cardinal Spellman's Dark Legacy," *New York Press*, Apr. 30, 2002.

34. James G. Wolf, ed., *Gay Priests* (San Francisco: Harper and Row, 1989); Robert Dawson, "Act-Up Acts Out," *Commonweal*, July 14, 1990; Donald B. Cozzens, *The Changing Face of the Priesthood* (Collegeville, MN: Liturgical Press, 2000); Michael S. Rose, *Goodbye, Good Men* (Washington, DC: Regnery Publishing, 2002); Lewis Whittington, "Priests and Gay Sex," *Advocate.com*, Feb. 23, 2002; Laurie Goodstein, "Homosexuality in Priesthood Is Under Increasing Scrutiny," *NYT*, Apr. 19, 2002.

35. Maureen Dowd, "Father Knows Worst," *NYT*, Mar. 20, 2002.

36. Paul Rudnick, *Jeffrey* (New York: Dramatists Play Service, 1998).

37. Bruce Bawer, *Stealing Jesus* (New York: Three Rivers Press, 1998).

38. Ibid., 59.

39. Ibid., 164.

40. Michelangelo Signorile, "Our Media-Made Martyrs," at http://www.advocate.com/html/stories/796/796_signorile.asp.

Chapter 6

1. "Lawyers Allowed to Hear Confession to Priest," *Houston Chronicle*, Aug. 10, 1996; Emily Eakin, "Secrets Confided to the Clergy Are Getting Harder to Keep," *NYT*, Feb. 16, 2002.

2. S. Robert Lichter, Daniel Amundson, and Linda S. Lichter, *Media Coverage of the Catholic Church* (Washington, DC: Center for Media and Public Affairs, 1991). The study is also found in Patrick Riley and Russell Shaw, eds., *Anti-Catholicism in the Media* (Huntington, IN: Our Sunday Visitor, 1993), 12–137; Mark Silk, *Unsecular Media* (Urbana: University of Illinois Press, 1995); S. Robert Lichter, Linda S. Lichter, and Daniel R. Amundson, *Media Coverage of Religion in America 1969–1998* (Washington, DC: Center for Media and Public Affairs, 2000); Bernard Goldberg, *Bias* (Washington, DC: Regnery Publishing, 2001). For a polemical account of media biases, see Marvin Olasky, *Prodigal Press* (Westchester, IL: Crossway Books, 1988).

3. William W. May, ed., *Vatican Authority and American Catholic Dissent* (New York: Crossroad, 1987).

4. http://www.creationspirituality.com/matthew.html; Matthew Fox, *Illuminations of Hildegard of Bingen* (Santa Fe, NM: Bear and Co., 1985); Matthew Fox, *The Coming of the Cosmic Christ* (San Francisco: Harper and Row, 1988); Matthew Fox, *Creation Spirituality* (San Francisco: HarperSanFrancisco, 1991); Matthew Fox, *Original Blessing* (Santa Fe, NM: Bear and Co., 1996); Matthew Fox, *Confessions: The Making of a Post-Denominational Priest* (San Francisco: Harper San Francisco, 1997).

5. Fox, *Confessions*; Patrick Allitt, "American Catholics and the Environment, 1960–1995," *Catholic Historical Review* 84 (1998): 263–80; http://www.creationspirituality.com; Don Lattin, "New Age Lecturer/Oakland Priest to Defy Vatican," *SFC*, Oct. 21, 1988. For the media glorification of self-proclaimed "heretics," see Philip Jenkins, *Hidden Gospels* (New York: Oxford University Press, 2001).

6. The *NYT* story is quoted in Lichter et al. in Riley and Shaw, eds., *Anti-Catholicism in the Media*, 25–27.

7. Ann Rodgers-Melnick, "Nun Who Ruffled Diocese to Speak Here," *Pittsburgh Post-Gazette*, June 16, 2001; David Van Biema, "A Nun's Dangerous Talk," *Time*, Aug. 20, 2001. For Chittister's response to the 2001 terrorist attacks, see Joan Chittister, "When Power Is Not Enough," *National Catholic Reporter*, Sept. 21, 2001 17; Joan Chittister, "A Time for Hard Decisions," *Sojourners*, Nov./Dec. 2001, 24–25; Joan Chittister, *Wisdom Distilled from the Daily* (San Francisco: Harper and Row, 1990); Joan Chittister, *Heart of Flesh* (Grand Rapids, MI: William B. Eerdmans, 1998).

8. Tom Heinen, "Nun Makes Plea for Equality of Women," *Milwaukee Journal Sentinel*, Apr. 20, 2001; Teresa Watanabe, "The Nuns Who Defied Vatican's Order to Be Silent," *LAT*, Aug. 5, 2001.

9. Stephanie Salter, "They Will Not Be Silenced," *SFC*, Aug. 19, 2001; Salter, "A Modern-Day Joan of Arc for Catholics," *SFC*, July 17, 2001.

10. Heinen, "Nun Makes Plea for Equality of Women."

11. Elizabeth C. Childs, ed., *Suspended License* (Seattle, WA: University of Washington Press, 1997).

12. Bill Peterson, "The Painting Pandemonium," *WP*, May 13, 1988.

13. Ibid.

14. Mireya Navarro, "In a Case That Parallels 'Sensation,' Cultural Leaders Took On Miami," *NYT*, Oct. 23, 1999.

15. Richard Bolton, ed., *Culture Wars* (New York: New Press, 1992); Marjorie Heins, *Sex, Sin, and Blasphemy* (New York: New Press, 1993); Steven C. Dubin, *Arresting Images* (New York: Routledge, 1994); Patricia Morrisroe, *Mapplethorpe* (New York: Random House, 1995); Marcia Pally, "Decency in the Arts," *Tikkun*, Nov./Dec. 1998, 58–60+; Michael Brenson, *Visionaries and Outcasts* (New York: New Press, 2001); Richard Meyer, *Outlaw Representation* (New York: Oxford University Press, 2002).

16. Janine Fuller and Stuart Blackley, *Restricted Entry*, 2d ed. (Vancouver, BC: Press Gang, 1996); Donald A. Downs, *The New Politics of Pornography* (Chicago: University of Chicago Press, 1989).

17. http://www.catholicleague.org/1996report/report96.htm. For a sympathetic view of the artworks in question, see http://www.voicesweb.org/voices/ae/quiltcrazy.html.

18. Erika Doss, "Robert Gober's Virgin Installation," in David Morgan and Sally M. Promey, eds., *The Visual Culture of American Religions* (Berkeley: University of California Press, 2001), 129–45; Christopher Knight, "Articles of Faith for This World," *LAT*, Sept. 9, 1997.

19. http://www.catholicleague.org/1998report/artists98.htm; John M. Glionna, "Catholics Slam Napa Art Exhibit," *LAT*, Jan. 5, 2002.

20. Lawrence Rothfield, ed., *Unsettling Sensation* (New Brunswick, NJ: Rutgers University Press, 2001).

21. The quote is from Lee Rosenbaum, "The Battle of Brooklyn Ends, the Controversy Continues," *Art in America*, June 2000, 39–43. The conflict is discussed by Stephanie Cash, "Sensation Battle Erupts in Brooklyn," *Art in America*, Nov. 1999, 37–39; Michael Kimmelman, "A Madonna's Many Meanings in the Art World," *NYT*, Oct. 5, 1999; Steven Henry Madoff, "Shock for Shock's Sake?" *Time*, Oct. 11, 1999, 80–82.

22. Philip Jenkins, *The Next Christendom* (New York: Oxford University Press, 2002).

23. Eleanor Heartney, "Postmodern Heretics," *Art in America*, Feb. 1997, 32–39; Heartney, "A Catholic Controversy?" *Art in America*, Dec. 1999, 39–41.

24. "Letters," *Art in America*, Oct. 1998, 29+.

25. Laura Miller, "The New Victimology," *Salon*, Feb. 17, 2001. "We just thought these were great images" is from "Female Jesus Draws Brooklyn Museum into Art Storm," Associated Press story in *NYT*, Feb. 15, 2001. "As in the real estate business" is from Michael Kimmelman, "Making and Taking Offense, Elevated to Art Form," *NYT*, Feb. 16, 2001.

26. Heartney, "Postmodern Heretics."

27. "Here we go again" is from Catherine Fox, "Demagoguery Threatens Arts," *The Atlanta Journal-Constitution*, Oct. 3, 1999; for the "culture wars," see Ben Cameron, "The Mayor and the Madonna," *American Theatre*, Nov. 1999, 4.

28. Cash, "Sensation Battle Erupts in Brooklyn"; "Anna Quindlen Joins Newsweek," *Salon*, Oct. 18, 1999.

29. Barbara Pollock, "Dung Jury," *Village Voice*, Oct. 12, 1999, 50–53; Stephanie Zacharek, "Sacre Bleu," *Salon*, Nov. 9, 1999.

30. Miller, "The New Victimology." For "Torquemada," see Bruce Shapiro, "Everyone's a Critic," *Salon*, Oct. 2, 1999.

31. "Female Jesus Draws Brooklyn Museum into Art Storm"; Katha Pollitt, "Anti-Catholic? Round Two," *The Nation*, Mar. 19, 2001, 10.

32. Karen Croft, "Using Her Body," *Salon*, Feb. 22, 2001; the *Daily News* interview is taken from Michael Kimmelman, "Making and Taking Offense, Elevated to Art Form," *NYT*, Feb. 16, 2001.

33. Steinfels is quoted from Ellen Willis, "Freedom from Religion," *The Nation*, Feb. 19, 2001, 11–16.

34. Norman L. Kleeblatt, ed., *Mirroring Evil: Nazi Imagery/Recent Art* (New Brunswick, NJ: Rutgers University Press, 2002); Sarah Kershaw, "Exhibition with Nazi Imagery Begins Run at Jewish Museum," *NYT*, Mar. 18, 2002; Dan Gilgoff, "Darker Visions," *USNWR*, Mar. 25, 2002, 42.

35. Michael Kimmelman, "Evil, the Nazis and Shock Value," *NYT*, Mar. 15, 2002.

Chapter 7

1. The "shark" cartoon was reprinted to accompany Philip Jenkins, "Celibacy for Beginners," *WP*, Mar. 31, 2002, B3.

2. Michael Rosenwald, "Protesters Target Easter Service," *BG*, Apr. 1, 2002; "Abuse Claims Against Archdiocese Mount," www.cnn.com/2002/LAW/05/05/boston.church.abuse, May 5, 2002.

3. For the clergy abuse crisis of the early 1990s, see Jason Berry, *Lead Us Not into Temptation* (New York: Doubleday, 1992); Elinor Burkett and Frank Bruni, *Gospel of Shame* (New York: Viking, 1993); A. W. Richard Sipe, *Sex, Priests, and Power* (New York: Brunner/Mazel, 1995); Thomas M. Disch, *The Priest* (New York: Knopf, 1995); Philip Jenkins, *Pedophiles and Priests* (New York: Oxford University Press, 1996); Stephen J. Rossetti, *A Tragic Grace* (Collegeville, MN: Liturgical Press, 1996); Anson Shupe, ed., *Wolves Within the Fold* (New Brunswick, NJ: Rutgers University Press, 1998): Thomas G. Plante, ed., *Bless Me Father for I Have Sinned* (Westport, CT: Praeger, 1999); Anson Shupe, William A. Stacey, and Susan E. Darnell, eds., *Bad Pastors* (New York: New York University Press, 2000).

4. Through the first half of 2002, the *Boston Globe* offered basically daily coverage of the scandals. The first major explosion occurred on Jan. 6, with a story by the *Globe* Spotlight Team (or the "SWAT team," as they are known within the organization) entitled "Church Allowed Abuse by Priest for Years." The article was researched by Matt Carroll, Sacha Pfeiffer, Michael Rezendes, and Walter V. Robinson. See also Investigative Staff of the *Boston Globe*, *Betrayal* (Boston: Little Brown, 2002). For the subsequent development of the scandals, see Peter Steinfels, "The Church's Sex-Abuse Crisis," *Commonweal*, Apr. 19, 2002: 13–19; Kenneth Jost, "Sexual Abuse and the Clergy," *CQ Researcher* 12, 17 (2002): 393–416.

5. The *Boston Globe* published the following stories on the Shanley case during 2002, among many others: Stephen Kurkjian and Michael Rezendes, "Calif. Parish Says Boston Kept Quiet on Accused Priest," Apr. 7; Michael Rezendes, "Newly Released Documents Show Church Officials Knew of Complaints Against Priest," Apr. 8; Eileen McNamara, "An Obvious Question," Apr. 10; Tatsha Robertson, "Shanley Couldn't Outrun Past," Apr. 19; Michael Rezendes and Thomas Farragher, "Letter Threatened Medeiros with 'Shocking' Revelations," Apr. 26. Compare Nick Madigan, "Sent to California on Sick Leave, Boston Priest Bought Racy Gay Resort," *NYT*, Apr. 15; Angie Cannon, "Is There Any End in Sight?" *USNWR*, Apr. 22, 2002.

6. Some major stories in 2002 included: Denise Lavoie, "Former Priest Convicted in Sex Assault Case," Associated Press, Jan. 18; Pam Belluck, "Papers in Pedophile Case Show Church Effort to Avert Scandal," *NYT*, Jan. 25; Walter V. Robinson, Matt Carroll, Sacha Pfeiffer, Michael Rezendes, and Stephen Kurkjian, "Scores of Priests Involved in Sex Abuse Cases," *BG*, Jan. 31; Stephen Kurkjian, "DAs Given Names of 49 More Priests," *BG*, Feb. 9; Walter V. Robinson, "Hundreds Now Claim Priest Abuse," *BG*, Feb. 24.

7. "Predator Priest," *New York Daily News*, Mar. 27, 2002; Nena Baker, "Church Hid Abuse, Victims Say," *Arizona Republic*, Feb. 10, 2002; Ken Thomas, "Fla. Bishop Resigns After Admitting Sexual Misconduct," Associated Press, Mar. 8, 2002; Donna Gehrke-White, "Church Money Silenced Sex Claims," *Miami Herald*, Mar. 20, 2002; Jim Salter, "Lawsuit Alleges Church Coverup," Associated Press, Mar. 23, 2002; Kim Baca, "Woman Stands by Charge She Was Molested by Cardinal," Associated Press, Apr. 7, 2002; Stone Phillips, "Crisis in the Catholic Church," *Dateline NBC*, Apr. 19, 2002, at http://www.msnbc.com/news/740606.asp-cp1-1; Rachel Zoll, "177 Priests Removed in 28 States," *WP*, Apr. 28, 2002.

8. Don Wright cartoon from the *Palm Beach Post*, reprinted *NYT*, Jan. 20, 2002.

9. Laurie Goodstein and Alessandra Stanley, "As Scandal Keeps Growing, Church and Its Faithful Reel," *NYT*, Mar. 17, 2002. One sign of a more critical media attitude was the appearance of emotive headlines and catchphrases to characterize the crisis. See, for instance, Bill Keller, "Let Us Prey," *NYT*, Mar. 9, 2002.

10. John Ziegler, "Cardinal Off Base on Pedophile Priests," *Philadelphia Daily News*, Mar. 5, 2002, reports a claim "that as many as 20 percent of priests could be identified as pedophiles." For claims that "between 2 percent and 10 percent [of priests] may be pedophiles," see Jules Crittenden and Tom Mashberg, "Experts See Familiar Pattern in Hub Archdiocese Scandal," *Boston Herald*, Jan. 30, 2002. For the Linkup, see http://www.thelinkup.com/stats.html; Kristen Lombardi, "Cardinal Sin," *Boston Phoenix*, Apr. 19, 2002.

11. Julia Quinn Dempsey, John R. Gorman, John P. Madden, and Alphonse P. Spilly, *The Cardinal's Commission on Clerical Sexual Misconduct with Minors: Report to Joseph Cardinal Bernardin, Archbishop of Chicago* (Chicago: The Commission, 1992). I have discussed the issue of assessing the numbers of abusive

clergy in *Pedophiles and Priests*, in which I particularly dispute the figures offered by Richard Sipe and Andrew Greeley.

12. Michael Rubinkam, "Phila. Diocese Finds Sex Abuse Cases," Associated Press, Feb. 22, 2002.

13. John Cornwell, *Breaking Faith* (New York: Viking, 2001), 147; http://www.catholicleague.org/pr0102.htm.

14. Mark Clayton and Seth Stern, "Clergy, Abuse, and Jail Time," *Christian Science Monitor*, Mar. 21, 2002; Michael Medved, "Catholic Bashing and Pedophile Priests," Mar. 25, 2002, at http://www.worldnetdaily.com/news/article. asp?ARTICLE_ID=26955; Richard Foot, "Catholic Clergy Far from Only Abusers," *National Post* (Canada), Apr. 12, 2002. For systematic abuse in other churches and secular institutions, see, for instance, Mike Echols, *Brother Tony's Boys* (Amherst, NY: Prometheus Books, 1996); Patrick Boyle, *Scout's Honor* (Rocklin, CA: Prima Publishing, 1994). To illustrate the diversity of complaints against religions, I point out some of the major abuse stories that occurred during 2001, that is, before the exclusive media concentration on Catholic horrors. For exposés about Jehovah's Witnesses, see Corrie Cutrer, "Witness Leaders Accused of Shielding Molesters," *CT*, March 5, 2001; for Mormon cases, see Gustav Niebuhr, "Sex Abuse Lawsuit Is Settled by Mormons for $3 Million," *NYT*, Sept. 5, 2001; for a non-denominational House of Prayer, see David Firestone, "Child Abuse at a Church Creates a Stir in Atlanta," *NYT*, Mar. 30, 2001; for a Mennonite church, see Zlati Meyer, "Places of Worship Face Tough Call: Screening Volunteers," *Philadelphia Inquirer*, June 25, 2001; for the Hare Krishna movement, see Peter Brandt, "Holy Abuse," *Salon*, July 2, 2001; for Baptists, see David A. Fahrenthold, "Sex Abuse at Church Shatters a Family," *WP*, July 30, 2001; for Jewish cases, see Andrew Jacobs, "Orthodox Group Details Accusations That New Jersey Rabbi Abused Teenagers," *NYT*, Dec. 27, 2000; Caroline J. Keough, "Boca Rabbi Enters Guilty Plea to Internet-Triggered Sex Case" *Salon*, Aug. 22, 2001; Julie Wiener, "No Longer Taboo," *Jewsweek. com*, Oct. 10, 2001. Of course this listing makes no attempt to be anything more than impressionistic.

15. Richard N. Ostling, "US Protestants Also Are Facing Scandals over Sex Abuse; But Cases Differ from Those of Catholics," *St. Louis Post-Dispatch*, Apr. 7, 2002.

16. "75 Years of Clergy Records Sought," Associated Press, Mar. 26, 2002.

17. Caroline Hendrie and Steven Drummond et al., "A Trust Betrayed: Sexual Abuse by Teachers," three-part series published in *Education Week*, Dec. 2–16, 1998, online at http://www.edweek.org/sreports/abuse98.htm; Caroline Hendrie, "'Passing the Trash' by School Districts Frees Sexual Predators to Hunt Again," *Education Week*, Dec. 9, 1998; Jane Elizabeth Zemel and Steve Twedt, "Dirty Secrets," three-part series in *Pittsburgh Post-Gazette*, Oct. 31–Nov. 2, 1999; Diana Jean Schemo, "Silently Shifting Teachers in Sex Abuse Cases," *NYT*, June 18, 2002. Charol Shakeshaft, *Sexual Abuse in Schools* (San Francisco: Jossey-Bass, 2003). The quote from the president of SESAME is from Chelsea J. Carter, "Teacher Sex Cases Overshadowed by Clergy Scandal,"

Associated Press story reprinted in *Sacramento Bee,* June 10, 2002, online at http://www.sacbee.com/state_wire/story/3155584p-4199203c.html. SESAME itself has a website at http://www.sesamenet.org; the estimate of a 15-percent abuse rate can be found at http://www.sesamenet.org/research.htm. See also D. Wishnietsky, "Reported and Unreported Teacher-Student Sexual Harassment," *Journal of Educational Research 84,* 3 (1991): 164–69.

18. Wills is quoted from "Priests and Boys: An Exchange," *New York Review of Books,* September 26, 2002. For the history of the concept of pedophilia, see Philip Jenkins, *Moral Panic* (New Haven: Yale University Press, 1998). My critical approach to the term pedophile has led some activists to accuse me of minimizing Church misdeeds. My most lurid critic was Garry Wills, who claims that since I have written about the "social construction" of problems such as pedophilia, sexual molestation, and rape, I must be saying that the behaviors themselves are trivial or nonexistent, and must not be criminalized. No social constructionist scholar of my acquaintance holds such a lunatic view, and nor do I. For a social constructionist, a social problem includes both an objective issue such as AIDS or child molestation, together with a subjective framework that people use to interpret it, and that framework changes over time. We can therefore say that the AIDS problem is socially constructed, though no responsible observer suggests that AIDS itself is nonexistent, or that society should respond to it with anything less than the utmost seriousness. Similarly, governments have the right and obligation to respond to other socially constructed problems, including (obviously) child molestation and sexual assault. See Garry Wills, "Priests and Boys," *New York Review of Books,* June 13, 2002, 10–13.

19. For the Cleveland story, see Francis X. Clines, "Diocese Questions Future Along With the Past," *NYT,* Apr. 14, 2002. For the Orange County case, see Gustav Niebuhr, "Dioceses Settle Case of Man Accusing Priest of Molestation," *NYT,* Aug. 22, 2001; Steve Lopez, "A Trail of Secrecy and Deception," *LAT,* Aug. 22, 2001; William Lobdell, Jean O. Pasco, and Larry B. Stammer, "Catholics Are Shaken by Molestation Allegations," *LAT,* Aug. 22, 2001; William Lobdell and Jean O. Pasco, "Judging the Sins of the Father," *LAT,* Nov. 10, 2001. The *Newsweek* cover appeared on Mar. 4, 2002. For the Weakland case, see "Former Archbishop Accused of Abuse Apologizes for Scandal," *LAT,* Jun. 1, 2002; Dirk Johnson, "An Archbishop's Fall From Grace," *Newsweek,* Jun. 3, 2002, 42. For heterosexual cases, see Jane Lampman, "A wider circle of clergy abuse; As US bishops meet, attention is drawn to female victims of priests," *Christian Science Monitor,* June 14, 2002; Sam Dillon, "Women Tell of Priests' Abusing Them as Girls," *NYT,* June 15, 2002.

20. Maria Russo, "Intro to Sex," *NYT Book Review,* Apr. 22, 2001; Stephen Holden, "Growing Pains, Without the Psychobabble," *NYT,* June 29, 2001; Judith Levine, *Harmful to Minors* (Minneapolis: University of Minnesota Press, 2002). In 2002, *Salon* published an article claiming that "[s]ex between teenage boys and older men is not always coercive—and it can be more ecstatic than traumatic." See David Tuller, "Minor Report," *Salon,* July 22, 2002. Social

attitudes to relationships between adult women and teenage boys are just as ambivalent. The 2002 film *Tadpole* lyrically depicts the sexual initiation of a fifteen-year-old boy by his mother's best friend. The review in the *NYT* found the film "endearing" with a "soulful heart", "a delicious bonbon of a film:" Stephen Holden, "Developing a Complicated Taste for (Older) Women," *NYT*, July 19, 2002.

21. Eric Lax, book review of *Mainly About Lindsay Anderson* by Gavin Lambert, *LAT*, Oct. 4, 2000; Stanley Kauffman, "Angry Young Man," *NYT Book Review*, Nov. 12, 2000; Andrew Curry, "The Geography of Perversion," *USNWR*, Apr. 1, 2002. For Oscar Wilde, see Vanessa Thorpe and Simon de Burton, "Wilde's Sex Life Exposed in Explicit Court Files," *Observer* (London), May 6, 2001.

22. The cartoon about color-coded threats is by Jimmy Margulies and was reprinted in the *Centre Daily Times* (State College, PA), Mar. 20, 2002. The "chaperone" reference is a Nick Anderson cartoon from the *Louisville Courier-Journal*, reprinted in the *NYT*, Mar. 17, 2002. The *New York Post* cartoon is described in http://www.catholicleague.org/02press_releases/pr0102.htm.

23. Johanna McGeary, "Can the Catholic Church Save Itself?" *Time*, Apr. 1, 2002; for the "wayward clergy," see *Newsweek*, Mar. 4, 2002, 3. The CNN story was broadcast on Mar. 23, 2002.

24. Thomas C. Fox, *Sexuality and Catholicism* (New York: George Braziller, 1995). These cartoons were reprinted in *WP*, Mar. 31, 2002, B3; William Saletan, "Booty and the Priest: Does Abstinence Make the Church Grow Fondlers?" *Slate*, Mar. 6, 2002.

25. "The Whole Story," *Commonweal*, Apr. 5, 2002, 5–6. For the problems involved in "remembering" abuse, see Jenkins, *Moral Panic*. Stephanie Salter, "Watch That Pedophile Priest Purge Not Become a Witch-Hunt," *SFC*, Mar. 13, 2002.

26. The cartoon appeared in the *Chicago Tribune*, Mar. 22, 2002.

27. Chuck Colbert, "Rome's 'No' Doesn't Stop Mass at New Ways Conference," *National Catholic Reporter*, Mar. 22, 2002. Compare Eugene C. Kennedy, *The Unhealed Wound* (New York: St. Martin's Press, 2001).

28. Burkett and Bruni, *Gospel of Shame*, 224; A. W. Richard Sipe, *A Secret World* (New York: Brunner/Mazel, 1990); Sipe, *Sex, Priests, and Power*; Sipe, *Celibacy* (Liguori, MO: Triumph Books, 1996); James Carroll, "From Celibacy to Godliness," *BG*, Apr. 9, 2002; Larry B. Stammer, "No Easy Solution to Priest Problem," *LAT*, Apr. 14, 2002.

29. Anna Quindlen, "Patent Leather, Impure Thoughts," *Newsweek*, Apr. 1, 2002, 74; Cahill is quoted in Anne Hendershott, "A Perfect Panic," *San Diego Union-Tribune*, Mar. 20, 2002; Katha Pollitt, "God Changes Everything," *Nation*, Apr. 1, 2002.

30. For "cloistered, arrogant fraternities," see Maureen Dowd, "Father Knows Worst," *NYT*, Mar. 20, 2002; for "stifling God-given urges," see Dowd, "The Vatican Rag," *NYT*, Mar. 24, 2002; for "Who knew that priests' dating," see Dowd, "A Clerical Error," *NYT*, Apr. 14, 2002. Her enumeration of the deadly sins is from Dowd, "Ire and Brimstone," *NYT*, Apr. 28, 2002.

31. For "the church subsidizing pedophilia," see Dowd, "Father Knows Worst"; for "Rome is in a defensive crouch," see Dowd, "Sacred Cruelties," *NYT,* Apr. 7, 2002.

32. Stephanie Salter, "Judgments Were Made"; *SFC,* Jan. 23, 2002; Dowd, "Vatican Rag"; Bill Keller, "Is the Pope Catholic?" *NYT,* May 4, 2002.

33. John William Draper, *History of the Conflict Between Religion and Science,* 5th ed. (New York: D. Appleton and Co., 1875), 285.

34. Eamon Duffy, *Stripping of the Altars* (New Haven: Yale University Press, 1994). For the concept of a "second reformation," see Alan Cooperman and Pamela Ferdinand, "For Catholics, Crisis of Trust Allayed by Faith," *WP,* Mar. 17, 2002; Ron Grossman, "Cardinal Law, Church Leaders, Preach Patience to Faithful Shaken by Scandal," *Chicago Tribune* story reprinted in *Centre Daily Times,* Apr. 14, 2002.

35. Dowd, "Vatican Rag."

Chapter 8

1. Gretchen M. Bataille and Charles L. P. Silet (eds.), *The Pretend Indians* (Ames: Iowa State University Press, 1980); Patricia Erens, *The Jew in American Cinema* (Bloomington: Indiana University Press, 1984); Vito Russo, *The Celluloid Closet,* rev. ed. (New York: Harper and Row, 1987); Karen Ross, *Black and White Media* (Cambridge, Mass: Polity Press, 1996); Vincent F. Rocchio, *Reel Racism* (Boulder, CO: Westview Press, 2000); Robert G. Lee, *Orientals: Asian Americans in Popular Culture* (Philadelphia: Temple University Press, 2000); Sarah Projansky, *Watching Rape* (New York: New York University Press, 2001); Jack G. Shaheen, *Reel Bad Arabs* (New York: Olive Branch Press, 2001).

2. "An industry largely financed" is quoted by Uma M. Cadegan in "Guardians of Democracy or Cultural Storm Troopers?" *Catholic Historical Review* 87 (2001): 252–82; Les J. Keyser and Barbara Keyser, *Hollywood and the Catholic Church* (Chicago: Loyola University Press, 1984); James M. Skinner, *The Cross and the Cinema* (Westport, CT: Praeger, 1993); Gregory D. Black, *Hollywood Censored* (Cambridge: Cambridge University Press, 1994); Frank Walsh, *Sin and Censorship* (New Haven: Yale University Press, 1996); Gregory D. Black, *The Catholic Crusade Against the Movies, 1940–1975* (Cambridge: Cambridge University Press, 1998).

3. I am thinking of classic Buñuel films such as *L'Age d'Or* and *Land Without Bread.*

4. The advertising campaign is noted as a turning point by George A. Kelly, *The Battle for the American Church* (New York: Doubleday Image, 1981).

5. For the change in media values, see Philip Jenkins, *Pedophiles and Priests* (New York: Oxford University Press, 1996), 53–76. Novello's Father Sarducci had originally appeared in 1975 on the Smothers Brothers' television show, but it was the *Saturday Night Live* appearances that made him a national celebrity.

6. Fr. Sarducci's pronouncements can be found at http://home.earthlink. net/~sarasohn/aboutgs.html.

7. For the Catholic League's response to the show, see http://www.

catholicleague.org/catalyst/1998_catalyst/398catalyst.htm; http://www.catholic league.org/1998report /summary1998.htm.

8. http://www.catholicleague.org/1998report/summary1998.htm.

9. Stephanie Zacharek, "Sacre Bleu," *Salon*, Nov. 9, 1999.

10. David Edelstein, "Dogma's Sacred Profanity," *Slate*, Oct. 4, 1999. The reaction to *Dogma* occupied a large proportion of Catholic League attentions during 1999; see http://www.catholicleague.org.

11. Russo, *Celluloid Closet*.

12. Jack G. Shaheen, "The Power of Film," *WP*, Nov. 15, 1998.

13. Richard Aloysius Blake, *Afterimage* (Chicago: Loyola Press, 2000); Lee Lourdeaux, *Italian and Irish Film-makers in America* (Philadelphia: Temple University Press, 1993); Andrew Greeley, *The Catholic Imagination* (Berkeley: University of California Press, 2000).

14. Larry B. Stammer, "The Messages That Bind," *LAT*, June 10, 2000.

15. William Diehl, *Primal Fear* (New York: Ballantine, 1996). Anti-Catholic imagery also ran riot in British films such as *The Baby of Macon* (1993) and *Elizabeth* (1998), though I am chiefly discussing U.S. productions here.

16. Philip Jenkins, *Hidden Gospels* (New York: Oxford University Press, 2001).

17. Steven W. Naifeh, *The Mormon Murders* (New York: Weidenfeld and Nicolson, 1988); Linda Sillitoe and Allen Roberts, *Salamander* (Salt Lake City, UT: Signature Books, 1990).

18. For "Mad TV," see http://www.catholicleague.org/98press_releases/ pr0298.htm; Alessandra Stanley, "Church Woes Are Invading TV Pilots," *NYT*, May 7, 2002. Details of *South Park* episodes are partly taken from http://www. catholicleague.org.

19. David Bauder, "'Ally McBeal' Episode Angers Catholics," *BG*, Nov. 5, 1998.

20. Christopher Durang, *Sister Mary Ignatius Explains It All for You and the Actor's Nightmare* (New York: Dramatists Play Service, 1999).

21. Steven Oxman, "Sister Mary Explains It All," *Variety*, May 28–Jun 3, 2001, 29, 33; review by Adrienne Onofri at http://www.oobr.com/top/volThree/ one/OOBR-Ignatius.html.

Chapter 9

1. Richard Slotkin, *Gunfighter Nation* (New York: Atheneum, 1992), 5–6.

2. Elinor Burkett and Frank Bruni, *Gospel of Shame* (New York: Viking, 1993), 178.

3. James Carroll, "A Human Humiliated Church," *BG*, Feb. 12, 2002; Kimberly Mills, "As Millions Succumb to AIDS, Ban on Condoms Jeopardizes Church's Position as Moral Leader," *Seattle Post-Intelligencer*, Aug. 12, 2001.

4. John Cornwell, *Hitler's Pope* (New York: Viking, 1999); Garry Wills, *Papal Sin* (New York: Doubleday, 2000); Gary Wills, *Why I Am a Catholic* (Boston: Houghton Mifflin, 2002); James Carroll, *Constantine's Sword* (Boston: Houghton Mifflin, 2001); James Carroll, *Toward a New Catholic Church* (Boston: Houghton Mifflin, 2002); Daniel Jonah Goldhagen, *A Moral Reckoning: The*

Role of the Catholic Church in the Holocaust and Its Unfulfilled Duty of Repair (New York: Knopf, 2002). The "book of the month" reference is from John T. Pawlikowski's review of David Kertzer's *The Popes Against the Jews*, in *National Catholic Reporter*, Feb. 1, 2002.

5. David I. Kertzer, *The Popes Against the Jews: The Vatican's Role in the Rise of Modern Anti-Semitism* (New York: Knopf, 2001).

6. William D. Rubinstein, review of Kertzer, *The Popes Against the Jews*, in *First Things*, Feb. 2002: 54–58.

7. Vincent Carroll and David Shiflett, *Christianity on Trial* (San Francisco: Encounter Books, 2001).

8. Philip Jenkins, *Hidden Gospels* (New York: Oxford University Press, 2001).

9. Anna Quindlen, "Patent Leather, Impure Thoughts," *Newsweek*, Apr. 1, 2002, 74; Chuck Colbert, "For Gay Catholics, Conscience is the Key," *National Catholic Reporter*, Jan. 16, 1998, 17.

10. "Celibacy of the Clergy," *Catholic Encyclopedia* at http://www.newadvent.org/cathen/03481a.htm; Peter Brown, *The Body and Society* (New York: Columbia University Press, 1988); H. C. Lea, *The History of Sacerdotal Celibacy in the Christian Church* (originally published 1867) (New York: Russell and Russell, 1957). The reference to "Priests were married" is from Jon Meacham, "Celibacy and Marriage," *Newsweek*, May 6, 2002, 29.

11. For Clinton's views, see Ann Coulter; "The Mind of a Liberal," *Human Events*; Nov. 26, 2001. For the myth and realities of the Crusades, see Philip Jenkins, *The Next Christendom* (New York: Oxford University Press, 2002). The extremely hostile picture of medieval Christianity vis-à-vis Islam was popularized through television documentaries such as *Empire of Faith*, broadcast on PBS in 2001.

12. Dave Hunt, *A Woman Rides the Beast* (Eugene, OR: Harvest House, 1994), claims that the Spanish Inquisition alone claimed at least 300,000 lives; see also Phil Porvaznik, "Dave Hunt and the Spanish Inquisition," at http://www.bringyou.to/philvaz/articles/num25.htm. For scholarly accounts, see Henry Kamen, *The Spanish Inquisition: A Historical Revision* (New Haven: Yale University Press, 1997); Kamen, *Inquisition and Society in Spain in the Sixteenth and Seventeenth Centuries* (Bloomington, IN: Indiana University Press, 1985); Edward Peters, *Inquisition* (New York: Free Press, 1988); James Hitchcock, "Inquisition," at http://www.catholic.net/RCC/Periodicals/Dossier/1112–96/column1.html. For the numbers of victims, see *The Myth of the Spanish Inquisition*, television documentary produced by BBC/A&E Network, 1994.

13. Carroll, *Constantine's Sword*, 37–39.

14. Carroll, *Constantine's Sword*, "the full and awful truth," 12; "corrupted the authors of the New Testament," 569; "Constantinian imperial Catholicism," 548.

15. Ibid., 22.

16. John Dominic Crossan, *Who Killed Jesus?* (San Francisco: Harper San Francisco, 1996); Jenkins, *Hidden Gospels*.

17. "You are of your father the devil": John 8: 43–45.

18. John 4: 21–23; Gal 2:15.

19. Carsten Peter Thiede, *The Dead Sea Scrolls and the Jewish Origins of Christianity* (New York: St. Martin's Press, 2001).

20. Carroll, *Constantine's Sword*, 604.

21. Mark Aarons and John Loftus, *Unholy Trinity* (New York: St. Martin's Griffin, 1998); Robert S. Wistrich, *Hitler and the Holocaust* (New York: Modern Library, 2002); Jose M. Sanchez, *Pius XII and the Holocaust* (Washington, DC: Catholic University of America Press, 2002).

22. Daniel J. Goldhagen, "What Would Jesus Have Done?" *New Republic,* Jan. 21, 2002, 21–45; Peretz is quoted in http://www.catholicleague.org/catalyst/2002_catalyst/3–02.htm; Ronald J. Rychlak, *Hitler, the War, and the Pope* (Huntington, IN: Our Sunday Visitor 2000); Rychlak, "Goldhagen v. Pius XII," *First Things*, June/July 2002, 37–54; Ralph M. McInerny, *The Defamation of Pius XII* (South Bend, IN: St. Augustine's Press, 2001); John Laughland, "A Visit with Father Gumpel," *Spectator* (London), July 20. 2002; Michael Burleigh, "Hitler's Pope Was Really a Friend of the Jews," *Sunday Times* (London), July 28, 2002.

23. Michael Bar-Zohar, *Beyond Hitler's Grasp* (Holbrook, MA: Adams Media, 2001). For the plan to kidnap Pius, see William D. Rubinstein, "The Devil's Advocate," in *First Things*, Jan. 2000, 39–43.

24. Rubinstein, "The Devil's Advocate"; Paul Blanshard, *American Freedom and Catholic Power* (originally published 1949), rev. ed. (Boston: Beacon, 1958), 286; Michael Phayer, *The Catholic Church and the Holocaust, 1930–1965* (Bloomington: Indiana University Press, 2001).

25. *60 Minutes*, CBS, Mar. 19, 2000; Saul Friedländer, *Pius XII and the Third Reich* (New York: Knopf, 1966).

26. Cornwell, *Hitler's Pope*, 241–67. Rychlak argues that even in Croatia and Slovakia, Pius's record was far better than has been claimed: "Goldhagen v. Pius XII," 49–50.

27. Goldhagen, "What Would Jesus Have Done?" 24–25.

28. Susan Zuccotti, *Under His Very Windows* (New Haven: Yale University Press, 2001).

29. Quoted by Sam Schulman, "Goldhagen to Christianity: Whatever You're Doing, Stop It!" *Jewish World Review*, Jan. 22, 2001.

30. Nathaniel Micklem, *National Socialism and the Roman Catholic Church* (Oxford: Oxford University Press, 1939). For the "Jew-loving cardinal," see Schulman, "Goldhagen to Christianity: Whatever You're Doing, Stop It!"

31. Rubinstein, "The Devil's Advocate." It has been aptly said that regretting Pius's alleged failure to attack the Nazis directly is like complaining that "the Declaration of Independence 'refused to name' George III, or that the Emancipation Proclamation 'refused to name' Jefferson Davis or the Confederacy": Justus G. Lawler, *Popes and Politics* (New York: Continuum, 2002).

32. Rubinstein, "The Devil's Advocate."

33. "Only slightly less vicious": Rubinstein review of Kertzer in *First Things*, 58; "You can be a Christian or a German": Cornwell, *Hitler's Pope*, 106. For

President Clinton's comments, see Dave Shiflett, "You Mean Hitler Wasn't a Priest?" *National Review Online*, Jan. 21, 2001, http://www.nationalreview.com/shiflett/shiflett012102.shtml. For the Nazi plan to destroy Christianity, see "The Nazi Master Plan," in *Rutgers Journal of Law and Religion*, available through http://camlaw.rutgers.edu/publications/law-religion/nuremberg.htm.

34. "Nazi-legitimizing": Cornwell, *Hitler's Pope*, 522; Frank J. Coppa, ed., *Controversial Concordats* (Washington, DC: Catholic University of America Press, 1999).

35. Charles Morris, *American Catholic* (New York: Times Books, 1997), 242.

36. Rubinstein, "The Devil's Advocate"; Kenneth Woodward, "The Case Against Pius XII," *Newsweek International*, Sept. 27, 1999, at http://discuss.washingtonpost.com/nw-srv/issue/13_99b/printed/int/socu/ov3013_1.htm.

37. Garry Wills, "The Popes Against the Jews: Before the Holocaust," *NYT Book Review*, Sept. 23, 2001.

38. Goldhagen, "What Would Jesus Have Done?" 29; Goldhagen, *A Moral Reckoning*. See the important counter by Rychlak, "Goldhagen v. Pius XII."

39. "The Church's anti-Semitism was the trunk": Goldhagen, "What Would Jesus Have Done?" 37; "evils of modernity," 25.

40. Goldhagen, "What Would Jesus Have Done?" 39.

41. Andrew Sullivan, "Goldhagen's Smear: Catholicism, Nazism and the Holocaust," http://andrewsullivan.com/main_article.php?artnum=20020117; Michael Novak, "Bigotry's New Low," at http://www.nationalreview.com/contributors/novak012802.shtml; Rychlak, "Goldhagen v. Pius XII," 54; Schulman, "Goldhagen to Christianity."

42. Goldhagen, "What Would Jesus Have Done?" 45.

43. Cornwell, *Hitler's Pope*, 295; John Cornwell, *Breaking Faith* (New York: Viking Press, 2001).

44. Wills, *Papal Sin*.

45. Wills, *Why I Am a Catholic*; Richard Eder, "A Doubting Catholic Affirms an Older, More Open Faith," *NYT*, July 12, 2002.

46. Wills, *Papal Sin*, 310.

47. Robert P. Lockwood, "Papal Sin is Palpable Nonsense," at http://www.catholicleague.org/research/papalsins.html.

48. Wills, *Papal Sin*, 133–36.

49. "This idol-goddess": Wills, *Papal Sin*, 211; David I. Kertzer, *The Kidnapping of Edgardo Mortara* (New York: Vintage, 1999).

50. Cornwell, *Hitler's Pope*, 345–46.

Chapter 10

1. These issues became acute over the question of gays in Scouting, and the Supreme Court's decision legalizing the exclusion of overtly homosexual Boy Scouts; see *Boy Scouts of America et al. v. Dale* (2000); Suzanna Danuta Walters, *All the Rage* (Chicago: University of Chicago Press, 2001); Chris Bull and John Gallagher, *Perfect Enemies*, updated ed. (Lanham, MD: Madison Books, 2001).

2. "Child-Rape Cases Prompt Lawmakers to Rethink Clerical Privilege,"

Associated Press, Aug. 1, 2001; Walter V. Robinson and Sacha Pfeiffer, "Senate Agrees to Widen Abuse Bill," Jan. 23, 2002; Kevin Cullen, "Reilly, DAs Pressure Archdiocese on Priests," Mar. 1, 2002; Michael Paulson, "Sex Abuse Reporting Measure Hits Snag," *BG*, Mar. 7, 2002; "House, Senate Divided over Clergy Exemptions," *BG*, Mar. 7, 2002; Richard Pérez-Peña, "Some in Albany Want to Make Clergy Report Possible Abuse," *NYT*, Mar. 16, 2002. The seal of the confessional has, however, been respected in recent Massachusetts legislation: Yvonne Abraham, "State Lawmakers Agree on Clergy Reporting Bill," *BG*, Apr. 24, 2002; Michael Powell, "Catholic Clout Is Eroded by Scandal," *WP*, July 6, 2002.

3. Kevin Cullen, "AG's Office Asks to Monitor Priests," *BG*, Mar. 8, 2002.

4. Michael W. Cuneo, *Smoke of Satan* (Baltimore: Johns Hopkins University Press, 1999).

5. Peter Casarella and Raul Gomez, eds., *El Cuerpo de Cristo* (New York: Crossroad, 1998); Ana María Díaz-Stevens and Anthony M. Stevens-Arroyo, *Recognizing the Latino Resurgence in U.S. Religion* (Boulder, CO: Westview Press, 1998); Jeffrey M. Burns, Ellen Skerrett, Joseph M. White, and Christopher J. Kauffman, eds., *Keeping Faith* (Maryknoll, NY: Orbis Books, 2000); Timothy Matovina and Gerald Eugene Poyo, eds., *Presente!* (Maryknoll, NY: Orbis Books, 2000).

6. Philip Jenkins, *The Next Christendom* (New York: Oxford University Press, 2002); Timothy Matovina, "Hispanic Catholics," *Commonweal*, Sept. 14, 2001, 19–21; Anthony DePalma, "Hispanics Still Backing Catholic Leaders, For Now," *NYT*, May 1, 2002; Daniel J. Wakin, "Ammunition in a Battle for Souls," *NYT*, May 22, 2002.

7. Charles Morris, *American Catholic* (New York: Times Books, 1997).

8. The poem can be found at http://ccat.sas.upenn.edu/jod/texts/cavafy. html.

9. Peter Viereck, *Shame and Glory of the Intellectuals* (Boston: Beacon Press, 1953), 48.

10. Andrew Greeley, *An Ugly Little Secret* (Kansas City: Sheed Andrews and McMeel, 1977), 14–15.

Index

4-03